"[HexCraft] is based on extensive interviews with local people who remember the practice of Powwowing and report it vividly. The author is able to show how ancient traditions merge, change and re-emerge in new and strengthened forms. This is exciting. The blend of Old Teutonic magic, Christian faith healing, Wiccan practice and Native American tradition that Silver RavenWolf presents is exactly the same sort of melding that gave rise to the Powwowing tradition in the first place, hundreds of years ago. And seeing the familiar charms and chants presented in a whole new way is grounds for hope that this timeless tradition will not disappear."

—*Yvonne J. Milspaw, Ph.D., Folklorist*

The roots of American Witchcraft can be found in a seventeenth century settler tradition comprising a variety of cultural and religious influences. Today Pennsylvania Dutch Country Magick has virtually disappeared, with few remaining to tell the real story of life in early America. Now, the history and growth of this tradition is brought to life in *HexCraft*. *HexCraft* revives the chants, charms, spells, and healing methods of a vital heritage that offered New World inhabitants spiritual respite, magical living, and political cover from reigning puritanical forces. "Pow-Wow" as it is also known, became a potpourri of traditions, practiced in as many diverse ways as there were people.

Through the vivid examples and rare testimonials from those connected to Pow-Wow, you can see first-hand how to bring this Earth-honoring culture to life for spiritual growth and practical gains.

HexCraft presents Pow-Wow's simple nature and easy implementation without a set platform. Individual interpretation and use is encouraged in this fascinating exploration of a 300-year-old folk tradition. More than a text book on magick or history, *HexCraft* will engage anyone interested in Early America, magick, spirituality, or freedom of speech!

About the Author

Silver RavenWolf is the Director of the Wiccan/Pagan Press Alliance, a network of Pagan newsletters, publishers, and writers. "It keeps me pretty busy," she explains, "but I adore it. Writing and publishing are important to the Pagan community. The editors supply the life line for growth, change, and acceptance of magickal people. Positive religions like Wicca are the heartbeat, but the editors are the arteries of the community."

Currently Silver works for a local newspaper and is active in her home town. She has been involved in various aspects of the Craft for twenty years. In November of 1991, she received her First Degree from Breid Foxsong of Sacred Hart and is on the rolls of the International Red Garters. Her Second and Third Degree initiations were conferred by Lord Serphant of the Serphant Stone Family and Lord Ariel of the Caledonii Tradition. Silver is now an Elder of the Family of Serphant Stone and the Clan Head of the Black Forest Tradition, which encompasses three states.

Silver teaches the magickal arts on a one-to-one basis in her home and provides group seminars during the summer months. Her open circle, Sisters of the Cauldron, works on healing requests from individuals all over the country.

Born on September 11, 1956, Silver is a true Virgo; she adores making lists and arranging things in order. She emphatically tells us that Virgos do not like housecleaning or laundry. Definitely a lady of the nineties, she's hard to pin down. "I spend a great deal of time with my four children," she says. "They come first in my life. Everyone else has to take a number and get in line after that."

To Write to the Author

If you wish to contact the author or would like more information about this book, please write to the author in care of Llewellyn Worldwide, and we will forward your request. Both the author and the publisher appreciate hearing from you and learning of your enjoyment of this book and how it has helped you. Llewellyn Worldwide cannot guarantee that every letter written to the author can be answered, but all will be forwarded. Please write to:

Silver RavenWolf
℅ Llewellyn Worldwide
P.O. Box 64383, Dept. K723-4,
St. Paul, MN 55164-0383, U.S.A.

Please enclose a self-addressed, stamped envelope or $1.00 to cover costs.
If outside the U.S.A., enclose international postal reply coupon.

Llewellyn's Practical Magick Series

HexCraft

Dutch Country Magick

Silver RavenWolf

1997
Llewellyn Publications
St. Paul, MN 55164-0383, U.S.A.

FIRST EDITION
First Printing, 1995
Second Printing, 1995
FIRST EDITION, REVISED
Second Printing, 1997

Hex symbols on back cover ©copyright Jacob Zook's Hex Shops, Inc., Paradise, PA.

Cover design: Anne Marie Garrison
Illustrations: Silver RavenWolf; hex symbols in Chapter 15 courtesy of Jacob
    Zook's Hex Shops, Inc., Paradise, PA
Book design and layout: Jessica Thoreson

Library of Congress Cataloging-in-Publication Data
    RavenWolf, Silver, 1956-
            HexCraft: Dutch country magick / Silver
            RavenWolf. -- 1st ed.
                p.   cm. -- (Llewellyn's practical magick series)
            Includes bibliographical references and index.
            ISBN 1-56718-723-4 (pbk. : alk. paper)
            1. Magic--Pennsylvania. 2. Pennsylvania Dutch--Religion.
            3. Pennsylvania--Religious life and customs. 4. Folklore--
            Pennsylvania. 1. Title. II. Series.
        BF1622.U6W65   1995
        133.4'3'09748--dc20   95-2100
                                                                                 CIP

Printed in the United States of America

Llewellyn Publications
A Division of Llewellyn Worldwide, Ltd.
P.O. Box 64383, St. Paul, MN 55164-0383

About Llewellyn's Practical Magick Series

To some people, the idea that "Magick" is practical comes as a surprise.

It shouldn't. The entire basis for Magick is to exercise influence over one's environment. Magick is an interactive process of spiritual growth and psychological transformation. Even so, the spiritual life rests firmly on material foundations. Magick is a way of life and must be lived, not just talked about, and that includes experiencing the wonders, pleasures and pains of material existence.

The material world and the spiritual are intertwined and it is this very interconnectedness that provides the Magickal Link, the magickal means for the spirit to influence the material, and vice versa.

Magick can be used in one's daily life for better living and in opening the doors to new worlds of Mind and Spirit. Each of us has been given Mind and Body, and it is our spiritual opportunity to make full use of these wonderful gifts. Mind and Body work together, and Magick is simply the extension of this interaction into dimensions beyond the limits normally perceived. That's why we commonly talk of the "supernormal" in connection with the domain of Magick.

The Body is alive, and all Life is an expression of the Divine. There is spiritual, Magickal power in the Body and in the Earth, just as there is in Mind and Spirit. With Love and Will, we use Mind to link these aspects of Divinity together to bring about change. We add to the beauty of it all—for to work Magick we must work in concert with the Laws of Nature and of the Psyche. *Magick is the flowering of our Human Potential.*

Practical Magick is concerned with the Craft of living well, in harmony with the cycles of Nature and the seasons of the Earth. We increase the flow of Divinity in our lives, and in the world around us, through the things we make with hand and mind. All our acts of Will and desire are magickal acts.

*Hear ye children, the instruction of a mother,
and attend to know understanding ...*

May we always walk together

ANGELIQUE

FALYNN

NICKOLAS

JAMIESON

Acknowledgements

When you finish writing a book there is a sense of relief, a niggling worry that you may have forgotten something, and pride in having completed a project that you hope will help to make the world a better place.

As I stacked the manuscript pages neatly in the center of my desk and carefully laid the title page at the very top, I thought back over the two years that it took me to complete the research and writing of a very favorite project and the many people who helped me bring the information into form.

"That is what a great deal of life is about," I thought to myself. "Sharing, learning, and giving—helping those in trouble, or simply taking the time to listen."

I'd like to take a moment to thank my husband of 14 years for putting up with a wife who has been either glued to her computer, involved with the kids, or taking care of strangers. Thanks for giving me the space to be me. I realize it was a long, hard battle for both of us, but in the end, I think each of us learned what marriage is really all about—and how to keep it fresh, loving, and survivable.

There were many people who contributed information, including Preston Zerbe, my Pow-Wow teacher; MaraKay Rogers, a good friend and wise counsel on the issues of ceremonial magick and life in general; Jean Kitzig, who listened to me fuss, fume, and complain when I thought I'd never get any information out of anyone; Wilma Clark, also a student of Preston Zerbe and an individual who offered to validate the information that Preston Zerbe did indeed teach me the art of Pow-Wow; and all those people over the age of 65 at the Dillsburg and York Springs senior citizen centers.

Yvonne J. Milspaw, Ph.D., Folklorist, also contributed to this manuscript in several ways. I have never met the woman in person, but through information she gathered for local seminars, her enthusiasm for the subject, and her kind review of the material, I was able to correct errors in historical sequence.

Special thanks to Trollwise Press, P.O. Box 080437, Staten Island, New York, 10308-0005, for all their research and the use of some of their material. Contact them for a compendium of Heathen information. Please use a legal-sized self-addressed, stamped envelope to ensure a reply.

I would also like to thank Nancy Mostad and Jessica Thoreson at Llewellyn Publications for their faith, guidance, support, and excellent work. I couldn't have made it without these special ladies. They are truly talented and unique. A special thanks, too, to Donald Tyson—I couldn't have done it without ya!

Other Books by the Author

To Ride a Silver Broomstick
Beneath a Mountain Moon (fiction)

Forthcoming

To Stir a Magick Cauldron

Table of Contents

Witches' Lucky Stars Hex Symbol
Designed by Silver RavenWolf

Preface

She rises at 6:45 AM and plans to get her children off to school with as little fuss as possible. Before breakfast is over and the last child speeds through the door, she has settled five squabbles, found a missing shoe, pulled a wad of bubble gum out of the six-year-old's hair, and answered three phone calls from grown-up people who need her help.

It's going to be another busy day. She had hoped to do a little shopping and go to the bank and maybe enjoy the sun a bit this morning, but it isn't likely. She should have listened to the lark on the patio. Three cries meant three visitors before noon. Well, so be it. After all, she is a modern Pow-Wow artist and there is no such thing as a smooth, quiet, normal day.

Past the noon hour the first student arrives for individual instruction. The Pow-Wow is a little tired from the healings she performed in the morning, but she has learned to relax, ground, and center herself. Her day catapults forward by answering questions and teaching her art. Occasionally she glances out the picture window in the living room. The day is brilliant and fresh, but immediately her mind snaps back to the tasks at hand.

As student number four bids farewell from the front porch, the school bus rumbles up through town. The kids are home and there are experiences to share, homework to oversee, and of course, dinner to make. The oldest has to go to Girl Scouts, the ten-year-old needs help with her social studies homework, the eight-year-old stopped up the toilet, and the little guy is in a spring concert and can't find matching socks.

The phone rings again. Her answering machine has registered 15 calls during the afternoon lessons. Sally wants to know how to keep that strange man from bothering her. Lisa is interested in bringing a friend over for a reading. Martha has a bad case of the flu; would she mind "trying" for her long-distance? Tony says he can't sleep; is there anything he can do so he doesn't have to take over-the-counter drugs? A new woman wants to learn how to do Pow-Wow; can she start right away? Her mother lost her glasses; could she use her knife to figure out where on earth they went? And so on.

She copies each message down carefully and separates them. Some go into the mesh basket over her altar in the dining room. Those requests will be worked on by her circle of friends who join with her every Thursday night to help those in need through prayer and magickal workings. Others she calls back, listens patiently, and deftly steers the callers toward the information they need. Her date book is always handy; she sets up appointments for the week for those in need.

She has regular calls, too, and more often than not, she finds herself pushing them aside to make room for the needs of total strangers. In fact, she muses, she's lost quite a few friends because of her lack of time for them over the past several years. There is a small sense of loss, but a bigger knowledge of pride in doing something worthwhile with her time. The television and telephone no longer are vehicles of idle time in her life.

Between dinner and Scouts she "tries" for the mailman down the block—it's his legs again. Why don't they buy him a moped or something? Between Scouts and the spring concert, a lady with an earache is on the agenda. Maybe tomorrow she'll get to the bank and the store … and go for a walk, if the weather holds.

After the concert, with all the kids tucked in bed, the phone rings again.

"Let the machine take it," says her husband. "You've had a long day."

The Pow-Wow smiles thinly, lines of age pronounced with fatigue. Her eyelids are heavy but her heart is light. She reaches over and picks up the receiver.

"Yes, tomorrow at 8:00 AM will be fine …"

Introduction

You teach best what you most need to learn.
—Richard Bach,
Illusions

The word "Pow-Wow" normally sparks thoughts of the familiar scene of a group of Native Americans sitting in a circle around a bright campfire. Perhaps Pow-Wow reminds you of a recent visit to a modern Native American gathering at a fairground or reservation. Your mind may conjure up scenes of strong warriors, beautiful landscapes, and vibrant American history. The word "Pow-Wow" does not normally tweak the imagination with the vision of a Pennsylvania Dutch person practicing faith healing. Especially not one who is into casting a magick circle, healing the sick, or dealing politely, but firmly, with a nosey neighbor.

You will now journey into a unique, almost defunct magickal system whose roots lie in south-central Pennsylvania. Pow-Wow is the oldest of the American magickal systems created by the European settlers. It stems from Pagan Witchcraft (commonly called the Old Religion) melded with Native American magicks. Oh, and let's not forget the dash of ceremonial practices dating back to the time of King Solomon that manages to float mysteriously between the two. The Pow-Wow system is part of the scientific aspects of the lost Old Religion. It is the root of American Witchcraft.

The Old Religion, or Witchcraft, is not evil in nature, practice, or design. It is a peaceful faith that celebrates all life on the planet and seeks to find enlightenment in universal love and peace. I ought to know; I am a practicing Witch. Throughout this book the religion of Witchcraft is often mentioned. Witches do not believe in Satan or condone violence or crime.

Thanks to a lot of bad press that has no basis in truth, Witches are often shunned by other religious bodies. Sometimes the Old Religion is called Wicca, meaning "craft of the wise." It is both a science and religion that uses elemental forces in harmony with belief in the Divine. Witches are monotheistic. This means they believe in a central, positive power source or energy. This single power source is divided into male and female archetypes, equal to each other. Real Witches are not involved with calling demons, killing animals, or other such nonsense. They are very enlightened and powerful people. They seek healing and harmony for every person in the world, regardless of their religious or political beliefs. You may be surprised to know that there are over three-quarters of a million magickal people in the United States, and this number represents a low estimate. More and more people are turning to alternative religious practices to find God/dess.

Unlike Witchcraft, which is experiencing its own rebirth, Pow-Wow is in the death rattle stage. Pow-Wow is the vestige of a lost religion. It is a healing art. It is a cunning man or wise woman. It is a magickal charm. It is Native American magick. It is a magickal system (no longer a religion) surrounded by a thick fog of mystery. Few practicing Pow-Wow artists of today will speak with the press. Their clients (those who they help) keep their existence very quiet. This is difficult to imagine due to the information age in which we live. Current Pow-Wow artists do not like to admit they are practicing Witchcraft techniques. Preston Zerbe, my teacher, believed he practiced on religious faith alone. He openly admitted he had no idea where many of the chants he used originally came from. His teacher taught them to him, they worked, and that was enough for him. To people like Preston, practicing magick is an unbelievable (and perhaps irreligious) idea. These people don't want to admit the true basis of what they are doing because they are afraid. They should not be. Life is magick. People are magick. Religion, if supporting positive actions, is magick. The art and science of magick is not evil or nasty. Magick is simply a force that is devoid of positive or negative connotations. It is how you use it, like fire or a knife, that designates the ultimate outcome as good or evil.

There is much discussion on the practice of magick these days in the Neo-Pagan and magickal communities in reference to what is ethical and what is not. Arguments of ethics are exactly why Pow-Wows don't normally admit they are practicing magick. To them, the practice of Witchcraft (and magick) is unethical. This view rises from their misunderstanding of the subject. There is nothing to fear in the archetypes of the God and Goddess—they will not whisk you away into the night. They have no desire to work with evil. It is amusing that those who practice Pow-Wow refuse to see the magick in what they are doing.

Introduction

Here is an example of an ethical argument for you. There are those individuals who feel that turning back any negative energy sent to you is wrong. Personally, I don't agree with this line of thought. However, I do not recommend using the art of Pow-Wow for negative purposes. It is better to search for a positive solution to a problem rather than throw bigger rocks at it and most likely create a larger problem.

Being a Virgo, my key words are "I analyze," and that is exactly what this book will do. Together we will analyze the history, strength, and passing of a magickal system. You will learn how to use it with positive results. We have all heard the saying "You learn by your mistakes," and it is true here as well. Major errors both in judgement and practice were made during the evolution of the system. These errors caused a backlash from which Pow-Wow may not recover. By acknowledging and studying these mistakes and the fallacies of thought they created, the Neo-Pagan population of today can benefit immensely. Pow-Wow doesn't have to die out completely. It can be reborn through the practices of its individual students. If you use the spells and rituals given, no matter what your choice of religion, you will be perpetuating the existence of this art. If you choose to relink Pow-Wow to the Old Religion, you will be practicing the roots of American Witchcraft.

Some areas of this text present theory; you are welcome to investigate and study the circumstances and history given. I encourage you to draw your own conclusions. By no means is my work the last word on the subject. Perhaps it will serve as an awakening, a catalyst for you to delve into your own family or cultural history. You may be pleasantly surprised—there might be magick hidden there.

The hands-on information of this text encompasses all religions. Most practicing Pow-Wow artists of today use Christianity as their religious base, but a growing number here in York and Cumberland Counties of Pennsylvania are again merging the practice with the Old Religion. Because religion is an item of choice and not all individuals practice the same beliefs, the charms and spells are presented for both mainstream and alternative religions. In the end, the source of Divinity is the same.

Everyone has a personal quest. My goal is to bring the techniques of Pow-Wow to as many people as I possibly can. I want to uncover and expose American Witchcraft for everyone to enjoy. I want to remove the fear, to smash the misinformation, to bring the God/Goddess into the Light, where they belong. It is my deepest desire to wake up the people of this country. They need to be shown that the Craft is not filled with a bunch of cult worshippers who spread mayhem and chaos wherever we walk. We don't want to steal your souls or eat your babies. We are not interested in your Satan (we don't even believe in him). In essence, we are sick of hocus-pocus accusations. It is time to set the record straight on both the Old Religion and Pennsylvania Dutch Country magick.

When I was 11 years old, my grandfather, Samuel Cornelius Baker, told me that my great-great-grandmother was a Pow-Wow artist. I have never forgotten the hot July afternoon when I peddled my bike to his home for iced tea and cookies. It was a favorite pit stop while I waited until the American Legion pool down the street opened its doors. My grandfather was 80 years old then (he lived to be 100), and I was proud that he could still take care of himself at the family homestead. We sat in his parlor—he in his rocking chair, me cross-legged on the floor. Together we sipped honey and lemon tea that only he knew how to make. I don't recall how we got on the subject of Pow-Wow. Perhaps I had asked about the braided rug that was digging into my swimsuit. This would lead into the subject of my grandmother, Lottie Knaub. She made the rug when my father was small. Then off we would go on a discussion of my paternal grandmother and her Pennsylvania Dutch background.

Lottie's life story is a sad one. When she was born, her mother died due to complications in childbirth. There was a midwife and a Pow-Wow present. The death of his wife caused a hatred so severe in Lottie's father that he couldn't wait to get Lottie out of his house, and from that day forward he plotted and planned how he could remove the child from his sight. For the entire family, all discussion of Pow-Wow and folk magick in general was banned from the home. I know that when Lottie entered school she could not speak English, only Pennsylvania Dutch, and that her childhood was a miserable affair. It is not an accident, I think, that when she turned 16, she met my grandfather and made plans to marry as soon as possible. Perhaps to force the issue—or if we are more romantically inclined, to cement her relationship with my grandfather—she became pregnant before she actually married him. Although they lived a long and happy life together, their road was filled with poverty. Many years later, when her youngest son was dying of cancer, Lottie sought assistance from a local Pow-Wow artist. It was her last resort. As was the case with Lottie's mother, the Pow-Wow artist was consulted too late. Her son died pitifully and her entire family, as well as the neighborhood, made fun of her for "such silliness."

Whatever the impetus of the conversation, Grandfather Baker looked me right in the eye and said, "You know, Pow-Wow runs in our family." At the time, I didn't know what the practice of Pow-Wow entailed. I asked him to be more specific. "They are healers," he replied simply. "Do you want more tea?"

It was getting late and I wanted to get to the pool to be with my friends. I also didn't want to embarrass him by refusing another cookie. He had made them that morning just for me. He often got the baking ingredients mixed up. As a result, I could find myself in the bathroom for the remainder of the day if I wasn't careful. He had a penchant for using heaping spoonfuls of baking soda in the cookie batter.

"Ah, well, so who was the Pow-Wow?" I finally asked.

"Well, it wasn't your grandmother's mother, it was her mother's mother."

"You mean," I said, thinking hard as my mother had schooled me closely on all this family stuff, including the once-removed bit, "that it was my great-great-grandmother?"

"Right. Would you like another cookie?"

Uh-oh.

"No thanks, Grandpa, I really have to go. My friends are waiting for me at the pool," I said hastily. I gathered up my swimming gear and headed toward the kitchen to put away my glass.

"Well," said Grandpa, "There is one thing you should know. It skips every generation."

"What skips?" I called from the kitchen.

"Pow-Wow," he replied.

I wondered at the time how Pow-Wow could skip a generation. Did it use jump ropes? My education on genetics wouldn't catch up with me until high school. That would be the same year I would enter the realm of the occult.

Much to my dismay, my grandfather never told anyone else about the Pow-Wow connection in my family. He did mention Pow-Wows often in later conversations, especially when relating memories of Dillsburg, Franklintown, and Churchtown, and the people who resided there. As I think about it now, it must be very sad to know you have outlived everyone you ever knew in the first half of your lifetime. Unfortunately, his memory was not the greatest. Most of the statements he made were vague, with only a few comments of clarity imbedded in his winding conversation. My living relatives today (save for my father) feign total ignorance on the subject. The few written occult records that existed were burned in a large backyard bonfire by my great-aunt before I was born. She was purported to have said, "There! It is done! There will be no more of this nonsense in this family. I have finished it."

I later found that burnings like this one were a usual practice in many farm communities on the eastern seaboard. Diane McDonough, a friend of mine living in Newville, Pennsylvania, has family in both New York and Pennsylvania. She supports this statement. "Oh yes, it was a very well known practice to burn the personal effects of the deceased, especially if they were not sure what the person died of or knew it to be TB or influenza. They would even burn the bed! My family burned all of my great-grandmother's possessions. They incinerated everything except the bell in the barn."

Many of the senior citizens I interviewed agreed with Diane. Burning was a common practice. In fact, our town still allows its residents to burn garbage on Wednesdays and Saturdays. You can fire up anything but toxics and tires. Personal possessions, records, journals, diaries that carry family secrets, you name it, are still thrown on the pile. My next-door neighbor, Jean Kitzig, decided to dig a garden a few years ago and found one of these old burn piles. We marveled over the odd bottles and other bits she unearthed.

Whether or not Pow-Wow is in my personal lineage, the thought instilled enough curiosity in me to begin my investigation into the art. During my research, I travelled all over the Pennsylvania countryside. I unearthed a treasure chest of information from individuals who frequent the senior citizen centers. It was through these gracious people that I pieced together much of the information presented here. I was able to verify many aspects of what was practiced in the realm of Dutch Country magick. Society overlooks much knowledge because it fails to respect the contributions of our senior citizen population. We push them aside. We are often too busy and we feel they don't understand us. When we look at an older face we foolishly see only the surface. We forget that the golden key to knowledge may be lurking behind their eyes and not within some techno-type gadget. Enlightenment often emerges from common sense and human memory.

Of course, I have not forgotten that there are readers who are more academically inclined than myself. This text does not claim to present detailed historical data on the rise and fall of the Pow-Wow Tradition, nor do I claim scholarship in this arena. To be fair to the subject in a historical sense it would be necessary to write a book on the historical aspects alone. This book, however, is designed to give you a feel for what you will be working with, nothing more.

Normally, because of the view of the word "tradition" in magical circles, I would hesitate to label the Pow-Wow system in such a manner. However, in this area of the country, Pow-Wow is viewed as a traditional practice, and called such by local historians and scholars.

Therefore, this book is dedicated not only to my children (who are learning the practice of Pow-Wow), but to my grandfather, Samuel C. Baker, as well and my Pow-Wow teacher, Preston Zerbe (who passed away at the age of 86, during the writing of this book). I would also like to acknowledge a special group of people—the over-65 crowd of the Dillsburg Senior Citizen Center, without whom this book would contain far less color and enthusiasm.

The Rebirth of Pow-Wow

This book is designed and tested for use in all religions and magickal communities. Your chosen divinity can be Wiccan, Christian, Druid, Native American, it doesn't matter. Many of the spells and charms give you the choice of which divinity you would like to use. If only one divinity is listed, don't have heart failure. Substitute the one you are comfortable with. If you like Jesus, then by all means, use Him. If you prefer the Goddess, substitute Her name, etc. The system will work as long as your belief is strong.

When I began teaching Pow-Wow to both my Wiccan and Christian students, we constantly ran experiments. We named various deities at the end of the chants. We invoked various archetypes. Yes indeed, we even learned to mix them effectively. We found that the system worked regardless of the positive divinity employed. The healing magicks contained in this work are designed for use by both adults and children. Jean Kitzig's 10-year-old daughter relieved her of a pounding headache within minutes of learning the Dragon chant. My eldest daughter, Angelique, has often employed the art, though she has some difficulties with the burn chants. She needs to reduce her own fear of looking at a burn to become more successful.

Some current Pow-Wow artists of the area will look at this book and say that this really isn't Pow-Wow because it is not exactly the way they practice. Historians may feel it is not legitimate because the material is not strictly geared to the Christian religious base. Pow-Wow techniques, as you have learned, are as varied as the people who use them. The information here is a collection of various eclectic uses of the system. I have not presented data from any particular teacher as the whole. This is both out of respect for those who have assisted me and to provide the reader/practitioner with a compendium of information from which to draw.

For over 200 years the local public has assumed that Pow-Wow is a Christian practice. In fact, we have now learned that the Christian overtones were added for the survival of the system. Christianity, though an acceptable religion to many, was not responsible for the birth of the Pow-Wow system; it was directly responsible for its secrecy, changes, and continuance.

I have gathered material that will teach you the techniques to stop blood, return stolen property, and heal burns. Some of the charms and spells are whimsical in nature, while others are adamantly serious. Never should any of this information be substituted for professional medical care. The author recommends seeking the advice of a physician on specific medical ailments in conjunction with the use of Pow-Wow techniques where issues of human or animal health are involved.

By using Pow-Wow practices, you will assist in prolonging the magickal life of the system. The author will be delighted to hear how the reader uses this information and is interested in both your successes and failures. No particular system works 100 percent of the time. If a charm, spell, or healing fails, look again at the issues of need, focus, and belief as well as your physical health. Any of these factors can result in an occasional failure or two. We all have them and they are nothing of which to be ashamed. One also must remember that magick follows the path of least resistance and not to count out coincidences. Finally, many situations are a part of destiny. Perhaps the failure occurred for your spiritual growth or for the growth of the individual for whom you are working.

After all, even the Pow-Wows themselves called it the art of "trying."

Good luck and bright blessings,
SILVER RAVENWOLF
aka Jenine E. Trayer
31 October 1993

Old World History

A Little Taste of "Once Upon a Time"

History is not boring if you can relive it. The idea of reliving it is to learn something by it. By looking at how things were, you can figure out why things are. In the 1990s there is a penchant for reclaiming what was, dusting it off, cleaning it out, and using it again to serve a useful purpose or idea. Using historical reference as building blocks, we are going to pull the practice of Pow-Wow out of moth balls, check it for holes, and patch it back together again. We will plow through the myths and history to unearth both the religion and the magick. Thanks to our efforts, living people and living history will reap the benefits of a revitalized magickal system. It looks like we are going to be doing a lot of work, doesn't it? I cannot blow life back into the system of Pow-Wow by myself, but we can do it together.

For you to take full advantage of the Pow-Wow system, it is necessary to relive a little history. This history will give you a foundation from which your magickal works will spring. I am not kidding—Pow-Wow is powerful stuff. I do not care if you are eight or eighty, Pow-Wow offers the opportunity for limitless change and empowerment. History isn't so bad if you face it with a fresh and open mind. For instance, let's pick an interesting time in American history. The Battle of Gettysburg will do as an example. It is July. The year is 1863. At this point the information you have is rather oblique. It is another piece of historical trivia to you. Should I test you on the subject two weeks from now, you may not remember anything about it. I did not give you any concrete (living) images to pull you into that setting and hold it in your head.

To live history, the scene needs to appear vividly in your mind. Likewise, to perform Pow-Wow (or any magick, for that matter), you must have the ability to let go and invent mental images as clearly as you see reality.

Visualize yourself on the battlefield at Gettysburg. You are wearing a wool uniform. The most welcome gift someone could give you is some corn starch. The heat of the day is enough to melt both human flesh and spirit. Although it is the Fourth of July, the furthest thing from your mind is a holiday mood. Last night, the moon was full and red. Now intricate streams of blood flow at your feet, soaking into the parched earth, feeding the broken fields of corn. Your ears vibrate with the whirring sound of cicadas and the screams of the dying. The hiss of bullets is but a recent memory, still ringing somewhere in your brain. Detached, you watch unskilled surgeons casually throw body parts out the window of the medical house. The bile rises with every beat of your heart and every sour breath you inhale.

You made a shocking discovery at the start of the day. Local residents set up a picnic on a nearby hill. They brought their parasols, blankets, and lunches. The battle of the day was to be their entertainment. You cruelly hope they had their fill. With sweaty fingers you dig in your pants pocket. Your clothing, spattered with dirt and blood, makes your pocket cling to your skin. After a moment of irritation, your fingers close over a familiar object. The conjuring bag your mother, a Pow-Wow, made for you is firmly in your grasp. Designed to protect you from the physical missiles of war, it does little for your torn mind. The battle over, your body is whole. For now, you stand in safety. You wish your mind would not insist on playing back the battle. You wish your mother could be with you—not for yourself, but for the thousands of wounded around you. She could have helped some of them. What was that charm for stopping blood? If only you could remember the right words, you know you could find the courage to walk among those in need. At this point, there isn't much you haven't seen.

You watch with horror as the vultures descend upon the dead and dying. One hundred and thirty years later a park ranger will stand in this very spot, wiping his brow as you do now. He will have a clean handkerchief from K-mart; you simply use your woolen sleeve. Before him will be sweating, camera-laden tourists. They see only rolling hills of grass and stone monuments where you see death. Their voices will drone through the heat of the day. They chatter about where they will eat supper. You can't possibly consider the intake of food. The ranger explains to the tourists that the vultures still return to the battlefield year after year, an instinct born of the carnage you now sadly view. Storytellers will gather all who will listen around summer campfires and relate the tales of the ghosts who walk the battlefield. Thanks to the magick your mother performed in her Pennsylvania kitchen, yours will not be one of them.

Living history reminds us that real people lived "way back when" with real and imagined problems, heartaches, and triumphs, just like today. Take your family as an example. You most likely know about your grandparents and how they spent their lives. This information has either come directly from them or through stories told by your parents (called second-hand information). You also have a good idea of how your parents have lived and what they have done. Although you were not alive 60 years ago, you still understand the living conditions of your grandparents or parents. You are familiar with the politics of the times, the state of health care, the popular music, food, entertainment, etc. You have a compendium of family anecdotes. Great Aunt Mary Lou gave birth to two sets of twins. Cousin George worked for the railroad all his life. Uncle Homer ran a farm in West Virginia. You can remember wonderful summer visits there before the farm was sold to a land developer.

You also know about the tragedies in your family. Perhaps Grandfather Howard, a coal miner, passed away of black lung disease before your birth. Though most of the family will not admit it, rumor has it that your great-aunt Sally committed suicide. She was only 22. Who knows what impetus spawned the tragedy? Family skeletons lurk everywhere if you know where to look. Your personal family history is your lineage. Your lineage and general historical information work together to bring an understanding of your past and influence your plans for the future. Your family history and the social circumstances in which you now live affect your life and color your views on society. This history sways many decisions you make without your conscious mind thinking twice about it.

The system of Pow-Wow also carries its own lineage, constantly affected by social circumstances. To tap into this lineage is to tap into raw power. We must examine historic events in the Old World (Europe) to understand the lineage and turbulent evolution of Pow-Wow. In seeking this lineage, we need to peer through historical cobwebs and actively live the past.

The Penn is Mightier than the Sword

Present-day Pennsylvania is an unusual state. As it was founded on freedom of religion, one does not need to charter a church here as in other states. There are no piles of papers, incorporation headaches, and no religious council to legitimize a faith. Call yourself a church, and legally, you are a church. William Penn, the founder of Pennsylvania, is the culprit of such magnanimous religous freedom. Without his beliefs and dreams, Pow-Wow would not have become an integral part of American history. William Penn must have been an odd duck in the flock of Puritan geese. I don't know about you, but I was very curious why, when everyone else in Europe did their best to be prim and proper, William turned out differently. In essence, he designed a safe haven for magickal people—the state of Pennsylvania. Why would he want a place where every man and woman could be free to practice religion without persecution? What led him to proclaim the fertile soil of Pennsylvania "the foundation of a free colony for all mankind"? To be forthright with you, had William Penn not created Pennsylvania, most of the family magickal traditions in the United States today would not exist. Many of these current traditions came in through Pennsylvania, moved up and down the wilds of the Appalachain Trail, then fanned out across America as she grew and prospered.

William Penn was born in London in 1644 to affluent parents. (Affluent here meaning upper middle-class.) Penn received his education in well-to-do schools, spending his adolescent years in Ireland. Christ Church College threw him out 1662 for his religious non-conformity. (Like him already, don't you?) Penn's father constantly fretted over him. Though the senior Penn was an important individual at the English court, political accidents could and did happen. Religious non-conformity was a risky business in those days. Hoping that his son would begin to think like everyone else, he sent William on a grand tour of Europe. At universities in France and Italy, young Penn immersed himself in scholarly studies. He returned highly educated, but continued to hold his odd ideas about freedom of religion. The Puritan political state did not consider this line of thinking a point in his favor. Witch burnings in the 1600s were frequent. Obviously Penn had a bushel of guardian angels.

Penn's father was an admiral and highly regarded in the political structure of England. He was privy to state information. You can imagine him wringing his silk tails every time William got on the freedom of religion kick. I'm sure he sent many prayers to the Almighty that William would be like everybody else. After all, being different meant being dead—not especially the type of "being-ness" humans want to get caught in.

With the knowledge you carry of your lineage and the society in which it evolved, consider what William Penn must have learned on his travels. Think of the tales he would gather, both delightful and monsterous. If he did not see the slaughter of innocent people, he couldn't miss hearing about it. That kind of gossip moves like lightning, whether it is the sixteenth century or the twentieth.

Although many historical sources portray William Penn as a poor Quaker, this is incorrect, nor was his intelligence in the country bumpkin category. Highly educated, he wrote copiously and spoke with eloquence. Penn often won his legal cases. Studying legalities means extensive research. Therefore, it is clear through the documentation on his own freedom of speech case (which he argued for himself in England and won), that he had examined material on similar historical cases—namely Witch Trials.

There's Nothing Worse than Bad Clergy

William Penn was born during the heat of religious persecution in England. He grew up in an age in which stoning children for lying was a normal procedure. It was believed that a woman did not have a soul; her main role entailed subservience to men. None of this sat very well with William, nor with his free-thinking friends. Everywhere he turned he saw murder, hatred, and intrigue. Are you jealous of your neighbor because everyone likes her and she gives herbs to get rid of your cold? Tell the authorities she practices Witchcraft. Did the baker's daughter turn down your bawdy advances? Tell the authorities she sold her soul to the devil and bewitched you. If you cannot abide your wife's sharp tongue, accuse her of dancing naked in the moonlight. Careful, though, they may whisk away your children. On to the burning pyre they would go. With your property condemned, the church would confiscate it and all your personal possessions. In essence, Europe was not burning real Witches (usually), it was practicing genocide. Both the clergy and the politicians approved of this wonderful money-making venture.

In 1667, at age twenty-three, Penn went to Ireland to manage his father's estates. The murder of two covens of thirteen Witches three years earlier (that we can only assume were the real thing) was still considered hot news. These unfortunate magickal people resided in Somerset. With this information available, Penn was well aware of the penalty for free thinking that befell the Somerset Witches.

William Penn, a renegade by nature, sought conversions to the Quaker message despite the bad press it generated. This organization was named the Society of Friends. The Puritans despised the Quaker theology of freedom and considered them as bad, if not worse, than individuals who practiced the Old Religion (Witchcraft). Other religious sects found the Society of Friends laughable. The word "Quakers" was adopted as the adherents of this religion "quaked before the Lord." Imagine Penn's father, thoroughly embarrassed because his son was tied up in a cult of quaking men and women. It was an eye-roller for the poor fellow, to be sure.

As a result, Penn's father threatened to disinherit him. Leaving this mentality behind, Penn put his education to work by attacking the religious and political system of the times. He made it a point to distribute his writing to the cliques where it would hurt the most. They were not amused and ordered him imprisoned for a year in the Tower of London. Upon his release, he campaigned hard for the right to trial by a free and uncoerced jury of his peers. In 1670 he was arrested again; during this trial, he skillfully exposed the unconstitutionality of the proceedings and convinced the jury to withstand the pressure of the judges who wanted to put him away for good. His father died during that same year, leaving Penn the heir to estates in England and Ireland, as well as his father's standing at court. Penn married Gulielma Maria Springett, a famous writer of Quaker mystical tracts.

King Charles II was now in power and he owed Penn a favor. It was repaid by granting Penn a large tract of land in the New World. Giving up on obtaining religious tolerance in Europe, Penn decided his "holy experiment" (a utopia of religious freedom) could only survive in the New World. It was time to turn away from a 600-year history of burning people. He had no reason to believe they would suddenly stop and declare the party over. In 1681, Penn became the proud owner of Pennsylvania (named dutifully for his father; the name means "Penn's Woods").

What Penn Left Behind

In Europe, surprisingly enough, the Witch trials did die down. Commerce among all but the very rich had suffered severely, crippled almost beyond recovery. There simply were too many persecutions and too few survivors left to tell about them. Accusations sidled close to people in power, giving incentive to put on the brakes. Male physicians of the time had eradicated their competition, the female healers. It was time for the doctors to cease their sneaky activities before they suffered the same fate as the wise women. Between 1700 and 1900, there are few female physicans mentioned in historical records.

The church activated the Witch craze to gain control over the population and destroy the Old Religion in the twelfth and thirteenth centuries. It progressed into a tool to eradicate any undesirables, whether in religion, family, or business. It ceased in England in 1736, when the statutes were repealed. Penn's personal involvement with the practice of Witchcraft is not the point. He saw the injustices done to the general population. He recognized an evil tool used by those in power, or by those who wished to gain it. Unlike many of his dandy peers, he chose to do something about it. However, I firmly believe that Penn knew he was inviting Witches when he encouraged people from up and down the Rhine to move to Pennsylvania.

The Rhine area was steeped in magick and mysticism, and the people had not progressed much further than their ancestral tribes in many of the areas Penn cultivated. I also believe he specifically worded the laws for his new experiment to include Witches. Citizens of Pennsylvania live in the only state in the Union in which we do not have to fight with the state government to practice our religion of choice. We do, however, stub our toes on local organizations and other clergy. Penn saw the Burning for what it was—a way to eliminate any type of competition. Incensed and frightened at the evil in his human brethren, he sought to stop it. He was outraged that those who called themselves Christians hid their murderous actions behind the cloak of their religion. Were he alive today, he would probably be astounded that the religious structure he fought against actually continues to hide and perpetuate persecution. Then again, maybe he would not.

In 1683, Penn wrote a promotional tract. As a result, fifty ships dropped their anchors in the Delaware River. They discharged persecuted souls from England, Ireland, Wales, and the Rhineland (now Germany). In all, 2,500 people came to Philadelphia (which means "City of Brotherly Love") and occupied 350 houses. We know the Witches freely came to the New World through Penn's marketing strategy. The proof lies in the birth of Pow-Wow; it flourished only in the Pennsylvania German settlements.

The Greatest Illusion

The occupants of the Rhineland ships are important in the Pow-Wow lineage. The original language of these people was German. The first stop, Philadelphia, became a melting pot of nationalities. By 1760, Philadelphia was the largest city in the colonies. Visitors were impressed by its well-lit streets and fine appearance (for which we can thank Benjamin Franklin). It boasted the first library in the colonies, most of its streets were cobbled, and of course, there were printed fliers and other materials not found in many of the other colonies.

Many settlers left the city after a short acclimation period and travelled deeper into Pennsylvania with others of their own nationality. The Germans in particular settled in Lancaster, York, Lehigh, and Burks counties where Pow-Wow is still found today. Wave upon wave of German settlers hit the interior of Pennsylvania during the early 1700s, while the Scotch/Irish wave commenced around 1720. Interviews I conducted around the original settlements further solidified Pow-Wow's German roots. My own ancestry and parentage is German (now called Pennsylvania Dutch), mixed with a smattering of Native American, Welsh, and a little Scots.

To my knowledge, never in public has anyone indigenous to this area linked Pow-Wow to the Old Religion (that of the belief in the God and Goddess); rather, it is erroneously linked to a bogus type of perverted Witchcraft (which isn't really Witchcraft at all). I have researched newspaper articles, videotapes, and old books. I have spoken to hundreds of individuals who related Pow-Wow experiences. Many eagerly tell a tale from their own family history, but none of these sources showed bravery in openly admitting the link between Pow-Wow and the worship of the God and Goddess of the Old Religion. My conclusion is they haven't the vaguest idea what the religion of the Craft truly represented. You will find the word "occult" referenced occasionally, or the words "folk magic" connected with descriptions of the system, but never an attachment to the religion of the God and Goddess of the Craft. It is clear that the Old Religion split in half after it came to the New World. This divorce represented the birth pains of Pow-Wow and the cloaking of traditional family Witchcraft. Although the Pow-Wow techniques used in the last fifty years apply Christianity as a religious base, these same techniques are, without a doubt, also the building blocks of the Old Religion.

The Craft Travels
to the New World

Piecing together historical information with the ultimate goal of accuracy is tougher now than it was one hundred years ago. These days we realize that in any situation, history is a creative result of the victors, not the victims. Obtaining a balance of what really happened is not as simple as reading an account of a priest/historian. We still dance over twisted histories, whether they are being composed now or are hundreds of years old. Unfortunately, there is still an enormous amount of information not available to us, either because it was lost by accident or by design. The public views knowledge as a valuable asset. Withholding it is often a way of showing power. The argument for suppression centers on the fallacy that the general population cannot tolerate the truth, especially in the realm of the occult.

To make matters worse, most academics refuse to look at either the spiritual or magickal sides of any history and feel that only dates and dry accounts of events are necessary. Today we do have folklorists who strive to find the truth about systems such as Pow-Wow, but if they are not magically inclined or at least open-minded, they do no better service to the community than the priests who burned volumes of spiritual and magickal information throughout the history of Christianity.

Fear suppresses knowledge, especially if that knowledge is going to drastically change the political, economic, social, or religious structure of the times. The religion of Witchcraft linked to the magickal system of Pow-Wow could change the religious philosophies of many people. Like a domino effect, these changes would touch economic, social, and perhaps political views of the people. Pow-Wow allows us as individuals to take control of our own lives without harming other people. That, I suppose, makes us dangerous characters indeed!

That Old Tyme Religion

Fear continued to suppress and corrupt the Craft, even as she sailed to the New World. To get here, she had to wear a disguise; in this case, a cloak of a different religious color. We know that Witchcraft came with the Germans. They immigrated from the Black Forest (located around the German and Swiss border) and the Rhineland. They had to be very careful, even while crossing the Atlantic. On the high seas, Witches were often hung to prevent the crews from rebelling.

Although Witch trials in the New World were not the norm, they did exist. Everyone knows about the trials in Salem, but there were others. The state of Maryland (which borders Pennsylvania) has a total of five cases on record between the years of 1665 and 1712 in which individuals were charged with Witchcraft. The death sentence was actually carried out in only one case. However, one is too many when your survival is at stake.

There are two recorded Witch trials in Pennsylvania in the late 1600s. In *Colonial Records of the Pennsylvania Provincial Court, Volume 1,* you will find the story of Margaret Mattson and Yeshro Hendrickson. William Penn himself sat in judgement. The defendants were two Swedish women accused of practicing the Craft for evil purposes. Margaret lived on a large farm along Ridley Creek in Delaware County. Locally, she was known as the Witch of Ridley Creek. Margaret pled not guilty to charges which included the act of casting spells on small animals owned by Yeshro and other small misdeeds. Margaret claimed she could bewitch cattle but she did not have the power to take on an ox. Her own daughter gave testimony against her (what a nice kid). Margaret then denied the whole affair.

Among those present were William Penn, his attorney general, a petit jury of 12 members, and a grand jury of 21 members. The jury (of which those in absence were fined 40 shillings) brought in an interesting verdict. She was declared "guilty of having the common fame of a witch." She was not guilty "in the manner and form as she stands indicted." Both ladies were given a sentence of six months and released on their own recognizance.

A year after the Salem Witch Trials, Robert Roman and his two sons were accused by the Concord Monthly Meeting of Friends in Chichester of practicing astrology, clairvoyancy, and necromancy. The Quaker government tried to dissuade Roman from his evil ways, and even visited his home several times. Eventually, a grand inquest seized many of his books and gave them to the judge as evidence of the family's involvement with Witchcraft and necromancy. A trial ensued and the order of the court required Roman to pay five pounds for all the charges and not to practice any more mojo. He was to "behave himself well for the future."

If you cannot practice your religion out in the open and you do not want to give it up, what do you do with it? There are only three choices, and none of them are all that great. You can stick out your tongue and say, "I'm going to do it anyway." This will give you a four in five chance of surviving (as in the Maryland cases). Or you can say "I'll practice in secret," and risk exposure, moving you back into playing the odds again. Or you can endanger the integrity of your religion and change it to suit society. It saves your skin and hopefully allows your family to live in peace.

Here lies the first mystery. What happened to the Witchcraft family traditions (often called fam trads)? A family tradition is a combination of the Old Religion and magickal skills that is passed down through a family lineage. This lineage includes oral teachings, written histories, and other documents. Pennsylvania was one of the original thirteen colonies and has some of the oldest settlements recorded in the New World. We know the Swedish ladies mentioned earlier were running around claiming to be Witches. Therefore, where are these Pennsylvania family traditions today? Are they underground? Did they fizzle out? Were they incorporated into other religions?

Pennsylvania settlements grew at the end of the European "Burning Times." Persecuted people whose religions did not match those of their Puritan neighbors flocked to the New World. Individuals who had lost favor with someone of importance in the Old World also joined the exodus. If the German Witches had hoped for freedom of religion here, they were disappointed. To survive in the New World, they needed the support of the other colonists. The trial of the Swedish women proved that. The Puritans, who were unceremoniously kicked out of England because they were so hard-nosed in their religion, influenced the colonies as far south as Virginia. Their beliefs spelled disaster for those practicing the Craft. Puritanism asserted the complete depravity of humanity and required total dependence on the sovereignty of God. They listed everything remotely fun in the sinful category, meaning no dancing, laughing, or parties. These things were *forboten* (forbidden).

The Puritans felt they were God's chosen and that this elite lineage gave them the right to run everyone else's affairs. The Craft was and is a happy religion. The ideas of karma and reincarnation are inherent to the belief system. Joyous celebrations, open fertility rites, and intrinsic faith in a female divinity are pivotal and directly opposed to Puritan theology.

The Puritans made no secret that they intended to govern as much of the New World as possible. They would do it according to God's will, as revealed in the Bible. In their minds, William Penn was destined for Hell. Obviously, they spouted, squawked, and pressured their way into local governments.

With all the hot air blowing around, the German Witches decided to disguise their religion. They would not choose Puritanism—it was simply too negative and too structured. They needed to find a religion practiced by the Germans that was closer to the Pagan belief system. Puritanism, after all, was basically English. The closest religion to the Craft was Catholicism, but there weren't enough of those folks around for decent cover. What faith, then, should they choose?

The Witches didn't just hop on a boat and sail over to the colonies without any sense of planning. Their choice of faith also needed to include a group (or groups) of people with whom they could comfortably travel after they arrived. The Witches carefully cemented friendships and an atmosphere of stability for their families with non-occult families. There were two main types of German settlers—the "plain" or pietist German sectarians and the "fancy" or Church Germans from which to choose. The plain Germans wore distinctive clothing and were made up of the Brethren, Mennonites, Amish, and Dunkers. During my interviews, I found some Pow-Wow artists who were Brethren (also called the River Brethren), Mennonites, and Dunkers. They practiced a form of Pow-Wow that borders on faith healing. The Amish alone did not, nor do they now, approve of hex signs, faith healing, or magickal practices of any sort.

The "fancy" Dutch or "gay" Dutch (which they don't call themselves now because of the connection with homosexuality) brought the ornate customs of Christmas and Easter to the region, including the Yule tree and log, colorful decorations, baskets, and bunny pictures. They also brought the hex signs and loads of superstition. Both have direct evidence of Craft influence. Many Witches chose to go undercover with the "Fancy Dutch." Wisely, people of the Craft infiltrated both the plain and fancy German groups, according to their personal preferences. This provided safe houses on both sides of the German fence. No matter which way they turned, there would always be someone to back them up, either through intermarriages or friendships.

In colonial times, the Germans (or Pennsylvania Dutch—Dutch being a bastardization of the German pronunciation of Germany, i.e., Deutschland) gained a reputation for being frugal, diligent, and productive souls. Men and women shared everything to such a degree that it often surprised their non-German neighbors. They harvested the crops together, took care of the animals together, and often worshipped together. The family and community structures were of the highest value. If disaster struck, your friends and neighbors would take care of you without regard to how much it might personally cost them. So competent were the Germans at farming that Pennsylvania was known as the "Bread Basket of America." Frugal but inventive, they fashioned the Conestoga wagons (the ships of the inland trade at that time) and were known throughout the colonies for their master craftsmanship.

The Craft Travels to the New World

In German, the words "Hexerei" and "Hex" mean "Witchcraft." The original Germans, especially those from the Black Forest, were tribal in nature, and called their magickal practices Hexerei. The German word, in the beginning, did not carry any negative connotations and was used often in the local colonial dialect. As the German Witch families became mixed with other religions through marriage, the meaning of Hexerei experienced perversion. Then, as now, people are suspicious of the magickal realms. However, "hex signs" (the English word "hex" being a derivative of Hexerei) retained their positive nature, and locals still love them.

That Sloe-eyed Mystique

"I can remember," said one lady at the Dillsburg Senior Citizen Center, "when the Gypsies came to our farm. I was a little girl. They came in their wagons with lots of children, horses, and mules. They spoke only German, like my parents. At the time, my family did not own our farm. We were tenants. The Gypsy lady told my mother that my family would eventually own the farm … and you know … my mother never gave up hope on that prophecy. It did come true. Some Witches did not choose to disguise themselves with the Christian doctrine, instead they disguised themselves as Gypsies. My mother knew that.

"My family came straight from the Rhineland," she continued. "My father was very superstitious. He forbade my mother to do wash on Wednesdays because he said it was bad luck. Well, my sister was grown then and needed help with her laundry because she had a baby. My mother did the wash but forbade my brother-in-law to tell my father. That night, as my father was bringing in the cows from pasture, his best heifer dropped dead, right at the gate! No one in the family ever told him my mother had done wash that day—he might even have blamed those Gypsies for it and my mother certainly wouldn't have wanted that! She was sure their visit had brought good fortune to our family direct from the Old Country, despite my father's reservations on the subject."

Through the disguise of Gypsies, a few Witches refused to give up their religion. Due to the superstitious nature of the local inhabitants, acceptance came grudgingly to their faces, but they were treated with little respect behind their backs. Most Witches, though, opted for community life with its beautiful sprawling farms and support from neighbors. Designing your own community does not mean you are fully free to practice your faith. Outsiders visit, perhaps even stay, so you have to create a front for the strange things you do. You also have to cut out some of the more bizarre activities, like running around with antlers on your head on Midsummer Night's Eve.

But What About the Native Americans?

During the interview process for this book, many area residents felt that a portion of Pow-Wow originally came from the Native American population. Most historical scholars do not support this theory. Anything historical scholars do not support ought to be delved into, don't you think? Enter now, please, the Native American.

The tribes indigenous to the south-central Pennsylvania area when the Witches first settled are the most unusual point of the Pow-Wow mystery. Some historians and locals feel that the Native Americans of the region had no effect on Pow-Wow. I don't believe they are blinded by historical rhetoric, but by historical prejudice. Unfortunately, the natives of the area were obliterated early in the 1700s, giving us little to go on. One of the most famous Pow-Wow artists in the Dillsburg area, known as Indian Peg, was obviously Native American. My grandfather Baker knew her and her husband, and spoke often of her powerful magicks and medicinal cures for the sick. There are several family trees in surrounding counties that show Native American heritage, with footnotes stating that these same individuals were Pow-Wow practitioners.

To give an accurate representation of an event, you have to allow for all the players to get on stage. If we write off the Native Americans simply because we don't know that much about them, we are unfair and egotistical. They were there. Some of their descendants are Pow-Wow artists, and there were more of them than most people think.

When I began my research on the tribes indigenous to the area, I kept running up against pockets of missing information. You can find reams of data on the Iroquois Nation, but practically zip on the Susquehannocks. There was a little more on the Delawares. All the information I obtained was colored by the ideas and the insights of the white people. Well, if you can't go to the mountain, I thought, find someone who represents the mountain. I contacted Chief Piercing Eyes of the Pan-American Indian Association, now located in Florida, and hit pay dirt.

"Part of my genetic heritage is Susquehannock," he said (at this time I was practically screeching with joy), "more fashionably known as Conestoga today. I've done a lot of research, but, as you doubtless know by now, it is hard to read between the lines written by bigoted observers from long ago. My people were comparatively rich and fashionable and lived in large palisaded cities." An example of what Chief Piercing Eyes is saying can be seen at the William Penn Museum in Harrisburg. Although enchanting, their Native American displays are dark, dreary, and give you the impression that the Native Americans were unclean.

"Along with the Hurons," he continued, "we monopolized the fur trade, collecting taxes at portages. This made us the enemy of everyone, but we bought cannons and hired Swedish engineers to build our forts, and held off the whole Iroquois League as well as the Delaware and the white folks until my people were cut down with European childhood diseases. The last ones were murdered at Conestoga [Lancaster] before the American revolution."

By 1676 (before Penn got to the New World) the Susquehannocks faced near annihilation by the Iroquois. This explains why white historical accounts are so vague. Eventually the small number remaining sought conversion to Christianity by the (mystical) Quakers. This small band was massacred in 1763 by a mob of white men inflamed over rumors of an Indian uprising. They thought, if you couldn't find the actual criminal, find someone who looks like him and plug 'em!

Chief Piercing Eyes told us, "Indians travelled widely in pre-white times through a network of rivers and trails. Many of the trails have been asphalted and are still in use today. White historians, for reasons common to the breed, insist there were few, if any, Indians in the area [by the time William Penn and his white settlers arrived]. Truth is, there were Delaware, Cherokee, Iroquois, Mingo, and other tribes in the area [south-central Pennsylvania]. The earliest identifiable Indians were the Beothuk, close relatives of the Innuit. Their settlements are recognized by unique crescent-shaped altars."

Chief Piercing Eyes also cemented the theory that the God and Goddess archetypes were waiting for the Germans long before they set foot on American soil. "The Susquehannock lineage apparently echoes my pet theory that Native American spirituality was brought here by the Europeans of the Old Way [meaning the Craft] who arrived here long before Columbus. The Mandan tribe was founded by a Welshman about 150 years before Chris got here. The Norse were here for 500 years—one travelled to Mexico and found some wretched people hiding there in a swamp and taught them how to fight. The rest is history, about A.D. 1000.

"Susquehannock pottery," he added, "had two faces in bold relief looking opposite each other, one male and one female. Bone hair combs were surmounted with male and female figures, the male bearing two short horns.... White settlers accused my people of devil worship, and not without reason. The idea of Our Lady and her feisty Consort would have had immense appeal to my warlike ancestors, but would be considered blasphemous to the Puritans."

Chief Piercing Eyes explained the relationship between men and women of the tribe. In discussing the Delaware and Mohawk, he showed us opposition to the Puritan approach to relationships and paralleled the Pagan ideology of sexual balance to that of the Native Americans. In Puritanism, a woman had sex with most of her clothes on and a blanket over her head. In general living, the Native Americans were like the pre-Christians. They functioned within a matriarchal system of living. "The woman owned everything," he stated. "Her man may be gone until spring, out hunting or going to war, or stealing from some enemy. He may not ever come back and she may never know what happened to him. Therefore, she acts as though he were already dead and carried on with raising the family, tending the garden, and making utensils and clothing. If he delays too long, she may even go out hunting. If it is obvious he must be dead or captured by an enemy, she will find another man to fill his place. At the time, the Susquehannocks were dying of childhood diseases. Droves of Iroquois warriors also died. We were home, so men, women, children, and farm animals died as well.

"Back in Iroiquoisland, the women went out beating the bushes for any husbands they could find for lineage purposes, no matter what the race or tribe. We don't talk about this anymore. The women let the men play church and play government, but if any [man] displeased them [the women], their council would unseat them, even to the point of putting them to death. Even the greatest of chiefs could be put down in this way. And much is still true today. In [the white's] efforts to assimilate the Indians, it could have been done if the women were hired instead of the men. The women would have been delighted to cut trees, build railroads, and do steelwork on skyscrapers while their men sat home playing cards. Everybody would have been happy except the damn Britishers who knew very well what was and wasn't God's way." Patriarchal society strikes again.

A Rose by any Other Name

The heritage of the Native Americans is deep and strong in this country. It is in the air we breathe, the water we drink, the soil where we grow our food. The Spirits are in the mountains, the lakes, the rivers, and the caves. Most importantly, it is not in the blood of a certain race of people. It is in all of us, simply because we were born here and are a part of this land. When your mother carried you, she drank of the waters here. She ate of the food grown here; she feasted her eyes on the beauty of the sunset and the sunrise. She gazed at the stars and partook of the beauty of the woods, fields, and forests. It was a part of her, and it is a part of you.

There are those historians who feel that "Pow-Wow" is a derivative of the English word "power," but in the area of York and Lancaster, residents say the word comes from an Native American word, *powaw*—meaning "he who dreams." The local Native American beliefs indicate that the tribe's Shaman received much of his power and healing capabilities through dreams and vision questing. Penn and many of his friends mixed with the Delaware tribe. We know that the remaining Susquehannocks converted to Quakerism, and we now know that the Iroquois women were hunting men "of any race or tribe" to continue their lineage. It is clear that the Europeans and indigenous peoples formed various relationships and that the exchange of survival techniques and family cultures created a new blend of knowledge. Together, the Native American and the Witch gave birth to a combined magickal system of their own—Pow-Wow—where the Craft of the Wise married He Who Dreams.

When the practice of Pow-Wow is performed by the magickal person, his/her aura vibrates like a drum beat. It pulses. Magickal people from all over the United States visit here in Pennsylvania. We often show them Pow-Wow techniques. They learn them quickly and carry them back to their magickal communities. Whether they have been in the Craft one year or twenty years, they all state, "I've never felt this kind of healing energy before. It is different from anything I have experienced." This is because it is a blend of two powerful lineages—Craft and Native American. Dutch Country magick is the root of American Witchcraft.

West
Water
Swift Movement
Designed by Silver RavenWolf

The Growth of Pow-Wow

If you have beauty in your life, know that it will attract
the dark as well as the light. Don't be surprised. Be prepared.
—Clarissa Pinkola Estes,
author of *Women Who Run With the Wolves*

Pow-Wows in the 1700s

Lancaster was founded in 1709, approximately 20 years after Penn came to the New World. York was founded in 1741. Little towns popped up along Native American trails at a steady pace. Today, the strongest pockets of Pow-Wow remain around the cities of York, Reading, and Lancaster. We are not talking about hundreds of people, but a mere handful. People living around these cities call this area the Hex Belt of Pennsylvania.

The Susquehanna Valley was excellent for farming, yielding rich and glorious crops and strong healing herbs. The prosperous farms in south-central Pennsylvania were large. The mothers and grandmothers of these families ran the main house. The fathers, sons, and often daughters worked the fields, both their own and those of neighbors. The Germans usually worked in a communal style. They focused on the good of the community as well as their own prosperity. The adult women, therefore, stuck close to home. There was the house to watch, the children to look after, and the small livestock such as chickens, turkeys, geese, etc. to feed. The making of all clothes and the planting of personal gardens, which included food to sell for market pin-money as well as healing herbs, kept those of the feminine persuasion working constantly. Extended family units were accepted and encouraged. Sons and daughters often built their homes right onto the main house of their parents. This assured the survival of the farm and the family. Ordinarily, the women acted as midwives to their kin and neighbors. They also doctored cuts, diseases, and broken bones. The actual practice of Pow-Wow was predominantly female until the mid-1800s. The damage to Pow-Wow began when the women lost control of the Pow-Wow system.

Pow-Wows of the 1800s

One lady I interviewed said that her great-grandmother (a woman of the 1800s) brought herbs with her from Germany to plant here. This way she had everything she needed to perform her art. There was no need to worry about learning the uses of plants that were new to her. Others traded cures and herbs with local Native Americans to increase their medicinal knowledge. Few indigenous people survived to carry on their lineage and practices. Those who did survive intermarried with the settlers. However, there were enough Native Americans around to relate the use of native herbs and flowers if one took the time to listen. Genuine Craft cures were often attributed to the local tribes as a cover. Who was to know if the information came from your grandmother or from the Indian woman who lived up the mountain?

In 1827, the *Philadelphia Gazette* printed an article on Pow-Wow giving us this information: "Pow-Wowing is a regular and well established business in the interior. Our readers are aware that this Pow-Wowing is what is designated in English as charming. The process is making certain gestures, turning round, moving the hands backwards and forwards, repeating certain words, etc."

The Wanna-bes

The self-proclaimed Witches made their appearance in the 1800s. Their practices grew in popularity until the fall of Pow-Wow in 1928 (which will be discussed later in this chapter). These individuals read books and visited real Pow-Wows, but they were never actual students of any particular person. These dabblers would then set up shop in their homes, indicating with much boasting their ability to Pow-Wow. Often they claimed that they had taken training from a living, breathing teacher whose identity they had sworn to keep secret. None of them were particularly skilled in magickal arts. A few managed sucess in minor healing techniques. These self-proclaimed Witches hadn't a clue about the true meaning of the Craft, wouldn't have understood the concept of the Goddess even if she had physically manifested in front of them, and had no idea that Witchcraft was really a religion, not a set of charms, chants, and spells. This is a scary thought. They perpetuated themselves for generation after generation on false information. They called themselves, as did their offspring, Witches or Pow-Wows, depending on how the thought moved them. In truth, they were so far from the original teachings and tenets of the Craft that they had managed to invent something unique and bogus—Witcherie. Those people involved in false magickal practices as Americans moved into the nineteenth century served to weaken the system to the point where both the magickal community and the general public saw only a confused mess of back-door occultism. This is why you can interview ten people on what Pow-Wow is in Pennsylvania, and no answer will be exactly the same.

During the compilation of this manuscript, one local authority questioned my use of the term "wanna-bes," and felt that my opinion may be more professional sour grapes than relating to accurate, historical phenomena. I thought about this for some time, but I will not change my ideas on the subject. Unless you are working within the magickal community for some time, it is difficult to discern the fakes from the real thing. Yes, some individuals are obvious tricksters, but others with hidden agendas are not so easy to spot until the damage is done. All walks of life have wanna-bes, and our society has a nasty habit of wearing blinders. In the world of magick, we take responsibility for our own actions, which includes our mundane lives as well. If I take responsibility for my actions, I do not look lightly on those who shirk their responsibilities, whether we are discussing magick or politics or anything else. So, as the Quakers used to say, "I stand against" wanna-bes. They exist and I'm not about to turn a blind eye toward them. Enough said.

Europe Comes Out of the Closet

As Pow-Wow grew in south-central Pennsylvania, the rest of the world was not standing still. Europe during the 1800s became a hotbed of occult activity, beginning with Alphonse Louis Constant (1810-1875), who wrote under the pen name Eliphas Levi. His most important accomplishment was bringing the Tarot under the eye of Western occultism.

Helena Petrovna Blavatsky (1831-1891) traveled to the United States around 1870 and founded the Theosophical Society in New York in 1875. Twelve years later, Dr. William Wynn Wescott, a Freemason, founded the Hermetic Order of the Golden Dawn in London with fake occult manuscripts said to hail from Germany. By 1900, Arthur Edward Waite, Dione Fortune, Aleister Crowley and a host of others were moving and shaking the occult circles in Europe. They were soon joined and followed by Israel Regardie, Margaret A. Murray, and of course Gerald Brosseau Gardner.

Not all Pow-Wows left were the folksie type. Many were interested in what was happening in Europe and followed the occult craze with a watchful eye. Both the Pow-Wows and the Hexmeister Doctors corresponded with these European occultists and incorporated some of the more ceremonial practices into their practices. Although you may wonder why I'm giving you European information, these facts are important. Pow-Wows were not hermits. By the late 1800s, they knew they were losing ground. They didn't understand the key loss of the Old Religion. The Pow-Wows took pains to strengthen European connections to better their skills.

The Pow-Wow Community in the 1900s

The strength of the Pow-Wow system lies in its healing techniques. These, above all other practices, survived the pummeling of the system. Here is an example. This story came from a volunteer at the Dillsburg library.

"Back in the seventies I was a private nurse. I was taking care of a lady with Alzheimer's disease. She didn't really know anybody anymore and kept thinking her son was her husband. One day I was making something for her on the stove and I burned my hand. I mean I burned it terrible. That lady grabbed my hand and said, 'Let me look at that.' I knew her state of mind and couldn't figure what on earth she was talking about. She took my hand, blew on it, and muttered words I couldn't hear accurately. Do you know she healed that burn, right then and there, and it never bubbled up? I never got a scar. Nothing. Later my husband said she'd Pow-Wowed for me. I didn't even know what it was. It was a mystery to me. How could this lady, whose mind was not functioning in reality, remember Pow-Wow? She remembered the technique immediately and accomplished a healing for me!"

In my interviews, I heard the following statement: "Never saw an Indian, but there was a white man who Pow-Wowed up on the mountain. He called himself a doctor. He said words I couldn't understand." I interviewed those who said, "She said the words so softly I couldn't pick it up," and "There was an Indian in Carlisle that did Pow-Wow and he may still be hanging around down there," or "There was an Indian woman up on South Mountain, but I never knew of any white women or men who Pow-Wowed," or "I think she was a lady of Indian decent but I know her daddy was Irish." I also heard "Strictly German, no Indian stuff with that man—all the Bible and holy words," and "No, no Indian, she was definitely German; my grandparents knew hers in the Old Country, but she's dead now." It was enough to make me throw up my hands and visit a graveyard, hoping a deceased Pow-Wow (because I was only hearing about the dead ones at that point) would pop up and make some sense of it all. Had I begun my research in 1929, I would have had about 1,000 possible Pow-Wows to interview. In 1990, I was lucky if I could find one.

Starting with a familiar base, I compared the rise of Pow-Wow to the growth of the Neo-Pagan community today. There are interesting parallels. Just as there are numerous magickal people now, many with their own styles and beliefs, so were there in the early 1900s. This explains why some of them appeared more Shamanic in nature. Others were more like Gypsies, and still others were more devoted to the Christian religion itself. There were a few who desperately tried to hang on to some semblance of the Craft. And, lurking around these people, were the wanna-bes.

American Witchcraft

Today, we Neo-Pagans pride ourselves in thinking we are the first individuals in the New World to exert our magickal prowess and theories of universal love and healing. We grapple with the ideology that we have no roots as magickal people in American soil. We envy those who reside in European countries who have lived with centuries of myth and magick and try to mimic them. We fail to recognize that the God/Goddess deity concept was here before our personal ancestors arrived. This concept of balance, already firmly established within the worship structure of the indigenous Americans, stood waiting. The God and Goddess, with their many myths and magicks, were here to greet our ancestors when they arrived. The true nature of the God/Goddess is omnipotent and omnipresent.

Why Pow-Wow Survived at All

Pow-Wow encompassed everything, as the Craft had done before. The Pow-Wow artist recovered stolen cows, protected the house and family, healed sickness, and set broken bones. She/he guarded against slander, controlled the weather, and used astrology for planting and planning most everything. He/she performed the tasks of doctor, lawyer, and police officer. Until the mid-1800s, the Pow-Wow practitioner was revered in the New World. As the immigrants ceased using their Germanic tongue, words like Braucherei (meaning Witchcraft, and later referred to as Using) fell from the vocabulary.

Pow-Wows evolved with a few unusual twists because its practitioners let go of the religious aspects of the Craft. At first, they taught their children the true meaning of the holidays, sigils, charms, and spells used. As more white Christians entered the area, people of the Craft put on a disguise to avoid possible persecution. Fewer parents were willing to tell their chattering offspring the truth. The disguise took on its own truth and the Craft connection met obliteration. By 1960, the public's awareness fell to only a few chants and spells peppered with farming by astrology. At the same time the public was fooled into believing that Witchcraft was Satanism, representing evil practices and deeds.

In colonial times, the Pow-Wows' popularity stemmed from their importance in the community. The skills of the Pow-Wow were needed and accepted. As long as no references blatantly tied the Old Religion to their practices, they worked without restraint. To further protect themselves, Pow-Wows added horrendously long prayers and incantations to the original folk spells. The Holy Trinity replaced the Craft deities who were usually invoked, and later on they added numerous references to Jesus. They also used Latin to hide what they were saying, since most local Protestant clergy were unfamiliar with that language.

Did their magick still work? Of course! Any magickal system will work as long as you connect with Divinity. In the 1900s, it has been linked to Christianity. As Christianity itself broke down into many derivatives, so did Pow-Wow. Moving farther away from York and Lancaster, the magick ceases and the system becomes strictly faith healing. From there it traveled down the Appalachian Trail. Witches who went north took on the name "Bone-Setters," and those who traveled further south were called "Faith Healers," "Grannies," and "Water Witches." By the time Pow-Wow reached Louisiana, where it ran into Voodoo, Witches up and down the East Coast were mixing magickal systems with fascinating results. Eclectic Witches, then, are not something new to the ball game of the neo-Pagan community. They were here long before the beginning of the current magickal community.

Additional Correlations to the Craft

Time may heal, but it also dilutes truth. Some information gathered here consists of primary sources. These sources include people who saw Pow-Wows for healing when they were children, and people who took their children and other family members to a Pow-Wow. There are also statements from practicing Pow-Wows. The material contains many secondary sources—what individuals remember that their grandparents and great-grandparents (should they have been lucky enough to live together) told them. Secondary sources are always less reliable. To compound difficulties, Pow-Wow was a tradition passed primarily by word of mouth. Studying any history (especially this one) is a gamble in logic and memory. To confuse the issue, the self-proclaimed Witches did irreparable damage to both the reputations of Pow-Wow practitioners and traditional Witches. They managed to muddy the scientific aspects of the system to the point where many source books discounted all acts of magick as wishful thinking and shyster claims.

Correlations between the Old Religion and Pow-Wow are obvious. For instance, both Pow-Wows and Witches believe in the "passing of the power." Many individuals relate that Pow-Wow was passed either from mother to son or from father to daughter. This is a Craft practice indigenous to the Old World in which only a woman could initiate and teach a man, and vice versa.

The Growth of Pow-Wow

In all fairness, however, there were those I interviewed who said they never heard of such a thing and that it had been passed from mother to daughter and from father to son, or even to a friend. I have even heard of passing the power through an inanimate object, such as a table, then having the student touch the table and receive the power to keep from breaking a tradition or oath. Germans were a tricky lot.

Teaching Pow-Wow and "passing the power" are two entirely different aspects of magickal practice. I would like to differentiate them for you right now, especially since there was such fuss about it between Pow-Wows themselves. You could tell a legitimate Pow-Wow from a wanna-be by his or her philosophy on training. Those who were not deeply into the mysteries thought that any person you trained directly sucked your power away. Those with Craft background knew that giving people spells, herbs, and incantations did not constitute the passing of power. Power is passed only through ritual and ceremony. The express purpose of that ritual or ceremony is to bestow a portion of your power upon the student. The number of these ceremonies performed by one person was limited to three.

If the power could not be passed (for any number of reasons) from one generation to the next, it did not necessarily die with the Pow-Wow artist. Many believed that the capability of performing magick was a part of their make-up (what we call genetics today) and would pass from generation to generation until a reawakening further down the genetic line occurred. I have heard rumors of these ceremonies. The catalyst to their performance centered on times of persecution. Perhaps the time of awakening is now.

Another correlation between the Old Religion and Pow-Wow lies in the colorful hex signs. They are testimonials to their Craft origin. The pentacle is an acceptable hex sign, drawn with stars between the points and a star in the middle. The history of hex signs is no secret. Created with magickal intent by occult practitioners, they served all sorts of human needs, from bringing love into someone's life to protecting the home and livestock.

Additionally, several Pow-Wow chants deal specifically with the Holy Mother (the last vestiges of the Goddess). One reviles a prostitute of biblical reference, and a few incorporate the aid of ancient temple priestesses. Pow-Wows conjured things and bound things. They made charms, talismans, and herbal sachets for magickal purposes. These items are today regarded as building blocks of the scientific aspects of the Old Religion.

To round out these correlations, most Pow-Wows were familiar with the "evil eye." They respected magick (done by others, of course), understood the difference between positive and negative uses of energy, and incorporated astrological and elemental correspondences in their workings.

The Casting Call in the 1800s and Early 1900s

Let's take a quick look at the active occultists floating around in Pennsylvania from 1801 through 1960. They made life interesting for the general population and bred wagonloads of superstition.

There were the traditional family lineaged Witches, who mostly called themselves Pow-Wow doctors or artists. The "W" word was a no-no. No one dared use the German word "Hexe," not unless one was talking about bad things and bad people. Trailing behind, but ever so vocal, were the self-proclaimed Witches. There also were the Native Americans who did their own type of faith healing and magick. There were the Gypsies who were travelling hither and yon, dragging their kids, horses, and fortune-telling techniques with them. Those of a more studious nature, such as the alchemists, Pagan theologians, ceremonial magicians, astrologers, and phrenologists (people who study the bumps on a human head) were present as well. Most of these people were positive in nature, and worked to assist others. A few scholars wrote this magickal information down, but not enough to give us a truly accurate portrayal of their closeted workings.

Unfortunately, nothing lasts forever. Along came a new fellow who spelled disaster for the Pow-Wows, Shamans, and Gypsies alike. He was the Hexmeister Doctor, and usually came from an affluent European background of bankers, doctors, or old money. His practices dipped into ceremonial magick. By 1901, the Hexmeister Doctor had far more occult knowledge than the average Pow-Wow. The training of the Pow-Wow by this time was ineffective in most areas of magickal expertise, save one—that of healing. No more was the Pow-Wow considered in contact with the more potent occult mysteries.

The Fall from Grace

By the 1900s, American society changed its footing on Pow-Wow. Medical doctors poo-pooed holistic healing and the church poo-pooed anything that even resembled the occult or sympathetic magick. The educated public stuck their noses up in air at magick and spit at superstition. The public made an about-face and sneered at Pow-Wow practitioners—which is exactly what the doctors and the clerics wanted. You can't run from a pack of philosophical wolves.

"We were like a bunch of Gypsies," said one woman. "If there was a new Pow-Wow around or we heard of a fortuneteller, we would travel miles to see them. We began to doubt their usefulness. It was like a game, a lark, something to do." Alas, magick in America was turning into a parlor game just when magick in Europe became a serious theological issue.

The Growth of Pow-Wow

Technology in the United States freed the farmer's hands and the men started getting into serious magick. The Christian motto of "an eye for an eye" and its patriarchal ideas twisted the magickal community. With the help of the self-proclaimed Witches and Hexmeister Doctors, the Pow-Wows fell from grace with a mighty thud. The public could not discern one magickal practice (or pest) from the other and promptly drew their mental shades down on the subect. The thought of a thriving magickal community in the midst of Christian philosophy was simply not conceivable, therefore it did not exist. The Pow-Wows were no longer viewed as folksy do-gooders. Respect for the Goddess fled from the Pow-Wow system. Her nurturing and wisdom withered from its practice, and all hell literally broke loose.

Hexmeister Doctors would throw hexes (evil spells) on anyone, for a price (naturally). Some of them were pretty good at it, and fear escalated. These Hexmeisters used the word "hex" to mean the act of doing magickal dirty work. It led the superstitious public to believe that Witchcraft was straight up evil. There was no room for discussion on the matter. Remember now, Pow-Wow teachers stopped telling their students that Pow-Wow incorporated the skills of the Old Religion. It is understandable that outsiders and Pow-Wow students automatically associated Witchcraft with evil! These Hexmeister Doctors (who called themselves Pow-Wows) often had skirmishes regarding who was more powerful than whom in York, Lancaster, and the surrounding areas. They hung shingles on their homes proclaiming themselves doctors of mind and body. They preyed on the fears of the residents, turning superstitions into a lucrative business. They sold fake cures, sometimes pushing people into doing criminal acts that they normally would never conceive on their own. Up and down the streets of York, Pennsylvania, you could find little signs and posters proclaiming the talents of these charlatans. Even the police of the times feared the Hexmeister Doctors. None of these practices had anything to do with real Witchcraft or the Old Religion, but Witches and Pow-Wows got blamed for it anyway.

Hexmeister Doctors (and some Pow-Wows as well) used the magickal texts attributed to Moses. These are more commonly called *The Sixth and Seventh Books of Moses* and *The Eighth, Ninth, and Tenth Books of Moses*. The information is said to have been passed down through Zadock, an Israelite priest who helped secure the throne for King Solomon after the death of his father, David. Although many biblical scholars denounce these books as utter fakes, we are all well aware that Moses was a magickal person. We are also aware that the Hexmeisters were successful, for a limited time, in their endeavors.

In itself, magick is not evil. Its use determines whether the outcome of a situation is good or harmful. Humans, however, fail to take responsibility for their own actions. With blind determination, they blame the tool rather than the human mind behind it.

The Murder that Killed Pow-Wow

The focus was York County, Pennsylvania. The year was 1928. The date was November 28, the time one minute past midnight, when a Pow-Wow artist by the name of Nelson D. Rehmeyer was murdered by three men who believed he put a hex on them. These men were 32-year-old John Blymire, a blatant example of a family tradition of wanna-bes; Wilbert Hess, age 18; and John Curry, who was only 14 years old. Although I did not agree with many of the statements in the novel *Hex* by Arthur Lewis (read this and you will see why magickal people do not appreciate writings by non-magickal people on magickal topics), John Blymire reminded me of the sort of person who haunts New Age stores, insists on repeated Tarot readings for the same problem, or calls a psychic hotline every evening, even for a stubbed toe. In my opinion, Blymire was a dysfunctional human being who needed psychological counseling. Of course this was unheard of in those days. William Keisling (in his introduction to a revised version of the *Long Lost Friend*, Yardbird Books, 1992) says, "The term 'Witch,' it should be noted, though used liberally by Lewis and others, is certainly offensive to most powwowers, who view themselves as following a religious calling of faith healing."

Nelson Rehmeyer's descendents claim that he did not practice magick. During my research, I found a 94-year-old gentleman at the Dillsburg Senior Citizen Center who remembers Rehmeyer and knew him. He said, "Why yes, he was definitely involved in Pow-Wow, and don't let anyone try to tell you different! I knew him! They called him the Witch of Rehmeyer's Hollow!"

The story goes that John Blymire travelled all over the tri-county area seeking the Witch who put a hex on him. His quest lasted for over 15 years. Finally, a 94-year-old woman in Marietta (called "the High Priestess") told Blymire to cut a lock of hair from Rehmeyer's head and burn it with his Book of Shadows. If John Blymire accomplished this task, the spell would be broken.

Nelson Rehmeyer was a very big man who did not take kindly to having his hair cut. A fight ensued and the three men beat Rehmeyer to death. To complicate matters, they couldn't find his Book of Shadows anywhere. Trying to hide the crime and destroy the book simultaneously, they attempted to burn the house. Only portions of the structure succumbed to fire. John Blymire, quoted by his accomplices, said "Thank God, the Witch is dead. The spell is off. I can't be hexed anymore."

You can still see the house today, in Rehmeyer's Hollow in York County, Pennsylvania. Amusingly enough, the area Jaycees run wagons through there for haunted hollow tours over Samhain (Halloween).

Whether Rehmeyer practiced Pow-Wow, was a Hexmeister, or was a self-proclaimed Witch is actually a moot point. The event provided ammunition for those already set against Pow-Wow artists, including the medical profession, the church, and the school system. Reymeyer's murder was not the only occult-related killing in the Hex Belt. There were many others over the years, adding up to about fifty. Unlike the others, the Reymeyer murder received a huge amount of press. It was featured in the *New York Times* as well as several European papers.

Ultimately, the educational edicts set down by the Governor of Pennsylvania dealt the death blow to Pow-Wow. He released a memorandum to all district personnel ordering superstition banished from every school in the state. The one-room school houses prevalent in the era were eradicated. The modern school system was born, including the procedure of busing. The prime intent was to murder the belief in magick. It worked.

"Needled into action by the press," wrote Arthur Lewis, "Governor John S. Fisher summoned Dr. Noll (Secretary of the York County Medical Society) and other officials of other county medical societies in the afflicted areas, then ordered his state police commissioner to take immediate action against the Commonwealth's legion of Witches. The investigation got off to an inspired start; evidence against hexers began to pour in."

Many residents of the Commonwealth wanted to crawl under a rock at the thought of their state becoming Occult Central. Instead of "You've got a friend in Pennsylvania," we could say, "You've got a friend in the Witch State." Both elite and middle-class citizens were not thrilled at the national coverage announcing a call to arms against Witches. Keisling says, "There came an easy truce. Practitioners kept a low profile, and modern society largely ignored them."

In 1940 (twelve years after the Reymeyer murder), the *Harrisburg Patriot* newspaper printed the following: "State educators declared here yesterday that hexerei, terror of numerous rural farm communities for many years, is being banished from Pennsylvania by the public schools. School authorities explained that instruction in the sciences, even in the lower grades, has proved the most effective weapon against the superstition. Court records show the 'hex' is responsible for many crimes, including murder and arson, during the past 50 years."

There is a rumor that in the 1960s, many of the Pow-Wow artists banded together to protect themselves. A loose network was formed to offer suggestions on how to handle various aspects of their specialties. Another function was to find ways to handle bad press. Records of interviews in the 1960s indicate the existence of individuals called "Pow-Wow Officers." This is a reference to a loose group or organization. Someone once told me that in such groups there was a specific person who threw hexes for everyone else. This person was called "the burner." I've not found anything to attest to this fact, but it is an interesting thought all the same.

In Pennsylvania today, unless you have heard about Pow-Wow through your family or spoken to someone who has been "tried" for (the act of using magick for another person), you probably have never heard of it. This then is fair warning to all alternative religions. Don't sit back and let the school system (or anyone else) dictate to your children. It is your place to make your feelings known about how you want their education manifested in their lives.

Hex

Perhaps the most interesting chapter of the Rehmeyer murder occurred in 1969 when Arthur H. Lewis published his book entitled *Hex* through the Trident Press. It was later turned into a movie bearing the same name. I did not read his documentation on the murder until after I had completed my research and written my second draft for this book. In fact, it was during the final tightening process of the manuscript that I even bothered to look at it. Something kept telling me that I was not going to like this book, nor was I going to agree with it. It was MaraKay Rogers, my consultant for many areas of this manuscript, who said, "Look, I understand your reservations, but you really should look at Lewis' book. There are many people who have read it and have seen the movie. When they read your book they are going to wonder why you didn't mention it." It was a convincing argument. (I might have known, she is an attorney by profession.)

My intuition was right. His book did not give me the thrill of a lifetime. In fact, I was very disappointed with it. The portions covering the trial were good and his information on the personal lives of both the criminals and victim was interesting. His thought processes, however, left me with the tantalizing thought of clawing the book to pieces. Mr. Arthur H. Lewis, for all his research, for all his plodding through historical documents and time-consuming interviews, failed. He fell into the same trap that many people do. Mr. Lewis never figured out that Witches do not worship Satan. It never dawned on him that traditional Witches do not conjure demons and practice black magick. There very well may have been individuals in the area who were practicing black magick, but they weren't the Witches.

Time and again Mr. Lewis connected Witches with Satanism and black magick. He could never prove the link he proposed. He always fell short. He implied, suggested, and used good prose, but he never met a Witch or Pow-Wow during his interview process who offered to throw a hex or cast an evil spell to cause harm to any person or animal. He also left the reader feeling sorry for the murderers. Excuse me? Every person is responsible for his or her own actions. Magickal people are well aware that we cannot blame social circumstances, our education, or our parents when we make mistakes.

My last and final argument on the validity of his book is the picture he paints of the Pennsylvania Dutch people. He leads you to believe they were stupid, superstitious, and sometimes vicious. There are times when the entire world could fall into that category. In my mind, he did a disservice to the people of the area and the beautiful and powerful magicks of the land and customs around them. Pennsylvania Dutch Country magick is indeed potent, but it is not to be feared, nor does it need that element to survive.

Recent Events

The Pow-Wow system certainly shakes up a variety of individuals. In 1984, the Pennsylvania Board of Medical Education and Licensure decided to take a peek at approximately how many individuals practiced Pow-Wow in Pennsylvania. Apparently they got more than they bargained for, panicked, and sent lawyers scuttling to separate the wanna-bes from the honest Pow-Wow practitioners. (Personally, I would like to know what sort of test one had to pass to be considered an "honest" practitioner.) Unfortunately for the attorneys, the state medical laws written in 1893 give a proviso for Pow-Wowers to practice within the confines of the law, as long as they do not misrepresent themselves or prescribe medication (this also includes herbs). The Witch hunt pooped before anyone got popped.

According to William Keisling, state and medical officials are turning a blind eye on the subject of Pow-Wow in the nineties. He called the Pennsylvania Department of Health, which didn't appear to care one way or the other about current Pow-Wow artists. The medical licensing board gave him a complaint number.

Keisling also notes that David Hufford, a professor of behavioral science and family and community medicine at the Milton S. Hershey Medical Center in Hershey, says, "My teaching shows that medicine now has an interest in such healing traditions." Accordingly, he discusses Pow-Wowing in his lectures and gives a coupon from a local palm reader and a local Pow-Wow artist.

Maybe we've come out of the dark after all.

The Thoroughly
Modern Pow-Wow

Is There a Witch in your Family Closet?

I cannot stress enough how difficult this research was to gather. At every turn, I would run into blank stares and dead silence. People did not want to talk about the Pow-Wows. I felt like a bad actress in a B-movie digging up information on a nest of vampires. I put an ad in the local paper trying to draw out some information, I got nothing. I tried calling the *York Daily Record,* a large paper in the area, and asked if they would do an interview on my research, thinking that it might encourage members of the public to come forward with fresh information. The paper flatly refused. When on the road, I often received adamant denials of any in-depth knowledge about the subject. I knew these people were lying through their teeth. Their eyes told me, their body language told me, and their attitudes told me. I was snubbed, laughed at, and once, spit at. You would have thought I was asking them if they masturbated. During an exceptionally frustrating week I screamed at my husband. "I'm sick of being polite when someone says they don't know anything, and I know that they do!" (Okay, so I don't have the sweet demeanor of Nancy Drew.) Luckily for me, my husband is the laid-back type. He laughed and said, "So what are you going to do, force them?"

I'd be lying if I told you it didn't cross my mind. Being a good little magickal person I figured that where there was a will, there was a way. I could have dressed in flowing black, pointed my broom in their direction, and uttered something unintelligible. Somehow, I didn't think that would have gotten me much. Well, maybe shot. (We are talking about a mountainous/ agricultural area, you know.) Instead, I put miles on my car, created a horrendous phone bill, and made many wonderful friends in the process. What I couldn't understand was why no one wanted to talk about a practice that was once acceptable. Even the history buffs shied away when I presented the subject. I would receive promises of information that never materialized. There were people who intentionally sent me on wild Pow-Wow chases and those who puffed with importance on how much they knew about Pow-Wows. Upon scrutiny, they knew nothing. (Elvis probably talks to those people.) Friends of mine agreed to check on stories they had heard from their parents. We found them unwilling to cooperate. Time and again people would say to me, "Oh, my husband (or wife) could tell you about that, but he (she) absolutely refuses to talk about it."

Witches of today are dealing with the Hollywood tripe peddled by various structured religious systems. The public, though now going through an educational process launched by the Pagan community, is still leery about the "broom set." The Craft is not a monster in the religious closet; it will be the catalyst of the future.

Methinks Thou Dost Protest too Much

The toughest nail to pry out of the secrecy coffin was placed there by the Pow-Wow artists themselves. They hiss at the mother religion right along with everyone else. They were careful, in some instances, to call negative magick Witcherie (meaning something bad or negative influences sent by a non-magickal person or a Witch wanna-be). Students of Pow-Wow who don't know "all" the mysteries innocently believe Witchcraft is bad. They agree with the rest of the community. In the past, they spoke out against the Craft, perpetuating the idea of persecution—if not the fact, the idea. Students who did know kept their mouths shut. One way to ensure the secrecy process was to threaten the student. Students were told that they would lose their power if they revealed the mysteries of their system. There are Pow-Wows today who still believe this and therefore refused to be interviewed! Others would not speak to me because they felt their practice was a "special gift"—in one person's words, "It is a gift from God not to be shared with the public." To me, the greatest injustice to humankind is to hide knowledge that would be of assistance to others. These people should be avoided.

At mid-construction of this book, one individual who indicated he had knowledge on the subject trotted out the "To know, to dare, to will, and to be silent" strategy. Ah, I thought—a valid argument. However, I've taken no vows regarding the information contained herein. In fact, I wrote a newspaper article about Pow-Wow and my teacher at the time loved it. Pow-Wow is a system without order. It is not a religion. Pow-Wow artists did not take ceremonial vows of silence. Therefore, I am not treading on any theological toes and the information is certainly not provided in an effort to harm anyone.

At the outset of my investigations, many Pow-Wows interviewed said they "hated" real Witches. We are not talking about a slight distaste here, but more along the lines of an ultimate spitting contest. I picked up a few chapbooks in Lancaster when I was visiting there and found them horrendously biased against Witchcraft and in favor of Pow-Wow. If that isn't the pot calling the cauldron black, I thought. I even wrote to the publishing companies of these books. I politely pointed out their errors but didn't receive a single note in reply. Not very surprising, is it? If one is making money off a misconception, why should one try to correct the errors?

This purported hatred stems from the false impression that Witches are devil worshippers, which they are not. As I have mentioned before, Witches don't even believe in the Christian devil in the first place. The concept of this fellow is as icky to Witches as it is to Christians. Setting the record straight on what Pow-Wow actually is would (and will) displease both religious leaders and tradesmen alike. Tough. I'm sure Lancaster and York County citizens would draw back in utter horror to learn that their area was actually the Witch Capital of the Americas. They may flutter and faint to know it is a hotbed of all sorts of magickal people now, as it has been for the last 250-odd years. Today, if you live around this area, you should consider it chic. This is the Avalon of the American Witch, where magick and reality live and prosper together. I can't think of a better place I'd want to be.

With the research performed, it is more logical to believe that, in later years, Pow-Wows disliked real Witches because anyone who had seriously studied the Craft would immediately draw the same conclusion as I (as well as many other Pennsylvanian Witches) did—Pow Wow *is* a cloaked form of American Witchcraft.

The Real Mystery

Earlier, I mentioned that there were all sorts of mysteries involved with Pow-Wow. Investigating its original religious base, its birth, the secrecy behind the practice, and even finding a Pow-Wow who practices today makes one think about hiring a private eye. An especially complex mystery lies around the Rehmeyer murder case. I personally think the actual murder was only the tip of the iceberg. Hysteria builds slowly. It is based on something such as a series of events, then takes off with such an impact that one only feels the effects. We forget about what the cause may have been. Perhaps there was a type of Witch War we never heard about. It may have been the age-old battle between positive magickal people and those who would prefer to promote fear. It emerged, flamed, and returned to the burning coals from whence it came, taking a human life with it.

In the 1920s, it was a favorite pastime of several wanna-be Witches to take money for psychic detective work. Their task was to find out who in a client's life was responsible for hexing him or her. No one ever thought events in their lives were bad because they made it that way. Uh-uh. It was far easier to believe someone put a hex on you than to take the responsibility of controlling your life. Local farmers and townspeople would make the rounds of all the Pow-Wows and Hexmeisters in the area until someone with a proverbial axe to grind pointed a finger. Sometimes this finger-pointing process resulted in murder. In milder cases, the Pow-Wow or Hexmeister would charge a fee of around 10 dollars to remove the hex from the client. None of these people— the Pow-Wows, the Hexmeisters, or, of course, their clients (naturally)— understood real magick. Any 101 Witchcraft student worth his or her holy water knows that you don't need a specific name to remove a hex. Also, hexes (especially long-term ones) are not that easy to cast and I highly doubt that there were as many powerful Hexmeisters running around as there were purported hexings. Plain old superstition was far more responsible for the triumphs and tragedies of country life than real magick.

In August of 1992, I took on a Craft student and began our one-on-one sessions as I normally do. Somehow we got on the subject of Pow-Wow. For half an hour I sat open-mouthed as he confirmed my suspicions about an actual Witch War that took place approximately 70 years ago. According to his account, it began in the late 1800s and ended with the inception of World War I. Of course, one must consider that the story is entirely hearsay because it is third-party information.

The story goes that a new breed of magickal people from the Black Forest in Germany came to Pennsylvania in the mid-1800s. They were not traditional Witches. Unlike their Protestant counterparts already established here, they replaced the Old Religion with Catholicism, bastardizing both religions to suit their needs. Another group emigrated to the Philadelphia area, while a third group, this one a Polish/Italian mix, wound up somewhere in between. Whatever their collective argument was, they brought the fight with them. Those who came from the Black Forest before the Revolutionary War (which is my lineage) were decidedly very unhappy about the newcomers. My people felt it was a healthy plan to lie low and watch instead of participate.

The origin of the dispute between the new clans could have been over something as trite as a rainstorm that spoiled a festival day. Maybe unusual lights seen in the sky were thought to be a power play. Who knows? They fought their battles with ceremonial magick as well as propaganda techniques. These Hexmeisters would tell their clients that other clans were casting hexes on them. They would then step back and let the chips fall where they may. That way the clients did the dirty work, acting on their fears. The Hexmeisters sat back and enjoyed the show. These new clans did not carry ethics close to their hearts and were absolute snobs. From the telling of this story, some indigenous Pow-Wows also joined the fray. No wonder the non-magickal community was all in a huff!

The new folks on the block called themselves "High Germans," meaning they were the elite such as doctors, rich merchants, and titled individuals. This does not mean they spoke high German; they frowned on their peasant counterparts and simply did not use the local flora for their work. Why bother? They were rich enough to have it shipped from the Old Country, which is exactly what they did. They also detested the Gypsies, and it is no wonder. Who else could rival their power base *but* a Gypsy? A few of these new, elite Germans were conjuring things all over the place, either by accident or by design. I believe a large portion of psychic activity was a result of uncontrolled psychic fall-out. When one works magick, he or she becomes a beacon that is seen in various planes of existence. Naturally, if there is a great deal of activity on the earth plane, various entities are going to be nosy. As a result, the increased psychic activity literally scared the you-know-what out of the locals. How much of it was real and how much imagined is open for discussion. The entire mess created a fear factor that has remained hooked to Pow-Wow for the past five generations. I also got the impression from this story (and no offense, fellas, because I understand women can be just as lethal) that the greater portion of the strife was male ego-oriented. Most of it involved mouth battles and propaganda plays. A lot like the Witch Wars of today—all hot air and no zap.

Many of the Pow-Wows and all of the non-magickal people rightly feared the new groups. Obviously, they didn't follow the "An it harm none, do what ye will" edict. Oh no. These people appear to have been power junkies; sadly, some of them were darn good at it. So how does this tale end? Influenza hit, killing thousands of people all over the country. World War I began. Rehmeyer was murdered and a truce was finally drawn. Essentially, the universe stepped in, figuring it was high time to do a balancing act.

Magick comes in many forms. You can try to squash it, hide it, and change it, but it never dies. Prayer is magick. Incantations are magick. Positive thinking is magick. Mother Earth is magick. Life itself is magick of the highest degree. Pow-Wows of today do not conjure demons. They do not sit around their kitchen tables talking to assorted astral nasties. I also believe that 90 percent of the Pow-Wows in the past did not operate on the dark side, but used their skills for the welfare of the people.

Magick is neutral. Electricity can fry you or heat your home. A knife can cut you or prepare your evening meal. Magick, electricity, and knives are merely tools. It is how you use them that is important. If you misuse them ... rest assured, you will pay a far higher price for it than you anticipated.

Belief

The charms, spells, formulas, and information offered in this text are by no means the complete scope of the Pow-Wow system. There is a great deal more to be discovered and unearthed in years to come. Individuals of all faiths can use the information gathered here with success; as long as you believe—and connect with your chosen divinity—the only person who can stop you is yourself.

"Belief," said my teacher, Preston Zerbe, "is really all it takes. It doesn't matter what religion you are."

Pow-Wow uses the process of sympathetic magick. There are no elaborate tools or ingredients. You can find most everything in your kitchen cabinet, sewing box, pantry, garden, or in your area or a grocery store. There are a few items that you may need to visit an herb shop to purchase. You need order nothing from an exotic island. Pow-Wow is inexpensive and practical magick. It is possible that the only money you will spend to perform it is the cost of this book.

Pow-Wow is and was eclectic in nature. This means that not every Pow-Wow artist operated in the same manner. Some used strictly faith healing, frowning upon those who believed in charms, spells, or herbs. Others had an array of medicinal cures, household baubles turned magickal, and specific astrological dates conducive to their work. There were those who leaned heavily on Indian chants, minor forms of hypnosis, and even a few tricks of sleight of hand. Others used Latin and quotes from the Bible. My teacher spoke special incantations in German. Like today's eclectic Witches, only Divinity and positive intent remain constant.

Magick and Divinity

Magick is concentrated thought fueled by a need, assisted by a tool, empowered by Divinity, trusted by the self, and cast into the void of the Universe. If the thought is not focused, the need not relevant, the tool inappropriate, the belief not strong, or Divinity not infused, magick will not work; or if it does, it will work badly. It is also wise to remember that magick follows the least path of resistance and is purely natural in effect. Often it looks more like a coincidence than a shower of thunderbolts. A student of mine once said, "I've been working and working like the books told me. For a while, I thought, 'Why am I doing this; nothing is happening the way I want it to.'

Then I sat back and really reviewed my life. I realized that all the changes I'd been working for had taken place, but they were so subtle that I hadn't even noticed!"

Some modern-day magickal people will tell you that you have to reach frustration level, where all mundane ways have failed, to do magick. I say this is a crock. To me, this is band-aid magick. It is like saying, "Gee, I let it get so far that now it's broken; guess I'd better run to my altar and do some magick to fix it!" This line of thought also tells me that the individual is only tugging at the link between Divinity and magick. One is not living a serene magickal lifestyle if he or she chooses to use bandage magick. In situations like this, the magickal person is constantly reacting to the outside environment that he or she didn't bother to control in the first place. As there is preventive health care, there should be some measure of preventive magick in your life. This is not to say you shouldn't learn the healing arts or how to catch a thief. We often get so focused on one aspect of our lives we let a few others trail downhill. Then we—myself included—need that magickal bandage.

Refreshingly, Pow-Wow has not faced corruption or sophistication by modern magickal practices. The tools employed are practical, such as the simple use of hand motions, your finger, your breath, or a piece of string.

The more times you perform magick successfully, the greater becomes your focus, the stronger becomes your belief, the more spiritually you link with Divinity, and the wiser you grow. In the end, your universe fills with love.

The Ego and Pow-Wow

Most individuals interviewed for this book agreed that the Pow-Wow artist was more religious in nature than his or her neighbors. The Pow-Wow made a point to live properly in regard to human ethics and was a good counsellor as well as a healer. They agreed that Pow-Wows followed their chosen religion closely, and had a strong belief in Divinity. They told their clients that healings did not spring from themselves, but from the Divine. The Divine had the "power," not the human.

Pow-Wow artists often agreed there was no room for ego and that the power came through them, rather than from them. If a Pow-Wow began to believe he or she was personally responsible for the healings or other magickal workings, his or her power was in danger of eradication by Divinity. Like a candle, the power could be snuffed out by the universe if the artist did not credit Divinity. In teaching my students, I tell them to imagine that the human is the engine and Divinity is the fuel. It is hard for people to think Divinity did it all and we didn't do anything, especially when you've been sitting in a healing circle for over two hours, churning out request after request. Humans like to get some credit for their efforts and I believe they should.

Although many interviewed felt that the patient or person being "tried" for should be a devout Christian (most likely due to modern church dictates) and that Pow-Wow would not work without this belief, there is much to disprove this theology. For example, many Pow-Wows were capable of long-distance healing. This is where the patient does not have to be present or know the Pow-Wow personally, which means the artist doesn't know the patient's religious affinity. Often all the Pow-Wow needed to know to work the healing was the patient's name. There are interviews recorded in which a person would telephone the Pow-Wow, give his or her name, and the healing would be performed after they hung up. Therefore, it is not the belief in any particular Divinity, but the combined faith of the Pow-Wow artist in Divinity and the faith that the patient has in the Pow-Wow. The faith leads them to subconsciously believe in the power of good over evil, which is what is essentially important. As in the case of the woman with Alzheimer's disease, the patient wasn't even aware of what was happening. She had no idea she was experiencing a healing until after the fact. This leads us to consider that in some instances the faith of the Pow-Wow artist or the patient's subconscious belief in good over evil is the only requirement.

Fear of Embarrassment is a Mind Killer

The biggest stumbling block in Pow-Wow today is embarrassment. One man said, "Oh, that stuff. My parents took me to one when I was a child, but I don't believe in such superstition." His tone of voice was angry and accusatory, as if he were trying to belittle his parents for their lack of education and their belief in the mystical. During various interviews, I asked, "If you had a choice between visiting a Pow-Wow and visiting your doctor, which would you choose?" About 90 percent of those asked said they would choose the Pow-Wow over the doctor. My second question to those who preferred the doctor was this, "If you could go both to a doctor and a Pow-Wow, would you do it?" All but one said yes.

While I was interviewing Pow-Wows, I was repeatedly asked not to release their names. One gentleman said, "If you do, I'll have them backed up all the way down the driveway again, and I don't want that." His teacher was interviewed by a newspaper reporter several years ago and she had released his name. "I had people all over the place!" he exclaimed.

Pow-Wows are also nervous about the medical community. Doctors have a bad habit of scoffing at holistic healing. Although they are serious about the welfare of their patients, they do force people to disbelieve in sympathetic magick. Instead of researching the possibility of successful healing techniques, they often spend their time campaigning for laws to persecute those who practice it. Health care today has become outrageous in price. Only the rich can remain healthy through paid-for medical treatment. The dirt-poor are paid for by the state. This leaves the rest of us floundering for medical care. A trip to the doctor for a simple cold can result in a $40 bill for 10 minutes of office time. A prescription can run over $30.

Not all doctors are money-hungry monsters, of course, and not all doctors disbelieve in holistic medicine and faith healing. In several interviews, I was told that people sought both the healing capabilities of the Pow-Wow and the physician and were pleased with both. Wilhelmenia Keefer, a resident of Pennsylvania, told me the following story. "My mother took me to the doctor for the wild fire [a type of skin infection that can eventually kill you]. They call it erysipelas [One Pow-Wow thought this affliction was directly attributable to the use of lye soap]. The doctor couldn't do a thing for me. My mother turned around and took me to the local Pow-Wow, who cured me using a series of hand motions, breathing, and rattlesnake oil. She cured me. When my mother again saw the doctor, she was embarrassed to tell him what she had done for me, but felt that because I had been cured he had the right to know how it happened. When she told him, he winked and said he was glad she had taken me to the Pow-Wow, and respected the cure. However, she wasn't to tell anyone he said that."

Rationality and Fear

Above all, Pow-Wows believe that not everything in the world is accessed through the use of the five senses alone. The Pow-Wows belittle those around them who insist on living in a non-expanding world. To support their beliefs, they quote from writings of famous philosophers throughout the ages. Most Pow-Wows, in their own manner, were and are egotistical. They had to be to survive. Both women and men carry a special air of determination and persistence and have a "Don't tread on me!" attitude.

"I can remember old Grandma Mary," reminisced one lady from Mechanicsburg. "Her family swore she could throw the evil eye. She was a good Pow-Wow, but it sure was a frightening thing. The neighbors were scared to death of her. In the morning, it was customary in town for every housewife to sweep the porch and sidewalk. Mary would wait until her neighbors got started. Then she would sashay herself out that door in her old-lady dress and her old-lady apron. She held her broom before her like it was the Ten Commandments and she would commence to clean her porch without looking left or right. As soon as her front porch door banged open, in their own doors would flit her neighbors as fast as their fat legs would carry them. They left their chores undone until she'd finished. Sometimes she would piddle around on purpose, just to upset everyone's day. She was a card, that Mary!"

Lessons in Sympathy

"If you set something in salt water, it will eventually take on some salt. If you set it in rose water, then it will emerge smelling like roses. This is two things growing in sympathy with each other," said Ruby in a stern voice. Ruby is 78 and resides in the city of York. "If a woman or man spends too much time with fearful people, they will become fearful themselves. That's what happened around here! Instead, they should surround themselves with those of strength and good virtue. Most of the ninnies don't understand that by controlling your surroundings you control yourself."

Most Pow-Wow artists believed that all issues were either black or white. Grey areas of thought did not exist and therefore were not an issue. "It was either this, or it was that," stated Ruby. "None of this in-between stuff like the young people are always hollering about!"

She held out her gnarled fingers and laced them together, then shoved them directly in my face. "For things to work together, they must be in sympathy with each other. When we heal, we are in sympathy with God and the land around us. This land here," she waved a boney hand at her luscious garden, "is full of Pow-Wow magick—God's magick! We take on properties of Him, and the act takes on properties of us, but, you give the credit to God. If you don't, your worst enemy will find you and take you way down deep." She waved a finger at me. "For every person, this is different. All things have natural enemies, even man. There is nobody who knows everything. If a body is a true Pow-Wow, they will admit that fact. It is when they get so high and mighty that the trouble comes knocking at their door. And it will come, mind you.

"Not one plant is better than the other, nor is one man better than his neighbor, or a woman better than her friend. You've got to have hot and cold to make warm bath water or you'd be miserable in the tub! These silly young people have forgotten a lot of this. Now, I've told you the principles of Pow-Wow. Git!"

The Retention of Power and the Elements

"Anything a Pow-Wow touches has the ability to retain power," stated Preston Zerbe, York Springs resident. "The Indian Pow-Wows believed this more than us faith healers. They had wolf skins, snake skins, you name it. They also used lots of plants and were big on salves. Rattlesnake was a favorite. Likewise, there was a belief that the elements provided by God, if used properly, would bring sympathy for healing. If you added emotion to it and concentrated real hard, the Pow-Wow could not be stopped."

Eloquence and Personality Traits

"A good Pow-Wow was an eloquent one," explained a senior citizen (who wishes to remain unnamed) from Hanover, Pennsylvania. "They found soft speech and slow, graceful movements created and held power. These were the strong ones. Often they didn't brag about how good they were. The real good ones could discern eye light. For instance, after you try for someone, you look into their eyes. A Pow-Wow can see the healing energy in the eyes. If the energy is strong and blue, then the healing has caught. If not, then you must try again. Some Pow-Wows see gold light instead of blue, but it's the light of God. If after the third time, it is evident the person doesn't believe, most Pow-Wows would refer them to another one down the road or in another town. If a person doesn't believe in Pow-Wow, you are playing the odds on whether it will take or not."

Timing, empathy, desire, courage, self-confidence, and a sense of stewardship were important personality characteristics of the more learned Pow-Wows. They often carried themselves with purpose and were careful not to underestimate the people around them. Hospitality was an important factor in their work. Although they offered none of the usual social amenities, such as food or drink, the atmosphere inside most of their homes was safe and peaceful. These qualities brought both respect from those they assisted and fear from jealous enemies. Many Pow-Wows realized that they were in the spotlight of the community. To live with ethics, balance, and integrity was important both for their personal spirituality and the continuation of the Pow-Wow art.

Legends and Lore

During my research I would muse to myself, "Why didn't I learn any of the colorful history of the state during my school years?" Myths, ghost stories, herbal lore, history—all weave an exciting tapestry of knowledge, waiting to wrap me in the veils of the unknown. The culture vibrates with frequencies most modern people never touch. Many of the mountains, roads, streams, or other natural landmarks are named after occult-related events or people. One rather colorful gentleman by the name of Charles "Doc" Dubson set a well-known place for himself in the realm of Pow-Wow. Practicing in Lancaster County, he Pow-Wowed for only two days out of each week, taking clients from several counties. A former Vaudeville acrobat, he specialized in hypnosis. Using what we would call the speed induction method today, he would place his hands a few inches from the client and draw the problem out, then cast it to the winds.

In Williams Township, Northampton County, lies a cluster of rocks named Hexenkopf. The translation of Hexenkopf is "Witch's Head." Supposedly (ahem) there are Witches who live in these rocks. Rising 800 feet over Stout's Valley, the hill is historically rumored to be linked to necromancy. Many today blame their misfortunes on the Witch's Head because the "powers" emanate from this point. If I were guessing, I'd say it is probably what we would call a ley line or junction of some sort. Historian Matthew Henry tells of Witches who dance with arms locked together, circling around an oak tree at the summit, complete with unearthly sounds and bouncing lights (see Adams, *Pennsylvania Dutch Country Ghosts, Legends, and Lore,* Exeter House Books, 1994, p. 21). One Pow-Wow artist, Dr. Peter Saylor, used the mountain as a generator, pulling power from and throwing energy to the Witch's Head.

In a paper titled "Hexenkopf: Mystery, Myth, and Legend," Professor Ned Heindel cited an 1863 article in a religious publication in which Rev. Charles P. Krauth recounted the legends of Hexenkopf, and further claimed that the Witches did not always escape with impunity (See Adams, p. 23).

A Williams Township widow was accused of committing wicked acts (enchantments, charms) against, of all things, a white horse. Although the woman's name is not given, she confessed (I shudder to think why and how) and was thrown in jail for one year. She was also to stand six hours in the pillory every four months. She should have used the following charm:

> As I walked before the house of judges
> Three dead men looked out the window:
> One had no tongue, one had no lung
> The third blind, sick, and dumb.
> Protect me from the county's legal scum
> In the name of the Father, Son, and Holy Ghost
> Amen.

The Tools of the Pow-Wow

Healing Tools

While I learned the art of Pow-Wow, my altar looked very different from a traditional Wiccan one. I tend to immerse myself in a magickal system to understand all its aspects. On my altar I kept a spool of red and black thread, a ball of red yarn, several lengths of red and black ribbon, two small, hand-made ceramic bowls, a dressmaker's seam ripper (no kidding), my creek stone (called a Divinity stone by some), and a flute of holy water. The colors of red and white were the basic power shades of the Pow-Wow, therefore my altar cloth and other decorations revolved around this. These are the basic tools of the Pow-Wow. Today I keep most of these supplies in my magickal cabinet. However, my Divinity stone rests on a silver stand and represents the South on my altar, no matter what system or tradition I am using.

The practical Pow-Wow stuck to earthen bowls, pieces of unbleached muslin, the kitchen table or desktop, and perhaps, if so inclined, a dowsing rod. In my magickal cabinet, I keep a supply of unbleached muslin bags and numerous herbs, white parchment paper, various acrylic paints, and round discs of balsa wood in various sizes. What tools a Pow-Wow incorporated in his or her work and the herbs he or she used (if any) depended largely upon training. I found that most of the remaining Pow-Wows, though they enjoy learning new techniques, do not incorporate them in their traditional work. What the teacher gave them is what they use—no more, no less. Of course, we could attribute this line of thinking to age. Most of the people to whom I spoke were over 65 years old. They had no desire to change or improve what had worked well for them for over fifty years. Who can blame them?

Within this text I have tried to keep as close to the original tools and herbs as possible, but I believe that the reader can take the system much farther than the skeleton remaining. I have tried to give you a system devoid of specific traditional overtones to allow you to use your own Divinity and chosen tools. Because Pow-Wow was a system that evolved year by year and changed from person to person, it would be downright silly and definitely close-minded to believe that "everyone used this and so ...".

Indoor and Outdoor Sacred Space

Christos (another word for Christians who work magick) Pow-Wows who used their homes to administer to the public did not have an "altar" on display where their clients could see it. Many Pow-Wows also used work tables or the cleared the kitchen table to sew and fill conjuring bags full of herbs and other items. In most Pow-Wow homes, the room used for assisting clients was an important place; its atmosphere (in most cases) must be correct and clean. This was the Pow-Wow's public sacred space. Those who used the Old Religion cleansed and consecrated the room and warded it against evil. Christos Pow-Wows hung pictures of Christ (the Last Supper was a favorite), crucifixes, and other items common to their religious base. Normally the Protestant Pow-Wows did not cleanse and consecrate the room unless they were working ceremonial magick. They did, however, believe in warding everything to the fullest. Private sacred spaces were a different matter, and the Pow-Wow used what he or she had available. Often they employed root cellars, out-buildings, or sheds to build their temples. They would erect complete altars there according to their magickal traditions. Those who did not understand the science of the sacred space simply decorated their entire house. Many Catholic Pow-Wows turned their bedrooms into shrines displaying statues of the Virgin Mary and collections of rosaries.

The garden and house yard often represented the outdoor sacred space to Pow-Wow practitioners. They spent a lot of time in their herb and vegetable gardens. Though the family might have a large farm, the house garden's products contributed extra money to the family budget and was a safe place for their magickal herbs. People who lived in town would line fence rows between the houses with needed herbs and special flowers. Those who didn't like their neighbors mixed pickling salt, vervain, and rue together, then sprinkled it up and down the fence row to keep any negative energies at bay. Be careful, though, because this mixture kills any plant life it touches. Trust me. I made a magick circle once to protect the house and killed all the grass in the line of a perfect circle.

A favorite Pow-Wow flower was the night-blooming sirius. They were very hard to get and would bloom perhaps once a year under the light of a Full Moon. "I can remember when the entire block would wait all summer for Mrs. Emmer's night-blooming sirius to open. Everyone would gather at the gate of the front yard to watch the momentous occasion," explained my father. "We always expected to see fairies when that flower opened, but never did."

"Town gardens were planted at the end of the yard, bordering the alleys," explained another fellow by the name of Lyle Becker. "It seemed that in every neighborhood there was one person who would canvass the gardens at night, looking to pluck the best produce for themselves. Our neighborhood had an old lady who did this. Although she had her own garden, she would rise early in the morning and sneak around town, taking the best peppers, tomatoes, and so on from neighbors' gardens. We found out who it was because a neighbor boy stayed up all night to see who was robbing his mother's garden and saw her. You see, that was around the Great Depression, and in those days, you worked hard just to eat. There was none of these fancy toys and cars. You were lucky to have dinner on the table.

"The garden was real important to the town family. It was sort of a sacred space to them. Well, that boy went to a Pow-Wow lady at the edge of town and asked her what to do. She studied him for a while, determining whether or not he was being honest with her. In the end, she told him to throw a bouquet of nettles and thistle on the lady's porch, as close to the sun coming up as he could. He did what he was told. Two weeks later, the thief lost her house and had to move in with relatives in another state. All those years she had been renting the property from a farmer down the road. When he sold out as a result of a lucrative deal, she had to move. Nobody in town would rent her a place. She had no choice but to go. I feel comfortable telling this story now because just about everybody's dead."

Fountains and Living Water

Pow-Wows found living water—such as streams, lakes, and creeks—important in their work. This element can be considered a valuable tool. Blessed waters from these natural sources found their way into healing rituals. Stones found in creeks and ponds were prepared for divinatory purposes. Natural items used to break hexes and remove negativity from a person or place were thrown into living bodies of water. The sounds of running water were important in healing as well. To remove stress and anxiety from a patient, a Pow-Wow would direct him or her to visit a favorite local body of water. Timing usually revolved around dusk, dawn, or midnight. There the person would find peace and prosperity in the sound and sight of the water.

North
Stability
Strength
Earth Element
Protection
Designed by Silver RavenWolf

We put a fountain on our property last year and employ it in many aspects of our magick. There is no limit to what you can do with even a small piece of property. Creativity and imagination, as well as good planning, figure into the creation of both indoor and outdoor sacred space.

Preparing Sacred Space

The Altar

If a Pow-Wow had a personal altar, it was certainly not anywhere the public could see it, or it was disguised as a shelf with a few candles and statues of either Jesus or Mary. While I was writing *To Ride a Silver Broomstick,* I had a fantastic wall altar made of tiered glass shelves. Unfortunately, I put my head up through it while I was cleaning one summer afternoon. So much for my wall altar. Rule of thumb, don't stick your head in your wall altar—better yet, don't clean! Catholic and Old Religion Pow-Wows did perform ceremonies of cleansing and consecration for various rooms in the house. The sacred space was prepared for magick by removing all negative energy that may have collected there.

One lady I interviewed remembered that her Pow-Wow grandmother had a huge statue of the Virgin Mary in her bedroom. It rested magnificently on a dressing table around which many candles could be seen burning every day. She would also add flowers, stones, and a few other items, such as pieces of amber, jewelry, etc. These items changed from day to day. I think we would be safe in assuming that her dressing table was her altar and that she most likely empowered her tools and jewelry there.

I keep my altar in my dining room, which is where I greet people and do my magickal work for the public. My altar, a stereo stand with a large slab of granite on top, is an integral part of my sacred space. The tape decks are on the second and third shelves of the stand, so I can play music to soothe any jangled nerves. During holidays, my altar matches my traditional Wiccan work. There are seasonal color illuminator candles set at the back, right, and left of the table. In the middle is my pentacle, carved on an agate and approximately six inches in diameter. Other holiday items include bowls of salt and water, an incense burner, athame, and items to represent the four elements. Because I practice the Black Forest Tradition, there are some items that relate only to that Wiccan sect.

During the rest of the year I do not normally keep open bowls of sea salt and holy water on my altar. At a flea market, I found a stand designed for two flutes of oil and salt and pepper shakers. The glass pieces are hand-blown with wooden caps and suspend from the stand in a neat group. This way I have everything together when I need it. In one flute, I keep holy water; the other contains rose water. In the salt shaker is sea salt from the Dead Sea, and the pepper shaker contains a mixture of pulverized dried herbs to add to my incense burner. These items make up my standard altar layout. On holidays, I will add ribbons, special cloths, flowers, etc.

Because Pow-Wow has so infiltrated my life these days, my everyday altar has changed considerably. Often I use tea towels with Pennsylvania Dutch designs, or scarves imported from Germany. I now have small ceramic candle holders done in hex designs for specific purposes. I employ Craft background, study, and practice with the system of Pow-Wow to round out the magickal elements of the system and give it the backbone that was removed in the 1920s.

My entire family and the women in both my open and closed circles also use the altar; it has come to be known as the "Temple Altar." Many Witches and individuals of other positive religions have worked on my altar as well. I don't feel this damages its energies at all. My students and I have found it to be a powerful springboard for faith, magick, and ceremony. During a dedication ritual, one of the ladies in my circle said, "Why is it whenever I come here and work with this altar I feel such power? When I work at home, I don't get the same feel." I could have been smart and told her it was a secret, or it was a great truth I would reveal in the future, but what the heck—I told her the truth. I work magick on my altar every day, I pray there, I weep there, I rejoice there. My children do the same thing, as well as several of the ladies who come here. The altar resonates power because pure love and intent goes into it each and every time it is used.

The Magick Knife and Your Hands

In Wicca, the magick knife is called the athame; it is used for ritual purposes only. It never cuts anything physical, nor does it let blood. The magick knife is only for use in the astral (as in conjuring a circle or cutting a door between the worlds) and in the preparation of holy water. The blade is six to eight inches in length and the handle is normally made of wood or bone. Often it is carved intricately with symbols belonging to the tradition of that person. Interestingly enough, more modern Pow-Wows (during the 1920s) often used kitchen shears instead of the magick knife. However, those who delved into ceremonial magick in the early to mid-1900s did indeed use knives and wands, as well as a standard altar.

Standard magickal objects, such as ornate chalices and wands and knives, were not normally used by the practical Pow-Wows. The hands were employed with far more intensity than in modern Wicca, where the knife is commonly used. From the practice of the Pow-Wows, we can learn to use

50

our hands to work powerful magick. By bringing the energy closer to our bodies, we learn to attune ourselves much better both to the world without and the world within. We begin to feel and then conquer complete control of energy. There is no better training than to dispense with as many tools as possible, and learn energy direction with our hands or feet as the tools. Practical Pow-Wow artists preferred using their hands and fingers to cast circles, work with elements, and empower objects. Kitchen knives were used as divinatory tools and spun on a smooth surface to find the direction of lost items, people, or animals.

Holy Water

Holy water is used for a variety of purposes, from cleansing tools, homes, and people to adding it to conjuring pouches and food. There are several ways to make holy water, yet three ingredients are standard—salt, water, and vervain. To make one version of (non-edible) holy water you will need sea salt, one cup of spring water or water from a flowing creek, some loose sage, ⅛ teaspoon vervain, and seven drops of rose water. You should also have a small glass bottle with a screw-on cap or cork stopper, and your magickal knife. If you prefer, you can use your finger in place of the knife.

Schedule five to ten minutes out of your busy day or evening when you will be alone and undisturbed. Check your almanac. The best time to make holy water is during the Full Moon cycle. However, should you run out for any particular reason during the month, you can make it under other moon phases. Just remember to add the statement: "May all astrological correspondences be correct for this working." The lunar eclipse, should you be fortunate enough to catch one, is a fantastic time to make holy water. My entire family made jugs of it the last time and passed it out to students and friends alike.

I prefer to have a white or blue candle burning while I make the water. Have all your supplies available. Often I cleanse the room with burning sage in a bowl. It only takes a minute or two and sets the scene for your work.

The first item on your agenda is to *relax*. Set yourself in meditation mode where the stress of daily living flows out of your body. Ground and center yourself. Most magickal people have a specific routine they go through when connecting with Divinity. If you are Christian, you might want to take this time to say the Lord's Prayer or read a few passages from the Bible. Choose something that reflects the open and loving aspects of the universe and God. If you are Wiccan or a member of another alternative magickal religion, you will most likely open the chakra centers, breathe deeply, and connect with Divinity in that manner.

You should keep in mind exactly what your purpose is during this ritual. You have the knowledge (that of how to make the water), the will (because you are sitting there in the process of doing it because you want to), and the intent (that of creating something that will help both yourself and others). The word "intent" is often magickally construed as "high emotion" or "strong feelings" on an issue or circumstance. Fear has no place with intent, nor does evil. Your intent should always be positive in nature. If you are angry or upset, forget it and wait until you have calmed down. This goes for any magickal procedure.

You can use "intent" if you are not emotional, but focused on what you are doing. I personally don't believe that you have to be at the point of hysterics or jumping with glory and joy to perform a magickal act. This energy can go off like a stray bullet if you are not grounded and centered. Conversely, if you are grounded and centered, you are not bouncing off the walls in the first place. The issue of "grounding" here does not mean that you are letting your personal energy soak into the ground. It is more like taking a magickal stance, where you are firm on your feet and connected to the Earth Mother. Take a moment to feel her energy move up into your body. It is helpful to visualize this energy as a green wave of soft, supportive light that connects you securely to the ground.

Take the container of water in your hands and hold it out in front of you. Ask your chosen deity to bless the water, to instill positive energy into it. Use your creative visualization techniques and imagine a golden light coming from the universe. Watch it change the water to golden essence. Don't get excited if your mind refuses to "see" the gold color.

Each of my students is required to perform an altar devotion that includes the making of holy water. During the exercise, one of my students squeakily said, "It's not changing. I can't get it to go gold. It's blue. Is it ready yet?"

From my vantage point I could feel her energy zinging all over the place and the water was literally pulsating with it. "No problem," I whispered. "Just keep going, you've got it." Her experience brings up a very good point. When do you know if the water is ready? Don't worry about it. Your intent is pure, therefore your water is ready when you feel it is. If you can't quite feel it yet, relax. These connections come with training. Many students expect bells and whistles to sound and it normally doesn't work that way. Energy is a subtle essence, and you need to teach your senses to acknowledge it.

Put the water down and pick up the salt. Again ask your chosen deity to bless the salt, to instill positive energy into it. This time imagine that the salt is turning to silver. Set the salt down beside the water. Take your magickal knife (or your finger), dip it in the salt, and balance some salt particles on the blade (or the end of your finger). Sprinkle it into the water. Your purpose here is to mix the positive energies of the universe together for the intent of healing and protection. Do this three times. If you are Christian, call out

Father first, Son second, and the Holy Ghost third. If you are Wiccan, call out the Lord, the Lady, and the White Light of the All. One can also use a chosen pantheon of deities or archetypes. Add the vervain and follow the same procedure. (Vervain was a favorite of Druids and Pow-Wow artists.)

Pour the mixture into a clear bottle. Hold the bottle in your left hand and the rose water in your right. Pour seven drops of rose water into the bottle. As each drop hits the contents, imagine it as a drop of light. Each drop is a blessing from the angels. Feel your own energy mixing with that of the universe. Set the rose water down and hold your bottle of holy water in both hands out in front of you. Raise your energy and watch the contents of the bottle begin to glow in your hands. Ground your energy in that water, not toward the floor. When you are finished, meditate for a few minutes. Relax, and thank the deities you have invoked for their service to humanity. Voilá! Holy water!

Many individuals have asked me if Catholic holy water can be used in place of making your own. This led MaraKay Rogers and I on a quest to determine how their water differed from ours. The answer is, not much. We basically use the same procedures in preparation. Their litany, of course, is much longer than the one we employ. We do not, however, recommend the ingestion of holy water sold in religious shops, nor should it be taken into a hospital environment or sprinkled on a sick person. There is a risk of contamination in this type of bottled water. If you are working with the sick, please make your own water or ask a Catholic priest to prepare it for you. Several of my students have volunteered to do the "holy water run" for their parents and grandparents because they know their loved ones are apt to drink the bottled water. These students either make a special trip to the parish priest or make the water themselves, refilling those plastic containers sold in religious stores with water they know is safe to drink.

Drinkable holy water contains only spring water and salt. Do not add vervain, rose water, or any other herbs in the preparation.

The Cleansing and Consecration of Tools

Protestant Pow-Wows from the 1920s on did not cleanse and consecrate their tools. Modern Christianity had taken such a hold that the practitioners thought it foolish. Most Protestants today do not believe in holy water or in blessing (in the old sense) anything other than what is done in the standard baptismal ceremony. However, I'm a firm believer that cleansing and consecrating everything, from the red thread used to the Divinity stone, is a necessity. Catholic and Wiccan Pow-Wows do cleanse and consecrate the sacred space and all tools, including their bodies. Serious magickal people believe wholeheartedly in cleansing and consecrating any tools or jewelry they use.

They also believe in making a "sacred space" where magick and healing can be performed. Protestant Pow-Wows did not think of these things at all—it would have been blasphemous. But I tend to go along with our old pal Shakespeare (who was quite a magickal character himself). In one of his plays, he writes, "There are more things in heaven and earth, Horatio ..." and we would be foolish to believe that the world consists only of what we can behold with the naked eye (especially when many of us require glasses, anyway).

The Pow-Wows used the Divinity stone, unbleached muslin, red and black thread, red yarn, and other items for healing and magickal purposes. Each of these items should be cleansed and consecrated before it is used. To cleanse and consecrate something is to remove any negativity from the item or place and fill it with positive, Divine energy. To do this you will need your holy water and items that represent the elements of fire, earth, and air. Your choices could be very simple. For instance, a candle flame for fire; a bowl of rice, corn meal, or dirt for earth; a fan, incense, or feather for air.

The ritual for cleansing and consecration is much like that with which you prepared the holy water. During the ceremony, you must pass the tool through each element, instilling it with positive energy and requesting blessings from the chosen deity and alignment with that element. Many Pow-Wows kept their simple tools—the thread, ribbon, the Divinity stone, the small earthen bowl, the magickal knife, and the yarn—in a wooden box painted in bright colors and delightful patterns. This sort of box is normally cataloged by most historians as the Bible Box. They also kept a seam ripper and a very small knife or scissors with their tools to cut string, thread, ribbon, etc.

The Divinity Stone

The basic function of the Divinity stone is to remove pain from the body of an animal or person. It is associated with the element of fire. It should be a little smaller than the palm of your hand so it can nestle comfortably in it. It is to be smooth to the touch. Neither the color nor the type of the stone is important.

Searching for your Divinity stone is a magickal endeavor in itself. My teacher, Preston Zerbe, looked everywhere for the "right" stone. For several weeks, he couldn't find what he wanted. None of the stones he picked up felt quite right. One day, he was working an odd job at a railroad that involved loading sacks of potatoes onto a box car. One of the bags split open and potatoes tumbled all over the ground. In the midst of one pile he found the perfect stone. It was round, smooth, deep brown, and about three inches in diameter. It looked just like a potato!

I didn't have much luck searching for my stone, either. I looked for weeks for the right one. Those weeks rolled into months and I still wasn't satisfied with anything I saw. We have tons of gems and stones around the house that we use for magickal work, but none were right. A friend of mine I hadn't seen for months knocked on my door one pleasant afternoon. She said, "I can't stay, but it has been a long time since I've seen you. I just wanted to let you know I was okay and things are going well. Oh, by the way, I picked up this stone about a week ago and it was just screaming your name. I think it belongs to you." And that's how I found my Divinity stone. It is pink and white speckled like an egg, smooth to the touch, and about two and a half inches in diameter. The stone practically pulses when I use it.

The Divinity stone is very easy to use. With specific chants, the pain is drawn into the stone, where it then dissipates into a void you create with your left hand. In some cases, students envision a hole in their left foot to allow the negative energy to flow into the ground. To prepare the stone, you should cleanse and consecrate it during the Full Moon cycle. At the end of the ceremony you should envision the stone as a black hole, and place this vision and purpose into the stone. Let it know its specific function—to remove and break down pain so it is no more.

I suggest sleeping with the stone for at least two weeks. It will be your friend during many healing sessions. The stone can be periodically cleansed by holding it under cold running water or placing it either in sunlight or moonlight. Unlike many tools, anyone can use your Divinity stone. It is of the earth and well-grounded. Its function is to absorb and then negate negative energy. You don't have to be afraid of it soaking up wild vibrations—that's what it is for. In working with and trading Divinity stones we have discovered some interesting points:

1. The stone works best for the person to whom it belongs. However, if a Pow-Wow uses your stone to heal you, it works the same as if you were performing the healing. If another person is using your stone to heal someone else, it does not work as vibrantly.

2. Each person should have his/her personal stone and bond with it for ultimate healing advantage.

3. Divinity stones are almost impossible to lose. When you need them, they are always available. Because they are not as delicate as gems or crystals, they can take a lot more psychic use. Like the famed Energizer bunny, they keep going and going. Divinity stones brave being carted around and left out in the yard by children, buried by animals, and whisked into hiding by pookas (little magickal, furry fellows that like to play astral jokes on you). The Divinity stone always returns "home," whether it be the altar or your lap.

4. Divinity stones are used for drawing out pain and infection. They are also good for moving energy through the body to break down energy blocks and pull out depression.

5. The Divinity stone is a tool of the element of fire and its cardinal direction is south. Clients are best served if they are positioned in the south during a healing session, especially if you are in the learning stages of this type of magick. Other items associated with fire work well with the Divinity stone, such as candles, images of a phoenix, smoke, oils, incense, herbs, etc.

Incense and Oils

The historical Pow-Wows did not use incense like we can buy today. Instead, they dried flowers and herbs indigenous to their area and added them to simmering liquid on the stove or burned them in an earthen or metal dish. Cinnamon and sage were favorites. Cinnamon is for good fortune and sage is for protection. Since the woman of the times spent a great deal of her waking hours cooking in the kitchen, she would often make her magickal items right along with the food for the family. When wood stoves were used, she usually had a special pan that slipped under the main oven where magickal items baked merrily away. Not many oils were employed by the practical Pow-Wow. Salves were another story. Using a lard base, herbs were pulverized and empowered to treat a variety of medical conditions.

String, Thread, Yarn, Ribbon, and Unbleached Muslin

These small items were used in conjunction with various chants and spells and are explained throughout the text as needed. Briefly, their uses involved removing negativity from a person and protecting the home and body, as well as preparing conjuring bags. To begin your studies in Pow-Wow, you will need a skein of red yarn, a spool of red and black thread, some lengths of red and black ribbon, and about a yard of unbleached muslin.

Magickal Voice

A great deal of Pow-Wow magick dealt with magickal voice—this is the tone, inflection, rhythm, and strength in the use of your vocal chords to bring about the correct vibrational frequency to enhance a magickal act. This takes some practice and decisions have to be made on whether to chant quietly or summon and command. If you are dealing with a client who is rather skittish, you should chant quietly to yourself or under your breath. If you are alone and doing long-distance work, then you can command the elements and intone the chants in a strong, clear voice. In a healing environment, you may wish to chant very fast and continuously to raise power. By doing it in a whisper you can go faster; as the sounds meld together, power is built. On a more personal note, if you flub up with a chant—and you will, everyone's tongue tends to have a mind of its own on occasion—no one will hear you. To the patient, it will be a jumble of sounds.

The Bible

The Bible and its verses became a tool for many of the Christos Pow-Wows as early as 1800 and grew in popularity until faith healing overcame most of the old charms and spells. Between 1966 and 1969, Pow-Wow and its faith-healing practices sparked the interest of several local magazine writers in south-central Pennsylvania. This was about the time when the country was gearing into "occult mode" when books by Ruth Montgomery and individuals like her would boom in the early 1970s.

Prior to that time, specifically between 1930 and 1960, there was little information published anywhere. By the sixties, in-depth interviews with local Pow-Wows showed that most had moved strictly to faith healing, using Bible verses that had been tried and found to work well. Although my teacher, Preston Zerbe, did not use the actual Bible, he certainly read from it when he was alone and used memorized passages, many derived from an out-of-print text entitled *Lessons in Sympathy*. He also, however, used Craft chants and spells, as well as German incantations handed down to him by his teacher, Gertie Guise.

The Himmelsbrief

The Himmelsbrief was a type of letter or testament carried upon a person or hung in the home for protection against evil people and deeds. Himmels-briefs were also known as "Letters of Protection" or "Letters From Heaven." The Pennsylvania Germans thought this paper to be as powerful as an invocation beginning with the Lord's Prayer. In 1918, the Aurand Press out of Lancaster, Pennsylvania received an order for printing copies of such a "Letter of Protection." It was subsequently learned that the copies were distributed to members of the National Guard and to draftees departing from several south-central Pennsylvania counties. During the 1920s and 1930s, Pow-Wow wanna-bes sold them at prices ranging from $1.50 to $10 a pop.

The Himmelsbrief came in a variety of forms, from a self-penned version to stuff in one's pocket to more elaborate documents, complete with hand-painted art work and ornate borders. Some included Christian symbolism, while others were more Paganized versions with magickal symbols. Some of these documents were not especially positive in nature. For example, one such letter, written in 1783, begins thusly:

> *Whoever works on Sunday is cursed. Therefore I command you do not work on Sunday, but devotedly go to church; but do not adorn your face;*

you shall not wear strange hair, and not carry on arrogance; you shall give to the poor of your riches, give plenty and believe, that this letter is written by my own hand and sent out by Christ himself, and that you will not act like the dumb beast; you have six days in the week, during which you shall carry on your labors; but the seventh day, namely Sunday, you shall keep holy; if you do not do that, I will send war, famine, pests, and death among you and punish you with many troubles.

It also says you are to knock off on Saturdays, too. It appears that the author was adding his own personal ideas of what constituted a no-no and what didn't. I personally don't think Divinity gives two ducks and a hen's tail what your hair, face, or clothing looks like. Only the last paragraph of this example actually gives the protection: "And that man who carries this letter with him, and keeps it in his house, no thunder will do him any harm, and he will be safe from fire and water; and he that publishes it to mankind, will receive his reward and a joyful departure from this world." Guess women didn't count in letters of protection.

On the top of this particular letter it states: "It was written in golden letters and sent by God through an Angel to him, who will copy it, shall be given; who despiseth it, from him will part." In other words, if you do not believe in being threatened, you will most likely lose the letter and the protection it brings with it. This example does nothing for me. Kind of reminds me of a young fellow I met once who claimed he could read angelic writing on everyone's forehead but he dared not speak of it because it would change their destiny. Uh-huh.

A second letter, more to my liking, comes from *Mysteries and Secrets of Magic* by C. J. S. Thompson:

Who that beareth it upon him shall not dread his enemies, to be overcome, nor with no manner of poison be hurt, nor in no need misfortune, nor with no thunder he shall not be smitten nor lightning, or in no fire be burnt soddenly, nor in no water be drowned. Nor he shall not die without shrift, nor with theeves to be taken. Also he shall have no wrong neither of Lord or Lady. This be in the names of God and Christ, Messiahs, Sother, Emannell, Sabaoth.

In my mind this is a much more positive approach. It was said to have been carried by King Charles I against danger and poison, and was originally drafted by Pope Leo IX.

The Magick Mirror

It wasn't until I learned the system of Pow-Wow that I was able to work with any success with the magick mirror. Magick mirrors were not the most used tools by the Pow-Wow as they smacked more of Craft than the Christian religion. These mirrors were simply constructed and instructions for making your own are found further along in this book.

Everyone works differently with a magick mirror. Some people actually see images floating around in the glass, others envision symbols; there are others, like me, whose mirror talks to them. When I made mine and used it the first time I called up MaraKay Rogers and said, "Ah, MaraKay, my mirror, ummm, talks to me. Is that right?"

She laughed and replied, "Well, if it talks like the one in Sleeping Beauty, hold on to it, we'll make a mint!"

"No! I mean, I hear things in my head!" I snapped.

She sighed. MaraKay is a lawyer. "Well, are you hearing good things or bad things?"

"I asked for advice on a problem and it told me what to do about it. The advice was sound," I replied.

"Actually, I use mine to contact entities on the astral to help me out," she revealed. "I'm not surprised yours talks to you, too."

Diane McDonough had quite the opposite happen with her mirror. "I was staring at it for the longest time," she said, "and I was really surprised when the entire image cracked, with little fissures running all over the glass. As the cracked image grew clearer it began to part. Out of the black depths rose the head of a bobcat with piercing green eyes. It was an astounding vision! Now, I wonder what the bobcat means ..." Diane did find about what the bobcat meant to her about a week later when events in her life led her to discover the truth on an issue that was disturbing her.

Summary

With this chapter you have learned that a Pow-Wow's tools were extremely simple in nature. From string to stone, special tools need not cost you your last dime. Layaway is not a necessity to get the magick right. Pow-Wow is a system that you can jump in and do without years of serious studying and mental machinations, or a packload of tools. It is light, simple, and it works.

East
Sacred Oak
Smooth Sailing Through Life
Intellect
Virility Symbol
God Energy
Designed by Silver RavenWolf

Pow-Wow Moons, German Foods, and a Taste of German Magick

Pow-Wow Moons

The phases of the Moon and position of the planets were important to the practical Pow-Wows. These concepts were also of use for the more elite German magicians. Directions for gathering herbs often went by the stars. For instance, gather sunflowers in August, during the Sign of the Lion, if you are planning to make a conjuring bag to catch a thief. Instructions rarely gave the correct terminology for the astrological signs. It was the "sign of the bull" or the "time of the crab," etc. Pow-Wows were mostly farm people. They depended on seasonal cycles, the weather, and the stars. When the almanac made its debut, people scheduled their lives with it.

The **New Moon** was a time to get things started, whether it was beginning to make a quilt or learning a new skill. Pow-Wows dutifully laid their money on a table by a window, thereby allowing their fortunes to increase during the month.

The **Waxing Moon** is the cycle in which the Moon moves from New to Full. Just as you wax a floor (and wax builds up), it was time to build a new project. Animals butchered on the Waning Moon were said to provide the best meat as it did not shrink while cured or cooked.

The **Full Moon** is for protective and healing matters. As the lunar energies move from Full to New, the cycle is called the **Waning Moon**. Waning can be remembered by thinking of someone's complexion being wan, or void of color. These two cycles are used to heal chronic disorders or non-threatening health problems, such as removing warts, corns, etc.

Three days before the New Moon is called the **Dark of the Moon.** This was a very special time to the Pow-Wow, a time to banish bad energies and turn back evil. The Dark of the Moon stood for the time of justice. It was also a time of practicality. Thoroughly sweep and clean your house during the Dark of the Moon to keep troublesome spiders away, whether they be of the human or insect variety.

Each Moon cycle lasts approximately seven days. It is best to purchase both an almanac and a large wall calendar that you can write on to help you keep track. This way you can schedule magickal endeavors and follow the Moon phases for the best success in your workings.

Full Moons, Their Meanings, and Their Recipes

Each Full Moon corresponds with an astrological sign as well as a seasonal sign. These correlations have been passed down through the centuries and they are nothing new. The birth of the correspondences lies in the movement of the seasons and how their calculated flow affected the survival of our ancestors.

Magickal cooking was no secret to the Pow-Wow. Empowered herbs for health and financial well-being were added to at least one daily dish. Food stirred in a clockwise direction facilitated the raising of a spiral of energy over each pot. On holidays, the entire meal would be laced with magick. The idea of saying grace was not just to thank the deity for the food, it was also a time to empower it with the circle of family energy. Holding hands while saying grace is far more potent than just sitting with poised fork, lovingly staring at the glazed ham in the center of the table.

Holy water (the drinkable version) was often added to dishes, and herbs were carefully sprinkled for both magickal and culinary intent. As you read through the following recipes, don't simply consider the dish. Examine the herbs used and what their magickal intent would be.

January: The Time of the Wolf

Wolves were a part of the Pennsylvania countryside, though the only ones you'll find here now are in cages or stuffed in a museum display. The elite Pow-Wow families had coats of arms they brought from the Old Country, often symbolizing some type of animal. The wolf, the lion, and the unicorn were popular motifs. During a few interviews, I was told they stood for totem animals of family lineages. The Pow-Wow chant for taming wild dogs was originally spoken to protect oneself from wolves.

The spirit of the wolf is called upon for teaching and protection. During the Wolf Moon, families would spend a lot of time in oral teaching around the fireplace or woodstove. January in Pennsylvania can be bitterly cold, with little to do outside. The spirit of pack life was welcomed within the home, but the animals outside were respected and feared.

The spirit of nurturing is important this month, whether it be children, mate relationships, or communication with siblings and other members of your circle. It is important to let all relationships grow and develop without being overbearing or insensitive to others' feelings.

One superstition holds that if New Year's Day is perfectly calm, many elderly people will expire in the coming year.

The idea of eating sauerkraut und speck (sauerkraut with pork) on the first day of the year to bring good luck is an old one.

Sauerkraut und Speck

4 pounds fresh arm picnic pork	1 teaspoon dried rosemary leaves
1 tablespoon salt	1 large onion, diced
2 quarts sauerkraut	2 cloves garlic
2 tablespoons brown sugar	Salt and pepper

Preheat oven to 325° F. Rub the pork with garlic and rosemary; sprinkle with salt and pepper. Place pork in baking pan, fat side up. Add enough water (about ½ cup) to keep it from baking dry. Roast pork for 2 hours, 15 minutes (or 30-35 minutes per pound). Mix sauerkraut, brown sugar, and onion. Mound mixture around meat, cover, and bake 15 more minutes. Makes 8 servings.

February: The Time of Storms

In Pennsylvania, February is usually when we get the most snow. Snow and ice are used to melt the cold hearts of lovers, friends, and obnoxious neighbors. Snow was put on a plate by the fire and charmed so that as it melted, the negative energy flooding from a particular person would dissipate. Icicles were hung above the cookstove for the same purpose. Hymnals, Bibles, birth certificates (taufscheine), pottery, cabinetry—all were engraved with magickal designs during the cold winter months.

Groundhog Day (February 2) has always been important in this area. If the groundhog sees his shadow on this day and returns to his hole, four to six more weeks of winter will descend on the area. If he doesn't see his shadow and does not return immediately to his home, spring is soon to come. Fellows who run along the short side in height are teased to stay inside, in case the spirits of winter mistake them for a groundhog, thus resulting in the commencement of a horrific snowstorm. Using resources with wisdom is important this month, and remember not to take too much too soon from new relationships.

Weather prediction was not always reliable, but blue flames in the fire generally meant a bad spell was coming. If the smoke from your fire refused to dance up the chimney, rain or snow was soon to follow, and if your familiar is sitting with its back to the fire—look out—heavy snows are on the way.

Schnitz un Knepp (Apples and Buttons)

1 quart dried apples	4 teaspoons baking powder
3 pounds smoked ham	1 teaspoon salt
2 tablespoons brown sugar	Pepper
A pinch of cinnamon	1 egg, well beaten
A few cloves	3 tablespoons melted butter
2 cups flour	½ cup milk

Cover dried apples with water and soak overnight. In the morning, cover the ham with water and simmer for 2 hours. Add the apples and water and simmer for about 1 hour. Add brown sugar, cinnamon, and cloves.

For the dumplings, sift flour, baking powder, salt, and pepper together. Stir in the egg, butter, and milk until lightly blended. Drop by tablespoonfuls into simmering ham and apples. Cover and cook over medium heat for 20 minutes. Serve hot. Makes 8 servings.

March: The Time of the Chaste Moon

Winter comes to a close with hoped-for speed. Agricultural pursuits are beginning. Spring Equinox falls within the month of March and is the first of the spring growth festivals. Easter may also fall here, with the customs of Easter baskets, egg rolls, and fire eggs (eggs with wax dripped on them to create a design and then colored). Spring cleaning begins with house blessings. On the nicer days, a few repairs to the house and barn are done. Yards are cleared if the snow has been light.

The Equinox was a time for celebration and fueling hopes for the coming warm season. Seeds are planted indoors. Slips of paper with wishes are put in the soil so dreams can sprout and grow with the seeds. March has a habit of blowing in extraordinary events in your life. You may find the month of March heralding major cyclical changes—a new job, new friends, new surroundings. March is a month to deal with releasing worn-out thoughts, ideas, jobs, even people from your life. The winds of change blow frequently, and let's not forget the Ides of March and its strong effect on the human psyche.

Funnel Cakes

1 egg, beaten	1 teaspoon baking powder
⅔ cup milk	¼ teaspoon salt
1¼ cups flour	Funnel with ⅜ to ½ inch hole
2 tablespoons sugar	Hot (375° F) oil

Beat the egg and milk together. Blend the flour, sugar, baking powder, and salt and add the milk to the mixture. Beat until smooth. Hold a finger over the hole in the funnel and fill the funnel with batter. Position the funnel over hot (375° F) oil as close as possible; remove your finger and drop batter into fat. Use a circular movement from the center outward to form a spiral cake about 4 inches in diameter. Close the hole again. Open the hole, then draw another spiral in oil. Remember that the batter puffs up, so don't crowd the cakes. Fry until the cakes are golden brown, then remove with a slotted spoon. Place on paper towels to absorb excess fat. Sprinkle with confectioner's sugar, brown sugar, or pancake syrup. Makes about 24 cakes.

April: The Time of the Seed Moon

April is definitely the time for sowing seeds, and most family activities revolved around that practice. Lighter clothes were taken out and checked for damage and needed repairs were made. Hex signs on barns were freshened on good days and more major repairs on buildings were completed. Wood from trees struck by lightning was never used as it was believed that lightning would strike the dwelling on which it was used. Animals were mated when the Moon was on the increase.

Magickal practices for the protection of the crops and home were increased during the April Moon. Fertilizer tabs were made in large cake pans, each cube inscribed with a particular rune or sigil for prosperity and protection, with the fertilizers being used when the Moon was in the third and fourth quarter.

Beans or peas were never planted on baking day. Peas and potatoes were planted when the horns of the Moon were up (Waxing Moon).

Rice Pudding

2 eggs, separated
½ cup sugar
2 cups milk
1 cup cooked rice

1 tablespoon butter, melted
2 tablespoons confectioner's sugar
1 teaspoon cinnamon
1 teaspoon nutmeg

Preheat oven to 325° F. Beat egg yolks and mix with the sugar, milk, and rice. Mix in butter. Pour into a one-quart baking dish. Beat egg whites until frothy; add confectioner's sugar and spread on top of the rice. Sprinkle with cinnamon and nutmeg. Bake about 35 minutes. If you like a sweeter pudding, increase the sugar to ¾ cup. Makes 6 servings.

May: The Time of the Hare

May is the Month of the Bull. Spring and the idea of procreation have finally arrived. Spring flowers are carefully harvested for their magickal and aromatic intent. Animals were bought when the Moon was in the first quarter, but never purchased over a Full Moon.

May is a delightful month, but it is one in which we tend to schedule too much. Plans for summer are heating up, and children are anxiously getting ready to leave the halls of learning and often pull a lame duck routine with both chores and homework. Adults aren't an exception to this scenario, either, and the child within is plotting with the adult self to drop that work and *play,* for goodness sake! Remember in this month to lighten up on yourself and enjoy the lusty month of May.

Hootsla (Egg Bread)

½ cup butter
1 bag stuffing or
   8 cups day-old bread, cubed
3 beaten eggs

½ cup milk
½ teaspoon salt
Pepper

Melt butter in a large pan over low heat. Add the bread cubes and stir until lightly coated with butter and beginning to brown. Mix together the eggs, milk, salt, and pepper. Pour mixture over bread cubes. Cook over medium heat until it sets and is golden brown. Makes about 6 servings.

June: The Time of the Dyads

June is the joining of opposites, when the months of winter give way to the months of summer. June is the month for romance and a time to complete the "twining process." Astral projection and more spiritual pursuits are thought to do well in this month. When looking for a husband, one odd belief was to put a drop of one's blood in your intended lover's drink. To discourage an unwanted suitor, a young lady would place feathers around the house. When finally married, the couple should step over a broom before entering their new home.

Schnitzel Beans

2 pounds fresh green beans, cut in 1-inch pieces
6 slices bacon, fried, drained, and chopped
2 large onions, diced
1 clove garlic, chopped
1 cup hot water
Cayenne pepper
Salt
3 medium tomatoes, cut into small cubes

Mix all ingredients, except for tomatoes, and cook over medium heat, uncovered, for about 1 hour. Add tomatoes and cook 2 more hours, adding water when necessary. Makes approximately 8 servings.

July: The Time of Mead

July is a remarkable month. The first of the harvests are coming in and there is much activity in the fields and the kitchen. More spiritual experiences may enter your life at this time than in any other cycle of the year. Magickal groups formed at this time have a good chance of balance and survival. You may find an unusual increase in people matters, including many phone calls, several unexpected visitors, and a heavier client load.

Smierkase

This is an easy one. Serve cottage cheese ringed with dabs of apple butter.

August: The Time of the Wort Moon

The Month of the Lion was a very magickal month for Pow-Wows. Any call for great power was done during this sign in August. Gates closed for centuries are more likely to be opened during this Moon phase than in any other.

"Wort" is an Anglo-Saxon word for herb. This was definitely the month for the harvest and drying of herbs that would continue until the frost came. Herbs were also empowered, hung to dry, and then mixed for conjuring bags. Marigolds were gathered and strung together, then hung by doors or over them, symbolizing the strength of the summer season and the power of the God.

Red Devil Cake

2 cups flour
1 teaspoon baking soda
½ teaspoon salt
½ cup butter
1½ teaspoons vanilla
1½ cups sugar or
firmly packed brown sugar

2 beaten eggs
3 (1-ounce) squares unsweetened
chocolate, melted and cooled
1 cup milk
1-2 teaspoons red food coloring

Preheat oven to 350° F. Grease and flour two round 9-inch layer cake pans. Sift flour, baking soda, and salt together. Set aside. Cream butter and vanilla together until softened. Add sugar slowly, creaming after each portion. Add eggs, beating well. Blend in cooled chocolate. Add flour mixture and milk alternately, beating until smooth. Blend in food coloring. Bake for 30 to 35 minutes. Cool and frost. Makes about 10 servings.

September: The Time of Barley

The Month of the Virgin was a time to work protective magick as virgins are said to have a great deal of untamed psychic resources. Seasonal spells worked in January, February, and March should now be coming full circle.

September has been associated with academics as most students, whether kindergarten- or college-bound, mentally gear up for the work ahead. Spells involving clarity, concentration, and general studious enhancements work well in this month.

Pickled Eggs

2 cups red beets
¼ cup brown sugar
½ cup vinegar
½ cup cold water

½ teaspoon salt
1 stick cinnamon
3 cloves
6 hard-boiled eggs

Boil beets until tender; drain. Boil remaining ingredients, except for the eggs. Add the beets to this liquid, cover, and refrigerate for 3 days. Add hard-boiled eggs to the liquid, cover, and place in refrigerator for 2 days. Makes 6 servings.

October: The Time of Blood

Sacrifices of animals and food grown on the property were numerous this month. The animals were prepared for the winter months and the vegetables and fruits canned or dried.

This was originally the Hunter's Moon. Firearms were blessed and consecrated and charms were intoned to protect the hunter throughout the coming year. Remember that to a Witch, October represents the coming of the New Year. October 31 is considered the last day of the wheel of their year. Magick was performed for good luck and protection. Divination was common this month, especially during the Full Moon and on October 31, when it is said that the veil between the worlds is the thinnest.

Acorns were gathered and strung in necklaces to promote spiritual growth. An acorn was placed in the pocket and carried for protection.

Ob'l Puffers (Apple Fritters)

1 cup flour	⅓ cup milk
1½ teaspoons baking powder	1 egg, beaten
3 tablespoons confectioner's sugar	2 medium apples, sliced thin
¼ teaspoon salt	Hot (365° F) oil

Mix the dry ingredients together in a large bowl. Stir in milk and egg. Fold in apples. Drop the batter by spoonfuls into the hot (365° F) oil and fry until golden brown. Turn fritters halfway through frying. Drain on a paper towel. Makes about 1½ dozen.

November: The Time of the Snow

Both flora and fauna were used to predict the severity of the coming winter. The winters in this area have become milder since I was a little girl. When I was small, it would be no surprise to see a good dumping of snow in October. The number of snows to come during the winter was often calculated by the number of days from the first snow in the fall to the following Full Moon. If the tops of the trees lost their leaves first, the winter was to be a mild one, but hold on to your long johns if the leaves fall first from the sides. Trees to be used for building purposes should be felled before December 1.

Corn Bread

1 cup flour	1 egg
1 cup yellow corn meal	½ teaspoon vanilla
½ cup sugar	½ cup canned corn, drained
1 tablespoon baking powder	3 tablespoons melted butter
¾ teaspoon salt	¼ teaspoon nutmeg and
1 cup milk	cinnamon mixture

Preheat oven to 425° F. Mix the flour, corn meal, sugar, baking powder, and salt in large bowl. Add the milk, egg, oil, and vanilla. Fold in corn. Pour in round 9-inch cake pan. Sprinkle with cinnamon and nutmeg. Bake about 25 minutes. Makes 6 servings.

December: The Time of the Oak

Dowsing rods were cut on Christmas Day or on Winter Solstice. A child born on the Solstice was considered to be a "bright one" and gifted throughout his or her life. It was also believed that the person would be able to talk to animals and see ghosts. December was the month for family celebrations and visiting, and for giving gifts, both magickal and mundane. The little acorns gathered in the fall were strung with popcorn to decorate the tree.

Apies Cakes

1½ cups flour	⅓ cup butter
1 cup sugar	½ cup sour cream
½ teaspoon baking soda	

Preheat oven to 400° F. Mix together the flour, sugar, and baking soda. Cut in the butter with a pastry blender. Mix in sour cream. Roll the dough about ¼-inch thick on a floured surface and cut into 2-inch squares. Draw bind runes (see Chapter 14) for good fortune and health. Bake on cookie sheets for about 7 minutes. Sprinkle with brown or white sugar. Makes about 2 dozen cookies.

The recipes here are the ones I remember from my childhood. There are many more. It was said that the Pennsylvania Dutch had the best cooks anywhere in the country. Small portions of the holiday meals were offered up to the God and Goddess and later to the Baby Jesus or a particular saint.

Pennsylvania Dutch cooking is inexpensive, yet tastes terrific. When times are slim, many of these dishes and goodies can be made without extra expense.

Boney Luther and the Boiling Water

One of my favorite Pow-Wow stories comes from Wilma J. Clark in Mt. Holly Springs. "When I was a child," she began, "my father worked as a butcher on his own property. There was a Pow-Wow fellow by the name of Boney Luther in the area. He lived on Mountain Road in Summerdale. Boney was a big man who really put the chill through ya when you looked him straight in the eye. As a kid, I was afraid of him. He lived in an olden house that had only two rooms. The floors were made of uneven wood. There was a cookstove in the corner of the main room and a long plank table on the north wall. Everyone around knew him. He would do the best for people and he would work the worst. I don't think he considered much about ethics. His mind ran more to the fastest solution. A lot of the local folks bartered for services.

"Early one morning, I guess about 5:00 AM, he was with my dad in the butcher shed. Daddy was getting ready to kill a hog. The fire was built high and the big kettles of water were on, but nothing was happening. The water simply wouldn't boil. Boney sat in the corner and told my Daddy not to worry about it because it just wasn't the right time to kill that hog. Boney said, 'Just be patient. The time ain't right.' My Daddy, though, was in a hurry. There was something else planned for that day, or else he had a lot to do. I don't really remember anymore. Anyway, he huffed and puffed around 'til Boney finally shook his head, got up, and walked over to the fire. His back was to me, but I know he uttered something under his breath and moved his one hand over the first kettle. It began to boil immediately. Then he moved to the next one and did the same."

Making water boil is not a hard task. Put a pot of water on medium heat. Hold your receiving hand over the water. Move your middle finger (the fire finger) in a clockwise spiral, imagining both the sight and sound of boiling water. After a little practice, you will be able to make any pot of water boil quickly. This is a good exercise in minor magick. If you would like to use a chant, simply say: "Boil and bubble, water double," as boiling water appears to double in level.

Hearth, Home, and the Little People

Every time my children visit Wilhelmenia Keefer, they pester her for a story. Last summer they voted her their adopted grandmother. Wilma is a fascinating woman who can take something as ordinary as a willow branch and turn it into a dancing dolly. Her stories follow the same pattern. "The Irish are not the only folks who believe in little people," she explained to my children. "My great-great-grandmother lived in a little house in the woods. Of course, almost everyone in those days lived in the woods. Anyway, there were a lot of kids in her family. Each child had to take a turn at watching the fire all night. If they let the fire go out, the family might die. It was winter, and they used the fire for everything from cooking to washing clothes to keeping the house warm.

"Well, my great-great-grandma had worked extra hard one winter's day and wasn't too happy about drawing fire duty. She was only seven or eight at the time. A big responsibility for a little girl. It got dark early and the family wasn't much on staying up. For hours she sat alone by the fireside, feeding the flames and minding that it didn't get too low. 'Twas around two or three in the morning and my great-great-grandma nodded off. She woke with a start to feel something tugging at her skirt. She looked down and there was a little man, dressed in green and brown, a-tugging on her dress. She claims he stood about knee high, but big enough for her to tell he was a person by candlelight. He motioned madly at the fire. Then she turned her head to look at the hearth and saw that the fire was almost dead. In her rush to stoke it up again, she forgot about the little man. After the fire was going good, she crept around the cottage looking for her rescuer. 'Course, he was gone.

"You know, she never forgot how he helped her and swore to her dying day that he was real and surely saved her life that night. Everyone else in the family made fun of her story, but she remained steadfast to her last breath on the existence of that little man."

Healing Magick

Nobility is not a birthright ... it is defined by one's actions.
—*Robin Hood*, the movie

In Pow-Wow healing there are many chants to learn, although they are simple. You cannot run for a book when someone is bleeding or screaming at the top of their lungs due to a painful burn. "Older people today understand a little bit about it," reminisced an 80-year-old Pow-Wow, "but there is not as much attraction because the older people are dying off. I had several young ladies in the area that showed interest in it. After they found out the amount of involvement required, they drifted away," he stated. "They weren't fascinated by all the work. Believe me," he laughed, "it takes a lot of hard work!"

All areas of Pow-Wow require practice and perseverance. When a Pow-Wow practitioner took on a student, the complete memorization of the chants, spells, herbal remedies, and any other information that was pertinent to that particular clan or family was required. Few of these traditions were written down, either because the Pow-Wow was illiterate or feared someone would steal them. Pow-Wows were a very superstitious lot and did not, as a whole, trust their fellow man or woman, though they cared for the entire community. After all, too much had happened to those of the Craft, and secrecy was a form of life protection.

Pow-Wow techniques and chants were memorized to perfection. You certainly could not take your "notes" with you when visiting a neighbor's home. They would either think you didn't know what you were doing or get snoopy. Remember that Pow-Wow was at its peak when professional medical care was either not available or too far away to be useful. At the inception of Pow-Wow, phones were not available to let the healer know the extent of someone's injury or sickness. Often a neighboring child or spouse would appear at the door, out of breath, with little solid information for a Pow-Wow to go on.

Remarkably enough, when the telephone did make its debut, there were many Pow-Wows who had no problem healing "long distance" over the phone. They would simply ask for the sick or hurt person's full "Christian" name and go from there. Asking for the birth name of an individual is a Craft-oriented procedure and Witches have always been trained in this type of work. One fellow I interviewed keeps all the full names and phone numbers of every one he tries for in a steno pad on his desk. "I check with them after a time to make sure they are doing all right and if they need anything else," he explained. "The book also helps me when they call about different problems. I can look back and see exactly what they were here for and when."

Some cures and remedies of Pow-Wow artists passed down through the ages are absurd, most likely given to the public to protect the true nature of the art. For instance, to cure a cold, take off your shoes and socks, run your fingers between your toes, and then smell your finger. One's first reaction is a wrinkled nose and some sort of guttural intonation. It makes the art appear nonsensical and weak. Who wants to try a magickal system like that?

"The greatest thing is belief ... faith ... it can be done," stated Preston Zerbe. "Faith in the Holy Trinity or your God is what counts. I ask everyone who comes in here for treatment if they believe in the Holy Trinity. Some do and some don't. Those that don't ... they may not admit it, but I can tell."

A female Pow-Wow related, "I had one person come in here from Harrisburg. She had a friend with her. After I treated this lady, her friend asked to see me and I took her into the kitchen. I was going to try [a Pow-Wow word meaning "work"] for her. Before I could ask her any questions, she said, 'Would you tell me whether my son is going to be successful in seeking a divorce from his wife?' I said, 'I don't do any of those sort of things.' That was one lady who didn't know what she was doing. That was just one example, and I've had some other weirdoes in here, too," she stated firmly, and winked. "You get them, you know."

As a researcher, I was uncomfortable with her thoughts on divination. By the time I had reached this lady for an interview, I had discovered the true roots of Pow-Wow. I was well aware of the various forms it took, not merely faith healing alone. Obviously this woman either did not receive schooling in the full realm of the occult sciences, or had turned away from all of the Pow-Wow skills originally available to her. She did tell me, however, that her teacher died before she had finished her training. I was saddened to again meet another person who only used a small section of such an interesting system. To my amusement, I didn't miss the safety pin in her sleeve, an old Pow-Wow/Craft practice used to ward off evil.

From the various interviews with healers, I discovered that the idea of "once and done" is often not applicable when performing a healing, especially if the condition is something that has taken months or years to surface. How your body absorbs energy may dictate how many times psychic healing may need to be repeated. Some conditions may feel "filled up" 10 seconds after you have applied healing energy. There could be numerous reasons for short energy absorption—the client may not believe in the procedure, the condition has gone unchecked too long and has built up its own negative energy field that must be slowly broken down, or there may be a psychological problem that underlies the condition. On some difficulties, you could theorize an entire day and night and still not discover "the reason for it all." "There was one man," said Preston Zerbe, "who went to my Pow-Wow teacher, Gertie Guise, eighteen times," he exclaimed. "That man truly had faith to go back that many times. But you know, on the nineteenth time he was fully healed.

"I'll read you a little bit," he said, settling back in his chair and adjusting his glasses. "I've used this booklet for the past 40 years, with great success." He began to read the preface, ending with, "I therefore recommend this work and hope the resulting blessings will be carried to many people everywhere." He looked up thoughtfully from the book and said, "This is an old Pow-Wow man that wrote this, years and years ago, and I use it faithfully. It's called *Lessons in Sympathy*. It says here that you should have faith and no doubt in your heart and that to succeed, your values and principles should be strong."

This information follows the basic rules for any positive magickal endeavor. Have faith, be strong, do not doubt, and trust in Divinity that your need will manifest to the benefit of the universe. Don't be impatient. If you are working to reduce a brain tumor or to mend a broken limb, don't expect to hunker down, run your hands up and down the person a few times, yap a couple of words, and *bingo*—instant healing. Jesus you are not.

As with all skills, proficiency takes practice. Just because you read this book once through and learn the appropriate methods and chants, don't expect to become an instant healer. There are individuals who have been gifted since birth, but often we need to reawaken our gifts and talents through practice and meditation to gain proficiency. When I began delving into this system, I was disappointed because it appeared that I had no talent for the healing end of Pow-Wow. I didn't realize that hands-on practice was needed to become at least semi-proficient. Like many others before me who gathered information as I had, I was disillusioned and felt the emotional tug of failure. Unlike many others, I didn't doubt the system (I had pounds of case histories to tell me it worked)—I doubted myself.

I am always up for a challenge. I decided that if my ancestors could do this stuff, then so could I. It was by accident (literally) that it dawned on me that the more you use it, the better you get. I have a nosebleed king and queen in my family (or rather, I had). No kidding—two of my children have gone through periods in their lives when it was common to have rivers of blood flowing from their faces. This can be very disconcerting if you are a person (like me) who has spent only a small amount of time around bleeding people.

At first, it took me up to ten minutes to stop a nosebleed using Pow-Wow (the chant and energy raising) and conventional methods (ice directly above the bridge of the nose, pressure on the bleeding nostril, etc). To my astonishment, after experience with ten nose bleeds over a three-month period, I found I could stop them in sixty seconds or less. In fact, the last time one of the children had a nosebleed, my daughter didn't get a chance to wrestle one ice cube from the freezer. The blood stopped that fast.

And it isn't just me, either. I went out on a quick errand one afternoon and left my oldest daughter in charge of the nosebleed royalty. When I got back she excitedly told me that her sister bumped her nose, and of course it resulted in a nosebleed. My oldest daughter promptly stopped it in less than one minute. To my amusement, they had used the stopwatch kept in my magickal cabinet, which got me to thinking just exactly how that nosebleed really did happen in the first place. I also learned that the more one uses Pow-Wow, the less you need to use it. Meaning, where before nosebleeds were a common occurrence in our family, now they are practically nil!

In April 1993, a friend of mine brought an acquaintance to my home for a reading. During our conversation, she told me that Gertie Guise (Preston's teacher) had Pow-Wowed for her when she was in her teens. "I had a very bad case of poison ivy," she explained. "And you know, Gertie Pow-Wowed for me and it cleared up just like that. Even more astounding, I have never had another case of poison ivy since that time!" Practice, then, definitely improves your skill level, and also seems to improve on the general health of the patient—but what about the basics?

Healing, Step-by-Step

Look at any prospective healing like a computer flow chart. There are different types of conditions, methods, and probable conclusions. Your task is to choose the best alternative in each of these categories. Let's look at general healings first, those that are not emergencies.

The Interview Process

Pow-Wow artists often set up a particular room, such as a parlor, in the house to interview clients, and performed the healings in a different space, one that had been cleansed and consecrated. Often a kitchen was used to heal as it was close to the elements of fire and water. In the early and mid-nineteenth century, some Pow-Wow artists designed and built offices extending from their homes. Others (especially those who used a compendium of herbs and other aids) converted garages or gardening sheds so they could set up a specific area for healing. One individual I know uses his den. It contains a file cabinet, a sofa, a straight-backed chair, a large wall mirror, and a desk. Unless you are attuned to magickal energies, you would never guess what the room is used for, or why the mirror is there.

Just like anyone in the medical profession, you should know the history and background of your patient, hence the use of the parlor to "chat awhile." Good communication with the client is necessary. The more the person feels at ease with you, the better chance you have of success. Likewise, the more information you can obtain before you begin, the more it will help strengthen the healing. If you understand the client, then a psychic link has been established. You must ask the client for details. Your mannerisms should be easy and calm. Take careful note of the client's body language. Have a pencil and paper handy to take notes and list items like allergies, historical family illnesses or complaints, etc. If there is unusual swelling, consider recent food intake, possible bites from insects, or perhaps sinus difficulties. Are you dealing with a new or old injury and what were the circumstances surrounding it?

You also must ask important questions that deal with pregnancy, addiction, and emotional outlook. Never make any judgements about what others share with you, if you are lucky enough to get the truth on these items. Your task, at this time, is not to be judge and jury, but to heal. Ask how the person is sleeping at night, if he or she is on any medication, what his or her diet is like, and of course, if the person is under medical care. If so, ask for how long, etc. Is the client satisfied with the treatment he or she is receiving from the doctor? If the person is not, you should suggest a second opinion from a qualified medical specialist.

If an individual tells you that he or she has not sought medical treatment, and the condition is either unclear or could be potentially harmful, you should suggest that the person seek qualified medical care. To be honest, I prefer working with people who have been to a physician and have a diagnosis both from their current medical practitioner and another who has been referred to them. With this advantage, you can direct your energy to a specific region of the body instead of hunting and guessing what may be wrong. This doesn't mean that you shouldn't trust your own judgement. You may find the medical diagnosis in error, or find something that has not surfaced yet in a medical report.

Unlike most medical professionals, you will find energy blocks in the body. However, never tell a client that his or her doctor is wrong. Instead, suggest that the patient re-evaluate his or her own condition. Mention specialists available in the area or the use of a second opinion program that does not recommend doctors in the same office building or practice of the original doctor. The final question you must ask is if the person requesting the healing believes in some sort of positive Divinity. This is vitally important to your work. Yes, yes, I know all about the healings that have taken place regardless of an individual's belief system, but these cases are a shot in the dark. I personally prefer a well-lighted view of what is (or isn't) happening.

If the person believes in Divinity, then you have an extra card in your hand toward a successful and relatively quick healing process. Also, if the person in question believes in your faith, meaning he or she is convinced that you honor your religion to the fullest, this will assist in manifesting a speedy healing. If the individual you are assisting usually exhibits balance in his or her life and shows good self-esteem, you are ahead of the game.

Getting the Client Involved

It is far better to get the person who wants the healing involved in what you are doing rather than having him or her as a silent audience. If the person is working with you, he or she will feel less self-conscious and will stop looking at you as if you have crash-landed from Venus.

When you feel comfortable with the answers you have received, take out a blank piece of paper and draw a stick figure on it. Ask the person to write his or her name on the top of the paper and circle the area on his or her body that is causing problems. Draw an arrow to the circled area and have the patient write beside the circle one of the four following chants:

Holy Mary
Mother of God
The Body is Whole
The Body is Strong

Holy Isis
Creatrix of all
The Body is Whole
The Body is Strong

Daughter of Diana
Aradia I call
To heal the body
To strengthen the soul

Eir, sweet sister of healing
I invoke thy assistance

To make my body whole
To make my body strong.

The purpose of giving four different invocations is to show that the Pow-Wow system works no matter which positive deity you prefer to call. The first chant is Christian in nature, the Second is Egyptian/Ceremonial, and the third is Wiccan/Strega/Dianic. The fourth is Germanic/Heathen in design. The original invocation would most likely be something like the fourth one, as most Germanic magick originally had a Heathen/Norse influence. Yes, Pow-Wow is the daughter of the Craft, but the Craft as the Germans knew it was the daughter of the Heathen/Norse beliefs, which are known today as Odinism.

The Energy Examination

Set the paper aside for the time being and ask the client to sit or lie down comfortably. Ground and center your own energy. If you have not thought to cast a protective circle around yourself before the individual entered the room, do so now. This is also a good time to call on a few angels or a deity to whom you have a close affinity for help. Use of the Lesser Banishing Ritual was not uncommon for those who have practiced before you, and you may well wish to use it yourself. Details for this short ritual can be found in the Appendix. You may do this silently or aloud.

With your hands approximately four inches above the body (it is not necessary to touch the person, and honestly, he or she may not want you to do so), run your hands up and down over the sick or injured area, then move to the rest of the body. Check for heat and coldness emanating from the body. Some people feel the sick or injured areas as dead spots; others feel an unusual surge of energy. Remember that the symptoms will cause energy fluctuations, too, and that symptoms are just that—warning signals. The problem may not be located near the symptom area. To treat the symptom is not healing the cause.

One by one, check the seven energy vortexes of the body, known as the chakras. They are located at the crown of the head, the third eye or forehead, the throat, the chest area, the solar plexus, right below the navel, and at the genitals. These areas are good indications if a psychic block is causing the difficulty. Once you have made your assessment, circle those areas on your body chart that you feel may need work, along with the injured or sick area already circled. You also may wish to ask some additional questions.

In the energy examination you may pick up a few odd readings. This is where the parlor chat comes in handy. Hopefully the client was honest with you when relating information on prescription (or non-prescription) drugs.

Drugs and alcohol will give off unusual readings depending upon the physiology of the body, the dosage, etc. I had a young fellow once who was under psychiatric treatment. He had been given drugs to "mellow him out." Surprisingly, I found the opposite in the energy examination. A large amount of excess energy was bottled up around his navel. It was so intense that my entire body began to shake in response.

If you don't feel anything, don't worry about it. Energy readings also take practice. You have to learn to enhance your psychic sense by shutting down input from the others. There are also individuals who are so grounded that you will barely feel anything. Don't exclaim, "I don't feel anything!" The person may believe that he or she is indeed one of the walking dead, or will consider you an utter fake.

Put on Your Thinking Cap

Now is the time to take a break and consider all the information you have gathered, but don't leave the person alone while you consider your options. Should you leave the room for any reason, it may make the patient nervous, especially if this is the first time he or she has had this type of experience. Offer to get the person a cup of herbal tea or a glass of spring water to give yourself time to think clearly. Sometimes you will know exactly what to do, but there will be times when you will want to take several minutes to get your thoughts in order. It is hard not to feel pressed by silence and the fact that the patient is sitting and waiting for you to "do something more." Be calm and smile. Lighten the conversation a bit, if you feel it is necessary. Playing soft music is also a good idea.

You always need to consider the possibility that the individual may be better served by seeking immediate medical attention and contacting you afterward. Keep a list of reputable psychiatrists, psychologists, and hot line numbers handy. Consider also the personality type of the individual. Will it help or hinder the healing? Should you involve the person in the healing by taking him or her through a guided meditation, or should you do the entire healing silently? Is a ritual required? Do you feel you need help with this one? Don't be ashamed to ask a magickal friend to help; it is the design of the universe for us to work together.

Many Pow-Wow artists were known for their scare tactics, some by design and some in error. There were those who were entirely too superstitious, usually students who never finished their training, those on power trips, and those who dabbled on their own, totally missing the philosophy and religion of what they were supposed to be doing. Several major religions base themselves on frightening people to conform to their views, which didn't help matters, either. You must not frighten the person you are attempting to help. Don't play scary music or make veiled remarks. Be open and honest.

Today, with the few Pow-Wows remaining (and most of them strictly faith healers), one finds an interesting mix of egoism and blind faith. Gone is the reasoning and true words of many of the healing practices. Don't ever go into a healing by telling the patient that he or she will walk out of your home or office 100 percent better than when he or she walked in. Instead, explain that you will "try" for them. This is an old Pow-Wow word meaning that you will do the best you possibly can—no more, no less.

If you feel that the condition will warrant more than one treatment, be up-front about it. Try not to put a time limit on yourself. For small things like swellings, bug bites, lumps, minor injuries, etc., the standard treatment is three times: morning, noon, and night. Some of the old Pow-Wow books carry the initials M.N.N. after the chant or spell. This abbreviation relates to the doctor's adage—three times a day and call me in the morning. If that doesn't knock out the problem, the next step is to Pow-Wow for three consecutive days. The second day you would Pow-Wow at the time when the injury originally occurred. On the third day, you would Pow-Wow at the same time again. For example, if I were stung by a bee on Friday at 6:00 PM, on Saturday and Sunday I would Pow-Wow for it at 6:00 PM. If the complaint arises within the next week after the last treatment, the process will have to be repeated. For something more significant, it may take 7 to 14 or even 21 treatments. Note that the treatments are done in consecutive patterns, using the magickal numbers three, seven, nine, and multiples thereof.

With all your choices made, you are ready to begin the type of healing you have chosen. Now you should again ground and center yourself. Centering is something entirely different from grounding. This is the ability to pull your energy into the navel area and make it float there like a medium-sized ball. It is where your personal power builds before you direct and release it. When you have achieved this state, you often feel calm and peaceful—in essence, centered. Your whole being feels serene and strong. It is your signal that you are ready to rock and roll.

Regardless of what chant, herb, or tool you have chosen to assist you in the healing, they work much in the same manner. You connect with Divinity (either through chanting or envisioning), then focus on the desired outcome in your mind. Begin to raise the power from the earth into your navel area and finally direct it out through your hands. Some Pow-Wows use their hands and their breath, feeling that both types of energy exhalations are sacred. If you are more comfortable directing out through your dominant hand, then by all means do so. However, if you like to stand to give the double whammy effect with legs spread firmly apart and arms outstretched, that's okay, too. Just don't scare the healing right out of the client!

Pow-Wow works in synergistic parts and the casual observer does not realize the many steps that are mentally performed by the healer. Before I take you further into the process you may find the following outline helpful:

    I. Interview
   II. Energy Evaluation
        a. Ground and Center
        b. Focus
  III. Healing
        a. Ground and Center
        b. Pull in Divine Energy
            1. Throat
            2. Third Eye
        c. Push out Negative Energy
            1. Hand
            2. Lodestone
  IV. Seal with the Sigil
   V. Ground
  VI. Cleanse

During my research, I was fortunate enough to take a very talented friend of mine, who specializes in auric readings, to watch a Pow-Wow at work. My vision of auras is limited. I see only a wavering around the body, much like a heat wave, and can discern the impressions of color with my third eye. There are times where I am able to see this energy (usually blue/white in color, filling the client's eyes, making them glow or waver to my physical vision). Sarah, on the other hand, is gifted with full-color vision and can relate both energy fluctuations and color during or after a magickal process.

With Sarah's reading, we discovered that a Pow-Wow uses the throat chakra for the entry point of divine healing, due to the nature of the chants. This is unlike their Witch counterparts, who normally use the third eye chakra as the point of Divine connection. She said she watched as pure white light entered his throat and traveled first into his left hand holding the creek stone, then funneled out through his right hand that was held slightly aside and pointed toward the floor. Around his feet, she said, was a huge pool of white light that eventually sunk into the floor. We also know, from other sensitive individuals, that the Pow-Wow energy fluctuates in a controlled pattern, like that of a beating drum.

Sarah's abilities have given us a clear picture of the visualization required during the Pow-Wow healing process. It is also important to understand that her presence was not intended solely for her to view the Pow-Wow's auric field and report what she saw. Her sister had requested the healing, with Sarah as chauffeur and me as navigator. It wasn't until we were in the car going home that I remembered her particular talent (one among many, I assure you) and asked her if she had seen anything in the way of auric impressions.

The Sigils

Pow-Wows used sigils to seal the auric field of the client after a healing. These sigils were traced in the air over the client three times, sometimes with obvious flourish, and other times so imperceptibly that the client had no inkling of the manifestation. The most favored by far was the equal-armed cross, a solar sign of healing and protection, with the pentacle a close second. Other signs were the crescent, done with the thumb and index finger spread apart to form a crescent; the Horned God sign, done by putting the index and little fingers up and holding the remaining fingers down with the thumb of the same hand; and of course, the runes (see Chapter 14).

Winding Up

When you have completed the healing, ground if you feel you have excess energy hanging around. In this type of grounding, you would run your hands under cold water, hold a hematite stone, or shake out your fingers. Some people put their hands on the ground and allow excess energy to seep into the earth. Often I have a bowl of holy water on the table and a white or red towel beside it. I will dip my fingers into the water and shake them out three times, then repeat this twice more. I will do this for the client as well. Occultists often ground their energy into their tools when they have finished a magickal endeavor, but this is not recommended in a healing. You are dealing with negative and perhaps chaotic energies, and unless you have a screw loose, you don't want to ground that type of energy into your tools. You would experience unpleasant effects and several misfires the next time you picked up your tools.

If you feel a little off-center, take a minute or two and collect yourself. Ask the person you are assisting how he or she feels. If you have created the necessary psychic bond, you will be able to extract honest answers. Too often we see people who go up the aisles in a tent revival-type atmosphere to receive a healing. They walk back praising Divinity until they get out the door, then turn to a friend and say, "I didn't feel a damned thing!" They don't speak up while they are inside because they feel it is their fault that the healing didn't work. After all, Pastor BoBo up there in his white suit with $25,000 altar, diamond-studded watch, and limo behind the tent must be doing something right because he is financially stable. Therefore God must like him and feel that the person in need doesn't deserve to be healed. Well, scorpion tails on that scenario! Everyone deserves to be healed. It is only personal choice or karmic debt that may defeat it.

I took my nine-year-old daughter to a local Pow-Wow because she had an odd lump on her neck. After the first treatment, I asked her how she felt. "Still the same," she said. However, that night she was able to get a full night's sleep with less pain. I didn't make a big deal out of it. I figured we would wait and together examine her reactions after the entire process was completed. After the second treatment, I asked her how she felt. The response was, "A little better." I noticed she could move her neck more easily and didn't walk as stiffly as before. Now, this is my daughter who bottles everything inside (not the one who will tell you she has a skin rash, a broken nail, or whatever), so I knew that what this daughter reported was accurate and to the point. I waited. With the culmination of the third treatment, the lump had disappeared and she was moving normally with no pain. When I asked her how she felt, she simply said, "It's gone."

My point here is that she did not feel a "rush of energy" or some other significant change either during or immediately after the first two treatments. Instead, the difficulty slowly slipped away, without her really being aware of it. There were no bells, whistles, or outstanding visions. Most non-magickal clients will not be aware of the energy raising in their bodies. If you are lucky, the person may feel a slight tingling. This isn't your fault. The individual has had years of practice setting up both mental and spiritual blocks to energy work. One sitting will not normally remove those blocks. There are some people from whom you will never manage to remove the blocks.

Continuing Client Involvement

Don't be shy while interacting with the client. Be serious when speaking with him or her. When it is time for the person to leave, be sure you have arranged for a return visit, if necessary. Give the person a white candle and the body chart you drew for him or her. Candles can be prepared long before the client arrives by carving runes or symbols related to the client's faith onto the candle. Others dress the candles in oils made from flowers and herbs known for their healing energies. Instruct the person to burn the candle that evening until it is consumed, with the candleholder placed over the drawing. Tell the person to remove the candleholder in the morning and burn the body chart, then take the ashes outside and scatter them in the wind.

In the old days, the Pow-Wow never asked the person in need to burn his or her own candle. The Pow-Wow did that long after the individual had left. The Pow-Wow did, however, provide talismans, charms, enchantments, etc., along with instructions on what was to be done with them. Candle burning rites were considered evil in nature by the pious of the community, so other solutions were given to the client. The candle-burning procedure was the duty of the Pow-Wow artist.

Every healing, every healer, every circumstance, and every client is different. You need to find your own style, your individual power center and sources. What works for the owner of the Mary New Age Crystal Store may not work for you. Just because you are different does not mean you are slated to fail. Each healing has its own network of probabilities. Each client has his or her own belief system. Each healer approaches the mystical experience in his or her own way. No one way is right for everyone. That is the delight of living on the earth plane.

The step-by-step healing format previously given can be tailored to your own style of healing. I suggest that you start with family members before working with strangers. Know your own skill level. Don't fool yourself, but don't cut yourself short, either. When you are ready to help the outside world, it will come to you. Impatience is a hard emotion to supress, but don't let it push you into a position that you are not ready to handle. Don't be surprised, too, if you go along just fine and suddenly an illness or accident hits you for a loop, and you fail in your healing attempts. Remember, the universe is aware of all things, and many events, such as birth and death, are pre-ordained.

Clearing Yourself after a Healing

The process of clearing your body after a healing depends upon each healer. If you are not an empathic person or you are a person who has learned to shield yourself well, little clearing is required. You may need only to sit quietly for a minute and imagine yourself under a giant cleansing waterfall. Some healers merely shake their hands and imagine that the negative energy is scattering into the earth. Others blow their breath into the earth, expelling any negative energy that may have attached itself.

If you are an extremely empathic person, you must take extra care. You are more vulnerable to residual negativity. An acquaintance of mine does healings and readings at psychic fairs. She is a very sensitive empath and has learned that the day's psychic debris winds up in her navel area. When she gets home, she must go through a clearing process that may take up to 20 minutes. If she does not clear herself, she may end up with a cold or experience other medical problems later in the week. Empaths may become ill if they do not shield themselves during their work and cleanse afterward. Interestingly enough, during emergency situations, empaths generate such productive energy that a personal shield gathers automatically, whether the individual has consciously remembered to protect him or herself or not. Panic turned and controlled is a valuable ally.

Pow-Wows and Angels

Pow-Wow artists firmly believed in angels and beings in the heavenly realms. It was thought that these beings were in existence to be of service to humans. Some Pow-Wows believed that summoning them firmly was the only way to get their attention. Others felt that assistance should be asked nicely, more as a favor granted to humankind. Archangels, such as Michael, Ariel/Uriel, Gabriel, and Raphael, were considered the most powerful and therefore the busiest in the "heavenly realms." You didn't bother them unless your problem was of a very weighty nature. These angels had control over everything except God. Angels in general were called upon all the time. There were those who gave wisdom, love, enlightenment, strength, protection, etc. Most Pow-Wows did not call them by name but invoked them by essence, either through chants or with passages from the Bible.

Terminal Illness and Healing

Many Pow-Wows would not touch terminal illness by themselves, but would call upon either their students or teachers to assist them in long-distance healing for the client. Others simply refused to work for it at all. This could be for one of two reasons—either they were not strong enough in their own belief, or a failure would be very bad for business and reputation. It is my opinion that the modern practitioner can work on terminal illness, either in a group or, if you so choose, alone. Though remember, there were a few Pow-Wows who felt that to cure the client he or she must first take the illness into him or herself, and then push it out into the universe. I don't agree with this, but it is a consideration. For terminal illness, whether it be in group or solitary workings, long-distance rituals were preferred over the laying on of hands. The correct direction of spiral energy is very important in terminal cases. It should always be worked widdershins (counterclockwise) rather then deosil (clockwise). Deosil energy will literally feed the cancerous cells. Work on banishing the illness with counterclockwise energy.

During the writing of this book, one of our circle ladies brought a request to our weekly healing ritual. "Blaze is dying of AIDS," she said. "He is really bad now, and they think they are going to have to put him in a permanent care home. His partner is very upset about it, but he doesn't know what else to do."

"I would like to work for him," I said to her. "Ask them if it is okay, then bring me his picture and something that belongs to him. I can't tell you he will be cured, but I will do the best for him that I can under the circumstances."

Our sister returned the following week with the needed permission, but did not have the personal items. The entire circle worked for Blaze for the next few weeks, but there was not much improvement; in fact, he got worse. In desperation, his partner sent along the needed items. "Do anything you can," he said, "even if it is just to make him peaceful and comfortable."

I placed Blaze's picture on my altar and worked for him myself for several days. A student of mine had never experienced sharing energy, so she worked with me to send positive, peaceful, healing energy to Blaze. That week there was no improvement, but he wasn't any worse, either. The report was that "he's so out of it, he doesn't know what is happening. But he is in no pain."

I kept the picture on the altar and continued to work for Blaze. So did our circle ladies. The following week we were sitting around my dining room table (all 14 of us), and I asked our sister how Blaze was doing. "Oh! You will not believe this!" she cried. "This week he got up, got dressed, drove the car down to the grocery store and did some shopping—all by himself! Just last week they were ready to put him in permanent care and had everything set, but now he is better—the hostel idea has been shelved for the time being!" So, in dealing with terminal illness, there is hope. We did not cure Blaze, but perhaps our intervention into his life with his permission allowed him peace, hope, and joy for just a little while longer on this plane. I personally don't think you can beat that.

Surgery and Healing

Pow-Wow should be used with professional medical care. When you are going in for surgery, don't think the doctor should take care of it all and leave it at that. There are several techniques you can use to heal faster and ensure a smooth medical procedure. First, for one to two weeks beforehand, meditate every evening on the surgery. I'm not saying you should worry about the surgery, but quite the opposite. Take several deep breaths and envision exactly how the treatment will go—smooth, serene, excellent, etc. Think of as many positive words as you can to describe the procedure. If you are afraid, take your fear and make it into an animal during meditation—like a wolf with fangs bared. Face your fear and grab the animal by the throat. Tell it you are not afraid of it and to "Get the hell out of my face!" Do this often until you are no longer afraid. Later on, you can encourage your fear to walk behind you, or beside you if you are in danger, but never in direct conflict with you.

Be informed. Know exactly what medical procedures will be involved. It is your body and you have the right to know what is going to be done to it. If you are nervous about having the procedure done, get a second opinion in another town or city.

Prepare a conjuring bag for yourself that includes specific charms for healing. Be sure to enchant the herbs before you fill the bag, and empower it after you have tied it up. Seal it with black or red wax.

If you have magickal friends, ask them to Pow-Wow for you before the surgery. If they are not magickal, choose those friends who you feel are strong in their chosen religion (or who love you very much) and ask them to pray for you. The morning before the surgery, do a cleansing or banishing ritual to release any negativity that has attached itself to your body. Use holy water or an herbal bath. Choose a favorite chant that can keep your mind occupied and reduce fear. Waiting for a procedure to be performed can be as stressful as the procedure itself. Besides, you have no idea what type of energy will be floating around in the room with you.

While you are waiting to go into surgery, whether it be outpatient or general surgery, be sure you have a blanket. There are times when the staff forgets, especially if you are going through testing and waiting in a hall in a hospital gown. Your body naturally goes into shock. Often the medical personnel are so concerned about the procedure itself that they forget that you get cold, which leads to being frightened. The blanket subconsciously gives you security.

Keep your conjuring bag with you and be sure you've stuck something in there for confidence, too. Fib if you must and tell the doctor that your kids or a niece made it for you for good luck—what do they care? I don't advocate telling a lie, but if that big old nurse insists you have to leave it behind, don't give in to the bully. After the surgery or treatment, draw the appropriate rune for healing as close to the area as possible—even if you are an inpatient. Use makeup that matches your skin, paint it on your cast, etc. Be ingenious.

After outpatient surgery, go home, rest, and if you have a magickal friend, ask him or her to sit with you for a few moments and Pow-Wow for you. If the person can't get to you, ask him or her to repeat chants or prayers for you every evening or morning. Continue your own chants and magickal procedures. Keep your conjuring bag with you until you are completely healed, then bless it, burn the spells, and return the herbs to the ground from which they came. Before your surgery, you should prepare a tape of healing chants (or buy a subliminal program designed for healing) to put on your tape recorder. It is best if you have the kind of recorder that constantly plays, not requiring you to take the tape out and turn it over. Put the headphones on your head and fall asleep with the tape running. If you are laid up for awhile, be sure there are plenty of batteries close by to keep the tape recorder running. Play the tape for as long as you are convalescing. If you can't operate the recorder yourself, have the person who is taking care of you monitor and handle the equipment. By using this procedure, I was completely healed two days after surgery. The doctors wondered just how I did it. Well, a girl has to have some secrets, you know!

If you are confined to the hospital, be sure to discuss with your physician that you wish to use the tape procedure and work out the details before you are stuck without it. Make sure it is on your chart that you will be using this healing procedure. Have a friend or loved one monitor your recorder for you if you are not aware of your surroundings for awhile. The more you use the method of healing, your chances of recovering faster than normal are greater than if you didn't bother to do it at all.

Emergencies

During my research for this book, all my children contracted the childhood disease of chickenpox. Near the end of the eight-week home epidemic, only one child had not recovered, and his difficulties were running the normal course. When one of my children is ill, I usually let him or her sleep on the sofa in the living room. I'm a night owl and my work area is in the living room, too. I feel better when I can watch over my kids while they sleep.

On the fourth night, I was happily typing away when Jamie sat up, gasping for air. From what we later surmised, the chickenpox in his mouth and throat swelled, cutting off his ability to breathe. It was almost midnight. My husband had gone to bed an hour before and all the other children were sleeping. It's a bizarre feeling when you are not medically trained in anything and you know that if you don't do something your child may never be with you again. All manner of thoughts enter your mind—the one in mine was "it only takes a few minutes to die."

At first, I was hoping that he was merely dreaming, or perhaps teetering in that half-awake, half-dream state where fears overtake normal reaction, but it became clear that he could not breathe, regardless of whether he had been asleep or not. I was petrified. I also understood that this was my son and it was up to me not to panic. I woke my husband (he's excellent in a crisis), but he was so groggy from his own dream state that what I was saying was not connecting with his brain. I rushed to the phone and called 911 (which I had never done before), and went back to my son. He was getting ashen and my husband was still rattling around in the bedroom trying to get his bearings together. (Actually, I think he was trying to locate his underwear in the dark.) I was alone with my son and he was in trouble. It was at that moment that I knew I must use the techniques I had practiced during routine healings in experimentation with the Pow-Wow system, with injuries such as burns, cuts, and bruises. However, with those types of injuries, you know the patient isn't going to drop dead on you. Therefore, you approach the patient with a calmer mentality than in a situation such as this. I grabbed my son in my arms, wrapped my body around him, and raised every ounce of energy I could muster. I transformed my fear into energy and called on the Goddess Diana (known for her affinity to children), then repeated a Pow-Wow chant in her name.

In less than five minutes, his breathing returned to normal and my house was filled with a variety of medical experts who had absolutely nothing to do but watch Steven Segal on television, peek at my computer, and stare at my son playing shyly under the covers. I can imagine what they thought, considering I have a banner on my bulletin board that says "Watch out! Witch at work!" In this case, so true!

I hope that you never have a situation like this one, but there are some things to remember in case of an emergency.

Do not panic. This can be very hard, especially if the injured person is someone who is close to you. If you cannot get a grip and think you are going to lose it, grab onto something solid, such as a chair or edge of a table. Take several deep breaths and visualize your fear melting like butter in a hot pan or freezing in place like the blob. If your visualization techniques are good, this will only take a matter of seconds.

Call or send someone to get appropriate medical attention. Better safe than sorry.

Do not yell or scream. Assuming that help is on its way, do not waste your time yelling, screaming, or crying. Instead, conserve that energy—you are going to need it—and channel it into your healing.

If you forget the chant or spell intended for the particular injury or illness, don't panic. Any charm or spell can be used, just change the phrasing to match the situation and keep it simple. If all words escape you, it's okay. Instead, visualize the divinity with whom you are connected and see him or her coming to help you and aiding the injured or ill person.

Follow appropriate first-aid techniques during the healing process. If you are alone, you will have to do first aid while you are working the healing. If there is another person with you, he or she may be able to render appropriate first aid and leave your hands free to do the healing. My oldest daughter and I often work in tandem. She rushes to acquire the appropriate first-aid supplies, herbs, stones, ice, etc., while I concentrate on the healing.

Call on the angels. Don't be shy here. Who the heck cares who is listening? Remember to invoke or summon the power and assistance of the "heavenly" realms. They will be delighted to help you, but they need your permission to interfere with your life.

Use your better judgement. Once expert medical treatment arrives and if the healing has not taken effect, or there is more damage than you are capable of handling, step back and allow the professionals to take over. Do not succumb to emotion, but continue the healing from the sidelines. You can use your skills if you are an onlooker and not a participant during a medical emergency or even a normal medical treatment. For instance, I watched as one of my children had a tooth extracted a while back and was getting a little nervous because there seemed to be some difficulty. I grounded, centered, called on the wisdom of Socrates, connected with Divinity, and *zip*, the tooth came out clean. And let me tell you, it was a monster tooth, still completely intact. Thank you, Socrates, very much! Of course, the expertise of the dentist was a contributing factor as well. If you are in the process of emergency healing and you wish to continue even though professional medical attention is being used, calmly and firmly indicate that you will stay out of their way but you will continue to do your work. As long as you do not jeopardize the medical personnel, you have every right to continue the healing process. If you are in full possession of your emotional faculties, you have a better chance of continuing the healing. If you stand in the way and begin to mouth off, I can assure you that you will be removed from the area. Instead, be quiet, calm, and firm.

How firm should you get? Only you can determine that call. "Ah am a healah," stated a southern friend of mine in a controlled voice as the ambulance personnel barred him from riding along to the hospital with his sick grandfather. "And you all will permit me to ride in that ambulance!"

They refused.

Again my friend informed him of his intentions to ride in that ambulance and assist his grandfather. Again, he was refused.

There wasn't time to quibble. He quietly stepped forward, pulled out a large pentacle medallion from under his shirt, looked the two burly attendants in the eyeballs, and politely informed them what would most likely happen to treasured parts of their anatomy should they consider refusing him a third time. Please also consider that my friend is slight of build, and normally would pose no threat to anyone's masculine prowess.

He rode to the hospital in the ambulance.

Was this ethical? He used the fear factor that has been floating around the Wiccan religion to his advantage because he wanted his grandfather to survive. Witches know that the pentacle is not a bad symbol. The five points stand for earth, air, fire, water, and the spirit of humankind. The circle around it represents the universal love of the cosmos. For some, this situation would be an easy call; for others, it would be a flagrant use of the fear factor. What would you do in a situation such as this? Think about it. No, I mean *really* think about it. Personally, I would have done exactly what my friend did.

Today, in the area of serious injury and illness, it is appropriate and necessary to dial 911. Foolish is the individual who believes that healing can only come from one source. In my mind, if I can have all the bases covered, it will be of benefit to everyone involved. It will also give you peace of mind that you have done everything within your power to help the person in need.

Healing Chants, Spells, and Tools: *Besprechen*

About the time I was ready to link my research together, I got very lucky—I found a Pow-Wow who agreed to train me. As is standard procedure, he asked me not to reveal his name to the public. He made me promise that I would not tell anyone in the media where he lived until after he passed away, whenever that would be. He said he was getting older and didn't want people all over the place. To give him credit, he didn't mind my donating our taped conversations to the local historical society. Yes, I hate reading books about Mrs. P. and Mr. X, too, but what can you do when you give your word?

On with my research I went, worried that no one would believe my sources since I couldn't name most of them. With a start, I realized that occult writers have been doing that for centuries, so why should I be any different? I know the magickal community is fed up with the stories of "my grandmother was a Witch" or "my Uncle initiated me." Here I was, with stories just as unprovable. I copied down on paper and taped my conversations with Preston with hope that I could someday verify part of the data I received. I would buzz home to get everything into the computer before I forgot it. Many of the healing chants in this chapter came orally from Preston Zerbe. I found several of the chants he knew in research material later on, and some I have not. On various afternoons, I would sit in his home, steno pad in hand, and write like crazy. Sometimes one of my children accompanied me, and other times we were alone. It was a nice place to be. I hoped once we got to know each other I could receive his permission to print his name. We never got around to it.

When Preston died, I was really at a loss. Although I had learned a lot from him, I knew there was more, and that I had missed it. I didn't grieve for Preston in the normal sense. He helped so many people in his lifetime. He earned a rest in his heaven. The day he died (I didn't know that he was in the hospital), I was Pow-Wowing for a young child with a cold.

"Do you believe in God?" I asked the child after I had finished.

"Oh, yes!" he responded with the wide-eyed innocence of an eight-year-old.

"Well, then," I said, "if you believe in God, then you will feel better very soon."

His mother patted his shoulder and he smiled, then said, "Thank you so much!"

At that moment I knew Preston was dead and that he was standing beside me. "Don't thank me, thank God in your prayers tonight," came flying out of my mouth. It was what Preston always said to his clients after a healing—and it felt so right.

Things were not so right with this book. "Now what do I do," I thought glumly as I stared at the material I did have. So far, everything I had amassed had been shotgunned (our word for tested in our Circle) and I knew the stuff to be good, but there wasn't enough research material to back it up.

I'm a big fan of talking to the dead and burning candles for them. If the candle flame burns high, the spirit you are seeking is in the room with you. No, I wasn't Catholic before I was Wiccan, but it is something I like to do. So I lit a red candle, sat on my dining room table (yes, call me Bohemian), and addressed Preston. About two months had gone by since his death, which is about right when you want to talk to a dead person. There seems to be (excuse the pun) a dead spot that occurs right after a person passes away. It can last from a month and a half to two months (or sometimes even three) where you can't "feel" them at all. It is like the person went on vacation.

"Hey, Preston," I said to the air in front of me. "It's Jenine calling here and I've got a major problem. If you have been floating around here, you know exactly what I do and that I'm interested in helping people." Naturally, there was no response; I'd probably have fallen off the table if there were. But I'm a persistent little bugger, so I went on. "You sort of left me hanging in the wind on the Pow-Wow thing. I don't know where to turn next. I'd be most appreciative if you could send some information my way because I don't, at this point, know where else to look. Please help me if you can, and send someone my way if you get the chance."

A few days later, information on Pow-Wow did start coming my way and has continued to wander in my direction ever since. It wasn't like a blast of lightning, but there were bits and pieces that I could add to the data I had already collected. Some information made things connect, encouraged my understanding into a broader sense, or simply confirmed information I had already received. Thank you most sincerely, Preston. I know you heard me.

Chants

Chants are vitally important to the healing process. Most charms and spells in Pow-Wow require the chant to be said three times. After each chant, the healer blows his or her breath three short times toward the client and often writes a sigil in the air or over the body. Remember, the healing energy comes in through the throat chakra. During this time you must focus, ground, center, and connect with a specific deity system. Whether you are Buddhist, Christian, Hindu, Jewish, or Wiccan, the chants will work if your faith is firm.

Several of the ladies in my healing circle experimented on their own with the chants. They used various deities to test the validity of the process. We found that whether you used the Christian closing of Father, Son, and Holy Ghost or preferred to use Maiden, Mother, Crone archetypes, the chants worked the same. We also discovered that if you concentrate on the imagery of the chant instead on the healing power you are trying to incorporate, it works better. Often two or three different chants are hooked together, depending upon the Pow-Wow artist and how they were taught. For example, Preston Zerbe used the following secondary chant after the primary invocation. This secondary chant works much like the chorus in a song. It comes from the Gospel of Mark 16:17-18.

> *(Begin this chant by repeating the client's full name)*
> *And these signs shall follow those that believeth in my name*
> *They shall cast out demons and they shall speak in new tongues*
> *And if they drink anything deadly, it shall not harm them.*
> *They shall lay hands upon the sick and they shall recover*
> *In the Name of the Father, Son, and Holy Ghost.*

The All-purpose Chant

If you don't know what is wrong with the person, this is the best chant to use. One Pow-Wow I spoke to says that he uses this one "just about all the time. There are many others that I have access to," he says, "but this is the best." This was the first chant I learned from him. It is for everything from bee stings, burns, and colds to unknown infections. Recite the chant three times. At each stanza, you must blow your breath at the wound three times in quick succession. You may end the chant with, "In the name of the Father, Son, and Holy Ghost" as Preston did, or you can end it with the connection to your own deity system. It will work either way.

97

I have provided two versions, one for those who are Wiccan and one for those who are Christian.

WICCAN VERSION

(Begin by saying the full name of the client)
Hast thou recovered health and Goddess
I will lead thee again to the Maiden, Mother, and Crone
Therefore so help thee our Goddess readily
And thou shalt be blessed as well as the sacred cakes and holy ale
Which Aradia offered to her followers before she left them.
Therefore so help you
Maiden, Mother, and Crone.

CHRISTIAN VERSION

(Repeat the client's full baptismal name first)
Hast thou recovered health and God
I will lead thee again to God, the Father, the Son, and the Holy Ghost
Therefore so help thee our Lord readily
And thou shalt be blessed as well as the cup of wine and holy bread
Which Jesus Christ offered to his beloved disciples on Holy Thursday
Night before he left them.
Therefore so help you
God the Father, the Son, and the Holy Ghost
Amen.

Chants and Timing

Repeat most chants at three- to fifteen-minute intervals, depending upon the seriousness of the problem. For example, a Pow-Wow may heal thusly:

1. Repeat the client's full name.
2. Say the primary chant once.
3. Say the secondary chant once.
4. Repeat the primary chant.
5. Repeat the secondary chant.
6. Repeat the primary chant.
7. Repeat the secondary chant.
8. Give the appropriate signage to seal the healing.
9. Wait three to fifteen minutes.
10. Repeat steps 1-8.

11. Wait three to fifteen minutes.
12. Repeat steps 1-8.

    The interval method allows the Pow-Wow to recharge his or her mag-ickal batteries. It also gives quiet time for a positive interchange between the Pow-Wow and client to boost confidence. Not all Pow-Wows use the break—some go straight through, taking up to 20 minutes to complete the hands-on healing.

Energy Drain

Many Pow-Wows report feeling exhausted after a healing session. This is nor-mal and nothing to worry about. The level of exhaustion depends upon per-sonal health, how much individual energy the healer expels, and whether or not you have grounded properly. When you exercise, you use up energy. Everybody knows this and expects to feel winded at worst or slightly tired at best. After you exercise, you need to take care of the body through food, drink, and rest. It is the same when you expel psychic energy. You need to per-form maintenance tasks to compensate for the energy drain. If you feel exhausted after Pow-Wowing for a simple burn, then you should review your procedures to determine what you did wrong. However, if you experience exhaustion after spending half an hour in consultation and an hour in the heal-ing process, you should expect to be tired. To put your mind at ease, the more you practice, as with exercise, the better your mental and physical bodies per-form. You become accustomed to holding high energy for longer periods.

    As previously mentioned, some believe that they have to "take on the ill-ness" before they can "pass it to God." This would be exhausting for the Pow-Wow's body. Pow-Wows and Christians aren't the only people who believe this. A Wiccan High Priestess, who I much admire, told me an inter-esting story of how her coven worked for a full year on an AIDS patient. His symptoms were very light, and finally, without the pain and horrid quality of life that many other victims experience, he lay down upon his bed and passed peacefully away. When I asked her how they had done it, she sighed and smiled sadly. "I don't recommend this procedure to be done by others, but this was a close friend of ours. We, as a group, took his symptoms into our bodies so that he could pass with little difficulty. It worked, but we are all emotionally and physically exhausted, and all of us have been very sick dur-ing this past year." Others, like Mr. Zerbe, said he did not have that problem. He believed his body wasn't taking on the illness. He said he was simply putting the matter in God's hands, and letting Him work out the logistics of how it got there.

If you are feeling overly tired after a healing, you should run your hands under cold water and take a breather. Plant your feet firmly on the floor and pull the energy of the earth up through your body to revitalize yourself. If you are very tired, put on some relaxing music and meditate for a bit. Use a subliminal programming tape designed for relaxation. Many individuals do the Lesser Banishing Ritual as I mentioned earlier in this text. You also can recite the Lord's Prayer or choose a special Psalm that you particularly like. One Pow-Wow (now deceased) from Berks County claimed that whenever he felt low on power he recited the following from the Bible: "And it came to pass on the day that Moses had fully set up the tabernacle, and had anointed it, and sanctified it, and all the instruments thereof, and had anointed them, and sanctified them" (Numbers 7:1). Although the original interviewer thought he got it wrong, and held his age (88 at the time) as being responsible for his confusion—he didn't get it wrong, the interviewer did. Every good occultist knows that all tools, including yourself, must be cleansed, consecrated, and charged to accept and work with Divine energy. He was not deaf, blind, or confused—he was using his instincts and they were right on the money. Another Berks County Pow-Wow fellow felt he preserved his power by reciting Numbers 6:24-27 as he watched his clients leave the house after a healing: "And the Lord bless thee, and keep thee; may He make His face to shine upon thee, and be gracious unto thee. May He lift up His countenance upon thee and give thee peace."

Don't worry if you have tried all these methods and are still tired—a nice nap, if possible, should do you up just right.

Energy Fall-out

If there are guests in the room while a Pow-Wow is working, they should not be allowed to stand in close proximity to either the Pow-Wow or the client. They must pick a place out of the way and stay there. They are not permitted to move, wander around the perimeter, or speak. In fact, if the visitor tries to walk behind the Pow-Wow, he or she will be asked to leave the room. The visitor may not sit in the "line of fire," should the Pow-Wow be of the type who "throws" the disease away from the client. The healer may specifically show the visitor where he or she is to sit.

There is good reason behind these precautionary measures. The healer is acting as a funnel, a whirlwind, a vacuum cleaner, even a hunter if you like that analogy. The prey is negative energy. The healer pushes Divine energy into the body and pulls the negative energy out. The healer dispenses with the negative energy, then fills the body with Divine light. The negative energy has to go somewhere. The healer normally directs it to a particular spot on the floor. Occasionally, the healer may carry a lodestone in the palm of his or her left hand to draw out the energy, pull it into the stone, and destroy it. If you were sitting under the left hand of the healer in the direct line of the negative energy flow, you most likely would suffer unfortunate effects.

Stopping Blood

I think there are as many chants for stopping blood as there are Pow-Wows. Although you may not believe it, it is one of the easiest techniques to learn and is often the first taught by a Pow-Wow. There are many people in my town who "can stop the blood" but know no other healing or magickal techniques. It was something handed down from their grandmother, like a favorite recipe for sugar cookies.

There are several chants that were (and are) said to still blood flow. Choose the one with which you are most comfortable and that is easiest to remember for you. The first chant listed here has never failed me. My family uses it for cuts, scrapes, nosebleeds, and deep wounds.

> *Holy Mary, Mother of God*
> *Who stoppeth the pain and stoppeth the blood.*
> *In the name of the Maiden, Mother, and Crone.*
> *So be it.*

> *Blessed wound*
> *Blessed hour*
> *Blessed be the day the Goddess came to power.*
> *Women's mysteries fine and strong*
> *Stop this blood through female song.*

> *Jesus Christ, dearest blood*
> *That stoppeth the pain and stoppeth the blood.*
> *In this help you (first name)*
> *God the Father, God the Son, God the Holy Ghost.*

Use the chant listed below in dire emergencies. It is good for all emergency medical situations.

> *Aradia walked before (the person's name)*
> *and She saw (the person's name)*
> *lying in blood and pain.*
> *She spoke and said: Thou shalt live, thou shalt live, thou shalt live*
> *And it was done.*
> *In the name of the Maiden, Mother, and Crone.*
> *And the Father, Son, and Holy Ghost.*
> *So mote it be.*

The chant also requires the healer to run his or her hands over the person three times. If you have chosen Christianity as your religious base, substitute the name Jesus in any of the chants.

In the name of Aradia
It shall not stand, not run, nor go further
Remain at the proper place
Not flow nor float
The bleeding be healed, divided rightly
In the name of the Maiden, Mother, and Crone.

The following chant is one of my personal favorites:

I walk through a green forest
There I find three wells, cool and cold.
The first spirit in the well is called courage
The second is called faith
And the third I call to stop the blood.

Many people have a great affinity for the Lord's Prayer. Here is a procedure to use it for stopping blood. Breathe three times upon the patient and say the Lord's Prayer three times until the words "on earth," and the bleeding will stop.

Healing Wounds

Now that you have stopped the bleeding, it is time to work on healing the wound. One spell requires four pieces of pine (if you have it), or another type of wood. The pieces should be of equal length. Tap each piece of wood (very lightly, of course) on the wound and say five times for each piece of wood:

Upon Golgatha, upon Golgatha
Upon Cypress, upon Cypress
Upon Arrorat, upon Arrorat
Thy pains shall flee
Thy pain shall sink upon the deep sea
As this wood burns, thy pain be sunk
Thy wounds be healed.

Burn the wood when you are through.

To Remove Bruises and Pain

No one likes the thought of being in pain, nor do they care for unsightly bruises. This chant has worked well for us for minor bruises. It is one of the better known chants.

> *Bruises thou shalt not beat*
> *Bruises thou shalt not sweat*
> *Bruises though shalt not run*
> *No more than the Virgin Mary shall bring forth another son.*
> *In the name of the Father, Son, and Holy Ghost.*

Repeat three times and move your hands from wound to fingers, or from wound to toes, whichever is closest. In this spell, you are given a condition that is finite in nature to visualize—"no more than the Virgin Mary shall bring forth another son." Some Christians believe that Mary had only one son, although there are those (my original faith included) who very much believe that Mary and Joseph had many children after Jesus. Despite this argument, no one believes that Mary is going to have another son now. Therefore, this is finite symbolism. It will aid your subconscious to connect the removal of the bruise to a finite thought. Mary can't have another son, therefore the bruise can't get any bigger.

I shotgunned this chant myself when I had some teeth extracted. I wrote it on a piece of paper and drew the rune Naud (Nauthiz) below it. Naud is a binding rune used to constrict and apply pressure. I put the paper in a conjuring bag with a few healing herbs and tied it to the belt loop of my pants. It was outpatient surgery in an oral surgeon's office. I knew I wouldn't have to remove my clothes (lucky me). I also asked to stay awake instead of taking anesthesia. I did this for two reasons—the first is that it's too expensive if you don't have any health insurance. Second, I'm a hard person to keep under and I can hear and remember what the doctors and nurses are saying. I personally think that all surgical procedures should be taped and played back for the patient should he or she desire to hear it. I bet that would cut down on the rude comments and negative attitudes!

During the surgery, I chanted a blood stopping charm to myself the entire time. When I got home, I intentionally didn't use ice to reduce swelling. Instead, I activated the conjuring bag by rubbing it between my hands, then took eye make-up and drew the rune directly on my cheek. Granted, my family thought I was incredibly stupid and my kids kept asking me what that "thing" was on my cheek. However, I was stubborn about it and ignored the "what if somebody comes?" comment. As a result, there was minimal swelling. Nobody said anything, as if they didn't want to admit that it worked.

The next day, my father asked to learn about runes and how he could use them for his needs. Obviously, my good condition was noticeable. I kept that conjuring bag with me, night and day, for a full week. In the next several months, I had a great deal of dental surgery. Each time I banished the room before the procedure began. I concentrated on my chants during the procedure, used the conjuring bag, and later drew runes over the surgical area. In each and every case (except the last) the doctors could not understand how on earth I could be healed completely two days later.

It was during my last and final surgery that I used pre-taped chants and subliminal stress-reducing tapes along with the other methods listed above. I knew the last surgery would be the worst and that the necessity of healing quickly was uppermost in my mind. The final surgery took several days longer to heal; however, I experienced no complications.

To Remove Sickness, Aches, and Pains from Bones

I think the most astounding chant in this book is the one below. In July of 1992, we began working on a brain tumor of a little boy. The first few weeks we used this chant and were told that his prognosis was good. We continued to work for the little boy each week until October of that year. At that time, he was scheduled for a second MRI—and guess what? There was no tumor, only scar tissue!

Since then many of us have used the chant for a variety of purposes, from bee stings to more serious medical conditions, including working with AIDS patients. Although I hate to sound like a nag, I'd like to remind you to seek proper medical treatment in tandem with healing magick.

> *(Disease/Injury) come out of the marrow into the bones*
> *Out of the bones into the blood*
> *Out of the blood into the flesh*
> *Out of the flesh upon the skin*
> *From the skin and into (name)'s hair*
> *Out of the hair into the green forest*
> *Out of the green forest into the dry sand*
> *As sure as the God moves within the Goddess and out into the land.*

When you are pulling sickness, pain, or disease out of another person, you should direct it out from your body and away from the patient's body. No one should be in the "line of fire," as previously mentioned. If there are other people in the room, it really is best if they leave before you begin the healing. The only exception lies in working with children who will need parental or guardian support.

This chant leads the subconscious mind of the healer in small steps through the healing process. It enables you to take one movement of the disease at a time. It allows your subconscious to connect with step-by-step imagery, instead of trying to blast it out of the body like a bomb, or using the jumbo vacuum imagery principle.

Pain

One of the most important tools of the Pow-Wow was a large stone that can fill the palm of your hand—the Divinity stone. It has to be smooth and it must "feel right" to you. It does not have to be a crystal or gem; a plain, ordinary stone will do nicely. The purpose of this stone is to draw out the pain, regardless of its actual origin. Although it is most often used for physical pain, it could also be placed near the heart chakra to relieve emotional distress. The chant used in conjunction with the stone is as follows:

> *Hair and hide*
> *Flesh and blood*
> *Nerve and bone*
> *No more pain than this stone.*

Follow this chant with the all-purpose one listed earlier in this chapter that begins, "These signs shall follow them ..."

Both chants are to be said three times. During the chants, the stone is to be held about one-half inch away from the painful area, and moved in a widdershins direction. I have also seen the sign of the pentacle (banishing) used, the rune Algiz (Elk), a two half-circle motion (possibly representing opposing crescent moons), and the sign of the equal-armed cross (which did not originate with the Christians, though the more modern Pow-Wows believe it to be a symbol of Christ's cross).

The crucifix is not a very good amulet or healing sigil, as although it invokes protection, it represents grief and sadness. The crucifix is historically an emblem of attack. Knights of the Church wore it on their smocks, shields, and banners into battle. I am sure some readers will scoff at my observation, but I have found that most of the people who wear crosses around their necks are primarily unhappy. Often they are filled with either remorse, grief, depression, or low self-esteem.

Several of my students have told me stories that are negatively linked to the crucifix. One fellow related the following. "I was at a party. It was cool, you know, no drugs or alcohol. There was music and dancing. I have this really beautiful cross that a friend gave me as a gift. It is gorgeous. I was wearing it under my shirt that night. Anyway, I walked up to this one girl and asked her if she would like to dance. She slapped me! It was really weird.

After that I noticed there was an unpleasant connection to my wearing that cross and other things that were happening in my life. I finally took it off, and haven't had any problems since." However, if you wear a crucifix and are happy as a lark, far be it from me to tell you to change it.

Ye pains I banish ye back
Let these limbs enjoy rest and peace
Be exiled upon the highest mountain
And sunk into the deepest sea!
In the name of the Guardian Angels!

Cures for Headaches

Tell the person who has the headache to focus on the pain. Instruct the patient to move his or her consciousness into the pain. It may be necessary that you guide him or her in through a meditation sequence. Once the conscious mind moves into the pain, the pain falters and dissipates.

There are two very short chants for headaches. The first is:

Tame thou flesh and blood
As our Lady tames the lion.

This chant could be in direct reference to Tarot symbolism, as most Tarot cards representing Strength depict a Goddess with a lion by her side. The following chant for the same purpose is obviously of German origin:

Von deine Kopf
Zu meine Hand
In Gottes Hand.

Translated, it means: "From your head/To my hand/In God's Hand." It is repeated three times in quick succession. With the first line, the Pow-Wow places the receptive hand on the head of the client. On the second line, he or she holds his or her hand outward, with palm cupped as if holding the pain. On the third line, the Pow-Wow does nothing until he or she has finished the chant. Then the Pow-Wow exclaims, "I throw it away!" and pitches the receptive hand outward away from both his or her body and the client's.

An all-purpose chant for general pain goes like this:

Dies Wasser und dies Feuer
Dies Wasser und dies Feuer
Dies Wasser und dies Feuer
Dies ist ein grosse Dinge

In dies grosses geheilige land
Unser shoene Frau Mari.

The translation is: "This water and this fire/This water and this fire/This water and this fire/This is a big thing/In this big holy land/Our pretty Lady Maria." As with the previous chant, you throw the pain away on the last line. Again notice the reference to fire and water, Heathen in origin. If you take "Maria" off, the chant becomes Craft. If you exchange Frigga or Freya for Maria, the chant becomes Heathen Germanic (which is probably what it was in the first place).

How to Cure Inflammation or a Simple Cold

Prepare the following:
   1 ounce tomato juice
   ¼ teaspoon black pepper
   ⅛ teaspoon cayenne pepper

Mix well and drink once in the morning and once at night. Repeat the following chant:

Inflammation lose thy color
Like Brutus lost his color when he betrayed Caesar
The lions roared and the waters ran
Stopped only by the Goddess' hand
In the name of the Father, Son, and Holy Ghost.

The imagery in this chant is strong. We've all seen movies on the fate of Julius Caesar and the traitor Brutus. It is said that lions ran wild in the city streets and the rain slashed the countryside on the Ides of March. Here, the Goddess takes Caesar into her arms and quells the disaster. Here is another chant for the same malady:

Inflammation lose thy color
As the betrayers of true Witches lost theirs
When fires rose high around the innocent
And those of cause went pale
In the name of the God, the Goddess, and the All.

or

Sanctus itorius res, call the rest.
Here the Goddess came to his assistance

Reaching out her snow white hand
Against the hot and cold brand.

Make three stars with the thumb each time (three) the chant is said. The chant must be done every three hours during the day and evening, then once again on the next day.

In the last chant, we could assume that the Goddess here is actually Frigga or Freya and "against the hot and cold brand" would be another reference to Heathen fire and ice.

A Cure for the Croup

This one was of special interest to me as my son, Jamie, continued to "get the croup" well into his sixth year. The croup is a modern parent's nightmare. If you have never suffered through this malady, it is difficult to fathom. I haven't decided who is worse for wear during the illness—the child who knows he or she is sick but little else, or the parent who realizes that his or her child cannot breathe. There isn't much you can do for the condition. Take the child out into the cold air to relieve the swelling in the air passages, run a vaporizer, sit up all night for at least the first two, and give the child antibiotics as prescribed by a physician. This procedure gets old quickly.

Milford Hess from Dillsburg, Pennsylvania, gives us the following treatment for the croup. Have the child stand (if he or she is old enough) beside a wooden door frame in your home, preferably the one that leads to his or her bedroom. Measure his or her height against the door and put a pencil mark on the frame to mark how tall the child is. Take a hand drill and bore a ¼-inch hole into the wooden frame right over the pencil mark. Cut some hair from the child's head and stuff it in the hole. Patch up the hole with wood plug. Have the child slowly walk back and forth past the patch three times while reciting Mark 16:17-18. The croup will be cured.

I followed Mr. Hess' instructions in the winter of my son's sixth year. He is eight now and has not had the croup since the afternoon I bored the hole in the doorway to his room, stuffed the hair in it, and sealed it up.

A Cure for Muscle Strain

Odin hung upon the tree of life
And his hanging did not do him any harm
Therefore (name)'s strain shall
Do thee no more harm that it did Odin.
In the name of Odin, Freya, and Frigga
So be it.

Removing Warts

Take several small creek stones (as many as you have warts) and rub each wart with a stone. Take the stones to a cemetery and cast them in a grave before the body is buried. This must be done at the decrease of the Moon.

In Pow-Wow healing, it was believed that if you could get something organic in "sympathy" with your illness, you could rid yourself of disease. Often vegetables or raw eggs were rubbed over diseased areas to "take on" the problem and then were discarded off the property. As the organic material decomposed, the illness or disease would be broken down and eventually disappear. Another cure for warts follows such a procedure. Cut an onion and rub both halves on the warts. Put the onion back together fastened with a pin and bury the onion where rain and water will reach it. You are not to look back after it has been laid to rest, and you should repeat a stopping blood charm to yourself three times.

A third way to remove warts is to draw half-circles on each side of the wart, starting at the point closest to the wart on the right and down. Then begin on the left, and down. Repeat "Father, Son, and Holy Ghost" three times.

Controlling and Banishing Fevers

Write the following words on a piece of paper, wrap it around garlic, then place it on the patient:

Potmat Sineat
Potmat Sineat
Potmat Sineat

General Remedies

There are certain remedies slated to be used when absolutely nothing else works—not doctors, not healers, not medicine, simply nothing at all. The Witches' bottle is one of them and is useful for a variety of difficulties. I have read or heard at least fifty ways to make a Witches' bottle. Here is a Pow-Wow version.

Find a wooden box that has a lock and key combination. Paint the outside of the box red and the inside white. Let the ill person, without speaking to anyone, put his or her urine in a bottle with nine new needles and nine new pins before sunrise. Seal it and lock the bottle in the box immediately. The key hole must then be sealed as well. The key for the lock is to be carried by the sick person for three days. No one else may touch the key or all is truly lost. When the sick person has recovered, the bottle should be removed and buried. A rider on this spell indicates that nothing from the house, premises, or person should be loaned out for nine days following the locking of the box. If someone does ask for a loan, he or she may be the source of the negativity that has affected the ill person.

Here is a charm to ease a fever that cannot be broken. Write the following on a piece of white paper and sew it on linen or muslin, then hang it around the patient's neck to be worn until the illness has abated:

$$\begin{array}{c}
A B A X A C A T A B A X \\
A B A X A C A T A B A X \\
A B A X A C A T A B A \\
A B A X A C A T A B \\
A B A X A C A T A \\
A B A X A C A T \\
A B A X A C A \\
A B A X A C \\
A B A X A \\
A B A X \\
A B A \\
A B \\
A
\end{array}$$

The remedy was first designed for children to reduce fever. The word ABRA-CADABRA is often used in the same manner. Both remedies are said to have originated in Rome and were believed to have been invented by Serenus Sammonicus, a physician to the Emperor Caracalla. Scholars believe that the inscription means "perish with the word."

Burns

It is a general consensus between Pow-Wows and other faith healers that neither ice nor water should be applied to a burn. They say it drives the fire into the bone and increases the chance of infection. If the burn is a bad one, it may take days or even weeks of hands-on healing to facilitate the healthy restoration process of the skin. Often, if done diligently, there will be little or no scarring of surface tissue.

To tend a burn, choose one of the charms listed below. Say the charm once while running your hand about an inch above the burn. Move your hand from the trunk of the body outward. As your hand moves out, blow on the burn, letting your breath follow the same path as the hand. Then repeat.

Here is one injury in which the sacred breath of the healer is important. You certainly wouldn't want to lay your hand directly on a burn. In this procedure, your hand pulls the negative energy (in this case, the fire) out of the injured area while your breath instills the positive healing energy. The full procedure is to be done at least three times over a minor burn and several more times for more severe burns. One faith healer visited a hospital daily to tend to a burn patient. The individual healed quickly and had little scar tissue.

It was also believed that you should never tie up a burn with heavy bandages, and dunking the burned area in water was a definite no-no. A light dusting of baby powder was used to absorb the liquid that came out of the burn and a light gauze pad was used to keep the dirt out. The redness around the burn indicates that the fire is in the skin. Pow-Wows believe that the fire must literally be taken out for the burn to heal properly. If the fire is not removed, it will take the injury longer to heal and the risk of infection is greater. It was also felt that doctors who ordered heavy bandages actually did the patient more harm than good, since the fire was pushed into the bone.

Chants for burns can be used for other difficulties, such as bee stings or rashes—anything where the skin is hot and is emitting an unusual heat pattern. Although there are many burn chants, this first one (from my friend in York Springs) works best for me. It is nonsensical, but it works for any kind of inflammatory condition and burns.

ALL-PURPOSE BURN/INFECTION CHANT (THE DRAGON CHANT)

The weed and the dragon tried to cross the river Jordan
The weed sank and the dragon drank
In the name of the Father, Son, and Holy Ghost
In the name of the Maiden, Mother, and Crone.

For a burn, say the chant in your head and keep blowing from the point of the burn closest to your body and out in smooth, even breaths. After each stanza, repeat the first chant in this chapter ("And these signs shall follow ..."). Two days after receiving this chant I burned myself on the stove, and the chant worked perfectly. Since then, my entire family has used it with success. This is one particular chant in which the three times rule does not apply. You should continue the chant and the blowing until the pain is gone completely. For first-degree burns, do not run cold water over the burn! Seek medical attention for second- and third-degree burns. Use the chant with proper medical treatment.

In reviewing this manuscript, Donald Tyson, noted Llewellyn author, had this to say about this particular chant: "Regarding the chant [of the Weed and the Dragon], 'weed' is an old term for a kind of perpetual fever (see the Oxford English Dictionary). The dragon is associated with fire, thus burning. Both of these (fever and burns) are defeated by water ('The weed sank and the dragon drank'), which is the elemental opposite of fire."

Our family has found that when this chant is used for first- and second-degree burns they do not fill with pus, but rather remain flat and turn brown. After a few days (or a week or so depending on the severity of the burn), the dark skin sloughs off during a warm shower or bath. For other types of pain, string magick is used with this chant and is described in detail elsewhere in the chapter.

Here is a chant for treating burns that comes from further south along the Appalachian Trail, and the faith healers who practice in that area.

There came an angel from the East
Bringing frost and fire
In frost
Out fire
In the name of the Maiden, Mother, and Crone.

This chant goes deeper than visions of an angel wandering around with fire and ice. In Teutonic/Germanic/Heathen legend and magickal practices, fire was fought with fire, and ice with ice. It is a type of power purification and aggressive defense. In the chant, you are combining two opposing energies to drive away the pain and promote equal balance in the healing fluids and tissues of the body. I wouldn't be surprised if the original deity here was Thor, wielder of those weapons, and not attributed to the feminine aspect at all.

You can try this chant for the same purpose:

Clear out brand but never in
Be thou cold or hot
Thou must cease to burn
May the Goddess guard thy blood and thy marrow and thy bones
And every artery, great and small.
They shall all be guarded and protected in the name of the Goddess
Against inflammation and mortification.

Dealing with Inflammation

The universal healing colors of the Pow-Wow were white and red. In this procedure, a spool of red thread, an earthen bowl, and a red candle are employed. Today, most Pow-Wow artists use a lighter instead of a candle. Before doing this ritual myself, I witnessed it performed by a Pow-Wow artist twice in 1992. The first time was for my son, who had a bee sting between his fingers that swelled up his entire arm to his elbow, making him look more like Popeye than an eight-year-old boy. It worked very well.

The second time was for a friend of mine whose face swelled up mysteriously. She had been both to a hospital emergency room and to the doctor.

Neither professional could tell her what was the matter with her face. I immediately called the Pow-Wow who administered to my son and asked for an appointment. When we arrived, she was taken to a small, unused bedroom and asked to sit straight in a hard-backed chair. The Pow-Wow went to a window ledge and from behind the curtain produced an ashtray and a lighter. He withdrew a spool of red thread from an old desk and unwound about three lengths of the thread. He cut it from the spool with a pocket knife.

He took the string between both hands and drew it taut, leaving two feet of thread extended between his hands. Taking his place to her right, he carefully lifted the string from her back, up over her head, and down over her chest in one smooth motion, intoning the following chant:

> *The weed and the dragon tried to cross the river Jordan*
> *The weed sank the dragon drank*
> *In the name of the Father, Son, and Holy Ghost.*

Then he brought it back over her head (keeping the string taut) and back down her side. He did this three times, blowing his breath three times at the end of each stanza. Moving widdershins, he stood behind her and repeated the procedure; then he moved to her left side, intoning the same chant. When he was through, he burned the thread in the ashtray and said, "We have eliminated it by fire." He rummaged again in the desk drawer and produced a large, smooth stone. "Now," he said matter-of-factly, "we are going to beat it out of you!—no, just kidding!"

I thought the young lady's eyes were going to pop out of her head.

During the entire procedure, we never heard what the Pow-Wow was saying. His lips moved and a whisper would now and then escape, but not even the lady in question could make out what he was saying. It was later, during a follow-up interview, that he told me what chant he used.

The young lady returned to this Pow-Wow for two consecutive days. After the third day, the swelling in her face disappeared. To this day, none of us know what was wrong with her.

Triple Charms

Several Pow-Wow charms fit into a category called "Triple Charms" or the "Three Lady Charms." Modern Pow-Wows begin the chant by saying "Three Ladies" or "Three Angels," or sometimes specifically name three of the Apostles. Thanks to research done by Thor and Audrey Sheil (*Old Norse Charms, Spoken Spells and Rhymes,* Staten Island, NY: Trollwise Press), we have a good explanation of the origin of these particular charms.

The Sheils feel that the three ladies represented are actually the three Sisters of the Wyrrd, those Norse weavers of Fate in legends, also known as the Norns. The ladies appeared on the eastern horizon and their task was to weave the tapestry of destiny. Each sister represented both a point in time and a color—past, present, and future corresponding to red, white, and black. The charms themselves denote a procession in time, beginning with calling the sisters into your subconscious, then journeying from past, to present, and on to the future.

These spells give no room for error and are clearly stated—it was that, now it is this, and it will finish up in a specific and positive way. The Three Lady Charms were not limited to healing pursuits and you will find several throughout this book that also deal with protection and hexing. Here are two examples (both from Thor and Audrey Sheil) of healing Three Lady Charms.

FOR STOPPING BLOOD

Three Ladies came from Jotun's land
Each with a bloody knife in her hand
Stand, blood stand! Letherly stand!
Bloody (whatever) in Odin's name, mend!

The Christianized version of this charm replaces "Jotun's" with "Jordan," a common mistake in many charms. The above charm is excellent if you are undergoing surgery or have been cut by a metal instrument. Thor and Audrey Sheil explain that "letherly" has no English counterpart, but that it could stand for "wound," in that it relates to an Old Norse term *(lesta)* for the same. The spell is from the Orkneys, an old Viking region, and some Old Norse words crept into the local dialect. Donald Tyson believes that the word is derived from "let," meaning to allow the escape of confined fluid, to shed tears or blood, or to emit breath or sound, thereby factoring down to the meaning of "flowing."

FOR BURNS, FEVER, AND INFLAMMATION

Three Ladies from the East had crossed
One brought fire, two brought frost
Out fire, in frost
Out fire, in frost
The fire is out!
The frost is in!

Summary

The process of magickal healing is many-faceted. If you need proof of this, you need only look at recent studies of cancer patients who use mind over matter. As Preston always stressed—with Divinity, it can be done.

Herbal Astrological Symbology and Earth Energy

Historical Background of Pow-Wow Plants and Herbs

Plants and herbs figured highly in Pow-Wow, both for their medicinal and magickal purposes. Until the 1900s, the Pow-Wow practitioner treated a patient internally with medicinal concoctions, and externally with magickal potions. With the availability of professional medical doctors and the fuss of the clergy, Pow-Wows gradually stopped dispensing cures for internal problems to individuals outside of their families. It just wasn't safe to treat a stranger or even the next-door neighbor any more. There were several cases in which family members took the herbalist Pow-Wow to court or accused him or her of trying to poison them. Such is the way of fear and superstition.

In the Dark Ages of Europe, many famous people were murdered through the ingestion of herbal concoctions. The use of poisons was a big deal and very popular. Old hatreds, as well as old formulas, die hard. Freely administered poisons to even the score are on record, and were viewed as commonplace. Familiarity with these herbal poisons was considered a magickal gift. The Pow-Wows and the communities around them are descendants of those people with this sort of herbal expertise. Eventually, herbal mixtures moved to the back of cookbooks and were passed along as "secret recipes." The discovery of digitalis by medical doctors came through the avenue of a family concoction. The power of an herbalist to kill was never forgotten and is encoded in ancestral memory, whether we believe it or not.

During the 1970s, many individuals turned toward holistic healing methods to avoid synthetic drugs and perhaps unneeded medical procedures. Publishing companies in the United States urged their authors to "hunt down those family remedies," and many were eventually printed. With the addition of respectable introductions written by medically degreed individuals, the trust of the public was secured. The Food and Drug Administration (FDA) nearly had heart failure, which has been proven by their attempt to pass bills through our legal system to outlaw over-the-counter herbs and leave them in the hands of physicians and pharmaceutical companies.

At the point when the Pow-Wows could no longer service their clients with herbs for consumption, some turned to the magickal lore of the herbs. Steeped in the Heathen arts of the tribal Germans, the Pow-Wow made a positive step toward increasing the prowess of the mind and psychic senses. The herbs were not consumed, but enchanted and used in conjuring bags or burned in earthen bowls. Other Pow-Wows dropped the use of herbs completely rather than face the risk of fines, incarceration, a lawsuit, or simple malicious gossip. Only in America do male doctors run the show. Even in the 1990s, medicinally untrained (by some standards) women provide most of the planet's primary health care. Again, only in America do we fight like mad dogs over herbals and question the idea of using them in healing and consumption, let alone magick.

The days of superstition and accusation are not over. Even non-magickal herbalists have difficulty understanding the nature of energy and magick in herbs. One herbalist I know found himself in quite a fix. Along with selling herbs and associated products, he also dabbled in palmistry. One of his customers accused him of doing a magickal no-no by using palmistry. There was no further explanation by the client on how one does such a no-no by the simple act of reading another person's palm. (We'll all have to guess on this one.) The client claimed this no-no hexed his marriage. He said his marriage had ended horribly. To cap this problem, the customer made big noises all over town and just about ruined the herbalist's reputation.

It appears that the herbalist was not trained in magickal operations. In desperation, the herbalist had a Pow-Wow friend do a spell of reflection using a bowl of inked water. The outcome, to him, was not only confusing, but devastating. He began to think that his Pow-Wow friend had deliberately hexed him as a result of the spell.

To show how one cause can have a variety of growing effects, the problem was not immediately resolved. The herbalist, not understanding Pow-Wow, decided that he would attack the local magickal community in writing, covering his behind with a smoke screen of, "here are the real bad guys, why are you looking at me?" By taking the easy way out of the problem, he unwittingly helped to create an even bigger one. Everyone was in an uproar ... and it all began with a simple palm reading by a dabbler.

So, you see how misunderstanding, misinterpretation, and muddling in other people's affairs can get you in deep trouble, even in the 1990s. To begin with, the individual who cast the spell with the ink water should have told our herbalist friend that when you ask for justice (which is what I assume was done, given the outcome), everybody involved had better have a clean slate as far as their own deeds are concerned. Justice is not blind, it simply makes everyone equal in accordance with their actions.

Unfortunately, people like to blame whatever is handy for the root of their problems, as long as it isn't themselves. A magickal act is easy to blame because it cannot be proven. Magickal people are prime targets—they are strange birds anyway. Neither the customer nor the herbalist wanted to take responsibility for their actions. Both, in their own manner, wanted to believe that they had been hexed. Both acted on the same level of ignorance and foolishness. Both ended up blaming magickal acts that were designed (we hope) to assist them. Situations of this nature led to the demise of the Pow-Wow practices.

The magickal person today must cast a wary eye on individuals such as those listed above—those who promote ignorance instead of study and common sense. There are people who rely more on superstition than the truth. Had our herbalist friend recommended a plant for ingestion that had made the customer sick, what would have happened then? For starters, a lawsuit. The moral of this saga is as follows: Never dabble. Never assume. Never point fingers. I have always found that it is often the finger-pointer who is responsible for various magickal messes, not the person at whom the finger is being pointed. End of lesson on responsibility.

Herbs and the Zodiac

Pow-Wows believed the herbs must be gathered in the proper season, at the proper hour, on the proper day, in the proper astrological sign, or else they would be of no use. The phases of the Moon were vitally important. Herbs whose magickal properties entailed only the above-ground portion of the plant were sown when the Moon was Waxing. Those whose properties were considered to be most powerful below ground (the root system) were planted during the Waning Moon. The Waning Moon is a time when negative forces are used to achieve positive ends, such as releasing yourself from a bad habit. All harvesting was to be done either on the Full Moon or immediately afterward (until the third day or so) if the plant was for immediate consumption. However, should storage be the main goal, then the harvesting was done during the Dark of the Moon.

What sign of the Zodiac the Moon was passing through was important not only for cultivation but also for magick. Don't feel bad if you are not "into" astrology. It's not one of my strong points, either. If you cover the basics, however, you can waltz right into Pow-Wow. Some guidelines for astrological correspondences and herbology follow.

Moon in Aries

Aries is a fire sign, and therefore considered dry and non-yielding when plants are the issue. When the Moon passes through Aries, it is a good time to dig up the garden or turn over the soil near growing plants to aerate the ground. Use your resources to say bye-bye to buggies, pests, and weeds. It is an excellent phase for gathering roots and leaves or flowers for magickal and medicinal purposes. Magickally, this is the time to use those herbs to banish sickness and other unwanted habits or nasties in your life. Aries is an aggressive sign. Linked with the Moon, it is a good time to push the harvest of something that you know is ready (such as an issue in your life, or getting Peggy-Lou to pay back that 10 bucks she borrowed six months ago). It is also a good time to "unearth" old projects that have been shelved due to waning interest. The Moon in Aries is a "big guns" type of magick in earthly matters. Aries is a strong and useful sign on this plane. Self-confidence, self-reliance magicks, and charismatic techniques are important here. Self-reliance magicks include those for health, success, opportunity, and creativity. Pow-Wows were considerably fond of the Moon in Aries.

The angels of this sign function primarily with pregnancy, propagation, and growth.

Moon in Taurus

Taurus is an earth sign and falls within the realms of fertility. When the Moon is in this sign, it is a good time to plant herbs, especially those in which the roots are of primary concern. As planting is the main theme here, magickal work would fall under the categories of seeding relationships, beginning new projects, and making that first move toward a goal you have set or a dream you have always wanted to pursue but never quite had the guts to do it. Taurus is both aggressive and patient, therefore magickal movements should involve those goals where you know darn well that time is not of the essence. Educational pursuits that require a degree of skill are best started during the middle of the Moon's movement in this sign. The Moon in Taurus works well with magick performed to look within the self.

The Angels of the Bull were best known for their assistance in business and career matters.

Moon in Gemini

Gemini is associated with the element of air, which has different textures and strengths. Moon in Gemini is like the dry winds of the desert. It is barren, and much like Aries, is a time for both harvesting and ground preparation or maintenance—and of course, getting rid of pesky things. Unlike Aries, Gemini carries a dualistic quality that should be considered when working magick. In Gemini, two halves make a whole. Therefore, dualistic issues take precedence here, like banishing negativity that is coming from two fronts or taking care of an individual diagnosed with two diseases or two distinct symptoms. Situations in which it takes two to tango (or disengage) should be worked on here, especially in the realm of communication. Moon in Gemini is also a good time to work on matters of choice in which you must pick either one or the other, and cannot have both. The Moon in Gemini works well for "freedom" magick—situations in which you need to disentangle either your mind or physical body from an issue, person, or habit. Gemini is the sign for travel, success, and opportunities. Protection magick for planned excursions should be done during this time.

The angels in Gemini are very busy indeed. They deal with communication; travel over land, sea, and cosmos; and love between friends and neighbors. Their most interesting function is to warn humans if they are in any type of danger from bodily harm, as well as protecting them from thieves.

Moon in Cancer

Cancer is a water sign. Moon in Cancer is associated with the aspect of fertility. It is the most fertile of the Moons. When taking care of an herb garden, this is the time to plant, plant, plant. Seed magick is at its best now. Cancer has the ability to make new issues and ideas flow smoothly. If a current project or issue has you stumped, this phase can be used to break the block with a new idea or approach. Insemination for child-bearing is most propitious during Moon in Cancer. Enchantments and fascinations were considered best worked at this time.

The angels who dwell in the house of Cancer rule over inheritances, treasures, and treasure-seekers. They are able to confer the gift of power and enlightenment through the written and spoken word.

Moon in Leo

Leo is another fire sign and likewise a Pow-Wow favorite. It is good again for putting the screws to those nasty buggies. Magickally, however, there is more to consider. With the Moon in Leo, this is the time to take care of that big mouth in your life (whether it is yours you need to snap shut, or someone else's). Leo is a proud sign and quite protective of its "domain"—family, home, etc. Therefore, protection and banishment of negativity for loved ones is a prime directive here, especially if the one causing the problem is rather famous or holds a powerful position. Leo is also a hunter and uses those skills in finding things that are lost, pouncing on truths (that up to this time have been rather elusive), etc. Magicks that involve social activities, romance, career, and change of your appearance are done during the Moon in Leo. Leo is a vital sign and Pow-Wows liked it for its performance qualities as well.

Angels in the house of Leo have the power to move anything, whether it be living or non-living. They are considered "watchers" and information unknown to you can be obtained through them. They render judgement in small matters, if they are permitted. The art of healing both body and mind is attributed to them as well.

Moon in Virgo

Virgo is a sign attributed to the earth element. Unlike Taurus, however, this Moon is not under the auspices of fertility. Surprisingly enough, Virgo is the influence of independence. Therefore, you can declare independence for your garden and assist it in seceding from the union of the bug patrol. Virgo's main forte is independence, logic, and service to others. Issues concerning such modes of thought should be worked on now. For example, someone who has recently divorced and has a bad taste in his or her mouth over it would use this phase to banish his or her grief or anger. The person would no longer yoke him or herself with depressing mood swings. It is a time to discreetly edit things out of projects or situations that have become burdensome or are stagnating. The Moon in Virgo is a good time for getting your house in order, whether it is your mind or your living establishment. Items of practicality with irritating loose ends should be dealt with here. These energies are effective when seeking guidance and giving advice.

The Virgo angels are regulators and could overthrow kingdoms should they be called upon to do so. They command evil spirits, grant perpetual health, and confer the art of music, logic, and ethical decisions upon the human world.

Moon in Libra

Libra is another air sign. In this phase it is semi-fertile. Gardenwise, this Moon is a time to plant flowers, vines, and plants in which the roots are important. Those plants where the leaves are most important, either for consumption or magick, should not be planted in this phase. Moon in Libra can magickally be used for the lighter things in life. It is not for those new projects that are intended to change your existence forever. Perhaps you want an answering machine (which would fall under the realms of communication and therefore air), or you wish to do a little friendly networking, and so forth.

Moon in Libra is an artistic sign. It is a good time to design a sacred space or make a new ritual robe or other magickal tool. Magick involving color is especially good during this period, as well as work for light romance and cooperation among friends. This is good time for contacting the muses. Art, poetry, writing, drama, etc. magicks are aided by this sign.

The angels of Libra hold as great a power as those of the Sun and Moon. They regulate friendship and the balance of harmony among all living things. Libra angels deal with items of justice, control wars, mediate among quarrelsome humans, and make rain when needed. Their gifts to humankind include mathematics, astronomy, and physics.

Moon in Scorpio

Scorpio is a water sign; this phase is almost as fertile as Moon in Cancer. Although most vegetation can be planted during this Moon, it is best for vines, like ivy or a flowering variety. When considering magick, Moon in Scorpio is rather unusual. It is used when you know your first actions will produce quite a few results. For example, if you were planning to begin a franchise, this would be the proper astrological correspondence in which to do it. If you wanted to begin a major networking organization or a project in which there will be many facets that must come together to bring a successful outcome, this is definitely the phase to use. Again, because Scorpio is a water sign, it can be relied upon to irrigate an existing problem with either one or several new ideas, therefore encouraging smooth sailing. Moon in Scorpio is an intense time and any magick done should be without malice, or else you might find yourself mightily stung. Scorpio is another sign for tying up loose ends, including introspection. Meditation techniques should be diligently practiced here. Working magick for your household budget also falls under the sign of Scorpio.

The Scorpio angels are by far the deadliest of the lot in the heavenly realms. They have power over suffering, fear, terror, and sin. They are the bringers of conscience to humankind and can force devils and demons to keep their bargains. They oversee the life and death of all living things and are responsible for both controlling and guiding dead souls. Their gifts to humankind include theology, metaphysics, and religion.

Moon in Sagittarius

Here is another fiery sign that is good for garden turnover. Onions, leeks, and garlic are planted now. These are some of the strongest plants for dealing with the banishment of illness and disease, as well as any other undesirables that may be floating around your house. This is a good time to banish outmoded or stagnant thoughts, as most people take a philosophical stance in this period. Laughter, along with emotional or mental stimulation, is the best type of banishment when the Moon is in Sagittarius. Work in theology and religious philosophy shines during this time. New paths to self-expression should be forged.

The angels in the house of Sagittarius control the four elements—earth, air, fire, and water—as well as regulate their use for various purposes. They are responsible for the protection of humankind when we migrate from country to country, or from planet to cosmos. The fertility and propagation of animals is also in their domain.

Moon in Capricorn

Capricorn is an earth sign and in this aspect is fertile, especially when planting for root properties. Magickally, the Moon in Capricorn was used by the Pow-Wow for projects where the result will stabilize a situation or in projects where each phase must be taken one step at a time to ensure a profitable and satisfying conclusion. This is not a good time to work major magick as Capricorn is a pessimistic sign, and definitely not a time for grand spiritual pursuits or breakthroughs. Personal advancement and recognition are keynoted with this sign, as well as ambition and cultivating one's dignity.

Angels in the house of Capricorn bestowed honors and virtue into the world of humankind. If you were very good, they would give you enlightenment, wisdom, and the ability to reason well.

Moon in Aquarius

This is another air sign and again we deal with the thought of the desert winds. For gardening, the same aspects that apply in Aries are used here. Magickally, however, Moon in Aquarius is not a "big guns" type of energy on the material plane. This Moon is better for banishing problems on the astral and getting rid of unwanted ghosts and elementals. Only little problems on the earthly realm should be tackled at this time. Aquarius is a talkative, social influence, therefore the process of changing small humanitarian issues can be taken up under this period. Imagination is strongest here and magicks to either control it or enhance it should be used. However, the sign of Aquarius was not a favorite of the Pow-Wow, most likely because Pow-Wows were highly secretive in nature. A garrulous ticket, like Aquarius, is not one they wished to write for themselves.

Aquarius angels present themselves to keep humankind healthy, contented, and out of danger through education. They can also teach a person about the mysteries in heaven and nature. Finally, they can order evil spirits to be subject to humankind and are able to protect those of pure nature from ultimate evils.

Moon in Pisces

Pisces is a water sign and here is fertile. Gardenwise, you can plant to your little heart's desire. Moon in Pisces seems to be a difficult time for many people; therefore, restraining the use of magick might be a good idea. Magickal works should only be undertaken if some type of divinatory tool is used. This is not a good time for magicks of practicality, but psychic work may be enhanced for the Pow-Wow under this influence. The knowledge could then be used for personal insight and improvement of character. The Moon in Pisces was not a favorite time of the Pow-Wow nor are there any angelic forces attributed to it in the Pow-Wow material.

The modern magickal practitioner is a busy person. Between a job, family responsibilities, magickal activities, and hobbies, there is little time for planting a garden. Even if you do have time to lay out a garden, other responsibilities in your life may take over to the point that you miss a particular cycle. You may forget to water your plants (and they poop out on you), or an army of snails invades your precious crop overnight (it can happen!). What do you do? These days it is not easy to follow the astrological guidelines for the cultivation of magickal herbs, especially if you purchase them instead of grow them yourself. How the heck are you going to know when a purchased herb was planted or harvested? However, if one empowers purchased herbs and asks that Divinity instills the correct astrological correspondences to activate its properties, the original intention, in most cases, will work the same.

Ah, you doubt me? Well, you are not alone. A rather well-known magickal person once told me he didn't much care for that line in my spell casting. "I don't think you should be teaching your students to align the astrological correspondences for what you want," he admonished me. I smiled sweetly and patted his arm.

"Spells are to be specific," I quipped. "True?"

He nodded his head. "Yes, true enough."

"And I am asking for specific correspondences, am I not?"

"True."

"And about 85 percent of what I spellcast for works. Right?" I asked.

"Ah, right. But I don't think you should be trying to realign the heavenly bodies," he stated.

"I'm not trying to realign them, I'm simply drawing on energies that have existed at one time or another. I'm certainly not making up anything new, and I'm not trying to change their paths. The idea is to use the correct energies by working without the boundaries of time. So, now tell me what don't you like about it." (Hands on hips time for me here.)

He grinned sheepishly. "Well, it's too simple."

Herbal Preparations

Usually herbs and plants were either crushed, used whole and placed in conjuring bags, or hung by the roots at strategic places in the home or barn—wherever air could circulate through the plant. Although some herbalists of today dry their plants in the oven or microwave, I don't agree with this as you are tampering with the natural order of the plant. For medicinal purposes only it is probably okay, but if you are planning to work magick, I advise against stepping up the drying time if you can help it.

Infusions were, and still are, very popular. They are ingested as teas, poured in bath water, or rubbed into floors and cupboards. Actually, a standard infusion isn't meant to be a tea at all because the herbs are soaked much longer in hot water and the results, of course, are much stronger. Therefore, steeping time would be different according to the use of the herb. Many herbalists refer to infusions as teas and interchange the two words frequently. The time it takes to make a tea would be small, compared to the time the herbs are steeped to rub into floors or cupboards, which would be the longest for that herb.

A traditional **infusion** calls for up to an ounce of the dried herb soaked in about a pint of boiling water from 10 to 20 minutes. If you are activating a fresh herb, you should double the amount used. If you are using the infusion for a cold remedy, you would also inhale the steam while you are preparing the brew. This will help open up clogged nasal passages and relieve chest congestion.

Infusions, as teas, do not taste very good and should be used immediately because of their short shelf life. Before a ritual of initiation or dedication in our Circle, we brew a large pot of chamomile tea and sweeten it with honey. It eliminates stress and nervousness and promotes a relaxing atmosphere with the steam that is produced as well as the tea that is drunk.

An herb must be studied before you make an infusion, so you get the water and the herb in the correct proportions for the properties of the herb.

A **decoction** is much like an infusion, save for two main differences. It is made from roots and barks. They are boiled for up to 20 minutes to activate the chemical, rather than steeped. As with an infusion, the measurement of the herb according to its properties must be studied and researched before it is used.

A **tincture** is an extract made with alcohol rather than water as a base. Tinctures have a longer shelf life but they are trickier to handle. They also are more concentrated in form. The standard formula for a tincture is five ounces of vodka, brandy, or apple cider vinegar and one ounce of the herb left to sit for six weeks. Use a sealable container—the mixture tends to ooze. Shake the mixture every few days and, as with all herbal concoctions, keep out of direct sunlight. Glass storage containers are the best, situated in a cool, dry place. A tincture should be respected. Large doses are harmful to small children and some adults. Again, the use, measurement, and properties of the herb should be known before a tincture is made.

Ointments were made with a lard base, though sometimes beeswax was mixed with the herb and a little olive oil in later years. Today many herbalists mix up to one teaspoon of an herbal tincture with one ounce of commercial skin lotion.

Poppets

Poppets (or dollies) are well known in magickal circles. A poppet is either a cloth or clay doll that is filled with an item belonging to the person the doll represents, along with herbs, stones, talismans, etc., to combat the problem—whatever it may be. In ritual, be it large and complicated or small and simplistic, the essence of the doll is melded to the energy of the person it represents. Unlike other magickal practitioners, Pow-Wows were very quiet about the existence of poppet magick. They didn't fashion clay dolls, sew ornate or even simple doll shapes, or use effigy candles. Instead, they took elongated conjuring bags, filled them with the necessary ingredients, tied off a head, stuffed that, and tied a top. One didn't want to be caught with an effigy doll. If someone got too nosy, you would simply cut the thread at the neck and the bag would assume its original shape. Herbs for these dollies were used in collections of three, seven, or nine.

Herbal Pendulums

Herbal pendulums were made by running red thread through the end of a root, flower, or nut. To answer questions of love, a rosebud was used—of sickness, a garlic clove. Pendulums are easy to use and fairly accurate with practice. Run an 18-inch thread with a needle through a garlic clove. Remove the needle and tie off the thread so that it hangs evenly. Sit comfortably in a chair and rest your elbow on a table. Suspend the clove by allowing the end of the thread to lay over the back of your hand with the clove end hanging across your palm. Your thumb keeps the thread from sliding. Suspend the clove about one inch from the tabletop.

Relax and breathe deeply. Then say to the pendulum (yes, you are going to talk directly to the garlic clove, and don't make any remarks about its odor), "Show me yes." Watch which way the pendulum swings. It may swing side to side, up and down, or in a circle to exhibit the yes answer. Now say, "Show me no." Watch the pendulum direction to see what represents a no answer. Finally, say, "Show me I don't know." Watch this result as well.

You are still not ready to ask a pertinent question. Instead, ask a question for which you know the answer to be yes. Does the pendulum response reinforce your knowledge? Go on to test the other answers as well. Once you have affirmed directional swing, you are ready to test the pendulum on a few real questions. A few tips when working with the pendulum: Don't be tired, frustrated, sick, or upset when you practice this type of divination. Often a picture or a map under the pendulum helps you to tie in to the answers you need. Above all, you must have patience for this work. It takes time and trust in yourself.

Herbal Precautions

Follow general guidelines if you are planning to use herbs for medicinal purposes. First, study the plant extensively and know its medicinal properties. If you have any questions, find a reputable authority who can answer them. If you have a chronic disease, be sure to check with your physician to make sure that it is okay for you to use the herb. Likewise, if you are pregnant, medicinal herbs are not suggested as the dose that would help you would most likely hurt the fetus.

Don't consume too much for too long. The American Medical Association is so hot against herbal remedies because those who take them do not always carefully consider the dosage. People make the mistake of thinking that if they use more they will get better faster. No, no, no! Like magick, herbs should not be considered a quick fix, but should be respected for their individual properties. Herbalists often do not recommend that you give medicinal herbs to children under two. Personally, I wouldn't give them to children under 12. Herbs should never be given to children without consulting a physician first.

In modern Germany, herbals are still very much respected. Although they must be proven safe before consumption, they are not forced to undergo the expensive and long-term testing required by the United States. In Canada, the Expert Advisory Committee on Herbs and Botanical Preparations has recommended a new class of drugs called "Folklore Medicines." As in Germany, the expensive tests normally required would not be needed as long as it was proven that the herb was safe and accurately labeled.

I personally like to use teas because you are less likely to poison yourself. An essential oil, sold over the counter, can kill you if you make one mistake and take too much. For example, one measured teaspoon of an essential oil could send you to the happy hunting grounds. Only a few drops of the oils should be used. Medicinal herbs are not to be used in place of professional medical care. Ideally, they should be used in conjunction with a physician's diagnosis and supervision.

Existing records of Pow-Wow remedies often used the folk names of the plant instead of its common or scientific ones. In most cases, I was able to match the folk names with herbs still used in this century, but I did come up with a few blanks. The best book I've found on the market today to match herbs with their folk names is Scott Cunningham's *Encyclopedia of Magical Herbs*. Pages 269 to 285 contain a complete listing for cross-reference purposes and is the best I have seen in any magickal or medical text.

Energy Levels and Harvest

Plants were chosen for their healing properties, vibratory energy, and their planetary, astrological, or elemental signs. Harvest was planned from the third day to the twentieth day of the Moon, and herbs were not to be harvested at any other time as the plant's energies were said to be weak or at a restful stage.

Once the correct plant had been determined for the need, the Pow-Wow would go barefoot into the garden and check the energy level of the plant with his or her open palm before harvesting it during the above mentioned time period. If the sensation was of a loving or warm nature, that plant would be chosen. If it was cold or unnaturally low in energy for the variety, the Pow-Wow would move to the next, and the next, until the right feeling became apparent. The actual harvest was made easier by following a few simple procedures. Always use the left hand (if you are right-handed) for plucking herbs, as this is your receptive hand and you wish to pull the energies of the plant toward you. If you are left-handed, then you would use your right hand for harvesting.

Do not face the wind during your harvest, as the element will blow the energies you need past you and you will not be quick enough to catch it. You must also never glance behind you. This is more for the aspect of focus rather than the idea of a threat around you. You need to be concentrating on what you are doing and not daydreaming.

Draw a circle at the base of the plant with a knife or stick and place a rune or star in the center of the circle. Cold iron (as in the faery tradition) should never touch the plant and if the circle is drawn with iron, you must be careful not to touch any roots as well. Actually, iron or steel should never be used in the harvest, as both metals will destroy any magickal properties the plant contains.

In your mind, call the plant by its folk name and explain exactly why you are harvesting it. A soft charm can be spoken, indicating your purpose and enhancing the enchantment. For harvesting the full plant, including roots, tell the plant that it is okay for it to release. Move slowly; remember that plants react to thoughts, sounds, and feelings, not physical sensations as we understand them. After you have experimented a few times, you will find that the plant will easily let go of the soil. Lay it on a bed of dried wheat, barley, or straw. If you are harvesting only leaves, do not use a knife if you can help it. It is far better to harvest plants and herbs with your fingers. Knives should only be used on thick branches.

After the herb was harvested and dried, it would be stored until needed. When it was time to use it, the Pow-Wow would enchant it by calling on the properties of the herb and expressing the desired outcome of its use in specific terms, whether it was to be used strictly for magick or only for healing. It was believed that most herbs kept their properties for approximately one year, or from one growing season to the next. Old herbs would be buried with honor and replaced by the new batch.

Medically, herbs have a shelf life of approximately one year and have no healing potential after that.

Planetary Correspondences

Although there is a great deal of information on astrology and planetary magick available, the following list can be used for choosing the correct correspondences when practicing Pow-Wow magick.

Sun

Rules success, ambition, career matters, healing, personal finance, government and legal matters, sports and athletics. Herbs of the Sun heal passions and griefs of the heart as well as cure impotency. Sun herbs were good for the eyes, lungs, and blood.

Corresponding day: Sunday—Start individual creative and positive works.

Corresponding angel: Michael

Astrological sign: Leo

Element: Fire

Colors: Gold and orange

Moon

Rules intuition, psychic powers, childbirth, women, travel by sea, the home, imagination, reincarnation, and dreams. Moon herbs take care of chest pains and stomach problems. The properties of Moon herbs vary with the phase of the Moon, thereby instilling it with either lesser or greater powers.

Corresponding day: Monday—Good for personal growth and inspiration.

Corresponding angel: Gabriel

Astrological sign: Cancer

Element: Water

Color: Silver

Mercury

Rules things that must move fast, communications, memory, teaching and education, writing and composing, the theater arts, finding lost or stolen property, and divination and the design of divination tools. Mercury herbs were made into plasters for speedy healing in wounds and used as an infusion for toothaches, mouth ulcers, and chest pains. Mercury herbs give one eloquence of speech and if you needed to ask a rich or powerful person for a favor, you would definitely carry a Mercury herb. These herbs were also said to dissolve kidney stones.

Corresponding day: Wednesday—Good for business deals and partnerships.

Corresponding angel: Raphael

Astrological signs: Gemini and Virgo

Elements: Air and earth

Colors: Yellow and silver

Venus

Rules matters of the heart, romantic situations, beauty, pleasure, marriage, twinning, friendship, music, and the finer aspects of the arts. Venus herbs dispel skin diseases and bladder problems. They are also used to reduce swelling. A Venus herb near one's crops was said to increase harvest; pinned to a baby's cradle, it would ensure that the child lived a joyous and happy life.

Corresponding day: Friday—Creating a union between opposites.

Corresponding angel: Anael

Astrological signs: Libra and Taurus

Elements: Air, earth, and water

Colors: Green, blue, and silver

Mars

Rules machines (all types), courage, manual dexterity, protection in dangerous situations, fires and volcanoes, lust, breaking hexes, protection, and sexual prowess. These herbs are linked with the signs of the Ram and Scorpio. The Ram herbs are good for headaches, where those of the Scorpio variety were said to handle lower intestinal problems and bleeding from the bowels.

Corresponding day: Tuesday—A power day. Raw activity and intense power.

Corresponding angel: Samael

Astrological signs: Aries and Scorpio

Element: Fire

Colors: Red and black

Jupiter

Rules material wealth, social standing, political strength, big business, gambling and games of chance, important friendships that may have a monetary value, and legal and insurance matters (including stocks, bonds, and estate transference). Jupiter herbs were used for skin rashes and blood problems, liver troubles, and difficulties with the feet. A Jupiter herb is worn to enchant women and bring them willingly to your bed.

Corresponding day: Thursday—Expansion and money matters.

Corresponding angel: Sachiel

Astrological signs: Sagittarius and Pisces

Elements: Fire and water

Colors: Purple and green

Saturn

Rules property, senior citizen interests, karma, death, immediate change, chronic ailments, agriculture, exorcisms, and endings. Saturnian herbs were used for leg and bladder pains. A Saturn herb placed in white muslin and delivered to an evil person would banish the nasty spirits that held him or her hostage. It is hung in the home to rid the residence of devils and given to children to strengthen their teeth. To carry a Saturn herb when traveling at night was to banish fear and protect the wearer.

Corresponding day: Saturday—Preservation and stabilization.

Corresponding angel: Cassiel

Astrological signs: Capricorn and Aquarius

Elements: Earth and water

Color: Black

The angels, along with their sigils, appear in the "Magical Elements of Peter de Abano" in *The Fourth Book of Occult Philosophy* (pp. 88-101), should you wish to use this information in your Pow-Wow magick.

In the seventeenth, eighteenth, and nineteenth centuries, Pennsylvania scholars were intrigued by the movements of the heavens above them. As the German court of Emperor Rudolf II studied astronomy and astrology, so did their German-American counterparts in Pennsylvania. The Germans brought with them the almanac, filled with astrological and astronomical symbology. In actuality, it was the Germans who brought printing and the skills for making paper, woodcuts, engravings, bookbindings, and so forth to the Pennsylvania countryside.

By the mid-1800s, there seemed to be a number of "secret societies" floating around in Pennsylvania that studied occultism mixed more with astronomy than astrology. These groups were decidedly male. There is evidence that two of these societies were the Rosicrucians and the Masons; the latter was often targeted in German-American publications, such as the yearly almanac. One anti-Masonic author, William Morgan, disappeared without a trace in 1826. Perhaps this marked the true beginning of the end of Pow-Wow, as a minor flood of literature attacking secret societies gave birth to an anti-Masonic political party. Future almanac covers would depict the stupidity and un-Godliness of dealing with the occult.

Quick Elemental Correspondences

Earth: Healing, jobs and career endeavors, money and property, fertility and growth, ecology, health foods, buildings, barns, general construction.

Air: Things that need to be "aired" out, mental agility, astral travel and visions, wisdom, dreams, psychic skills, organizing and organizations, groups, theory.

Fire: Passion, strength and courage, breaking hexes, exorcism, revitalizing health, competitions, dowsing, war, banishing illness, the military.

Water: Things that need to flow, meditation and sleep, romantic love, close friendships and marriage, family, hospitals, medicine, restoring cell growth, beauty, negotiations.

Herbs and the Land

The country Pow-Wows used those plants that were indigenous to the area, while people of the higher ranks (later called High Germans) had many of their herbs imported from the Old Country. In time, some of these plants were shared with neighbors and flourished in many a non-Pow-Wow garden. The herbs were not only imported for their medicinal or magickal qualities, but they were also brought here in hopes that the power of the land from whence they came would travel with them.

Tribal Germans (as well as the Brits and Gauls) believed in deity differently than most of us imagine today. The idea of idols is a Roman one, not a mindset belonging to the ancient tribal peoples who gave birth to Pow-Wow. To a German, everything was magickal, whether it be a star, a tree, or a bug. All was considered to be connected with the Source, today thought of as God/dess. Each part of the Source was known to have its own power. Hence plants, trees, stones, and animals each had their own magickal properties (or power) given to them by the Source, and of course, their own legends. Therefore, the land where a person lives has its own power, its own being, yet everyone knows it is ultimately connected to the Source.

This strong belief led to the legends of a particular area. In time, only the wise held the legends together and told them around the hearths to the children, a few of whom were magickally inclined and kept the legends alive through generation after generation. In a new land, though, local lore was non-existent as far as the settlers were concerned. There were no local devas, fairies, or particular energies to contact by name. What to do? Many of the new generation did not even know how the legends began in the Old Country, and they were not aware of the need to connect with the new ones where they now lived. Many people (except those who worked with the indigenous peoples of the area) simply assumed there weren't any. Hoping to connect with those legends again (they understood there was a source of power there), they would write home and have boxes of earth, plants, and seeds shipped to the New World. Now you know where the idea came from of Dracula bringing the earth of his homeland with him wherever he went.

Many magickal people of today fail to understand the connection of humans to the earth power around them. Oh yes, they talk about Wicca being a nature religion, but how many of them actually learn to network and build upon the power centers in their local areas? Not many. I have never read of instructions on how to build a power matrix in any modern magickal text, although many are specific on telling you how to build a physical circle or altar site. They then instruct you to call in archetypes that are native to a country across the sea, and not your own backyard.

Most magickal instructions of today tell you how to cast a circle and how to call in the Divine to manifest or banish something. This is fine. Most people also intone the quarters, but haven't the vaguest idea why they are calling in the element in the first place. The idea of calling in the element (earth, air, water, fire) is both to touch its characteristics *and* to connect with the local power source, whether you know the local legends or not. Some older traditions associate local archetypes and totem animals directly with the element. To name them with titles indigenous to the area is to draw specific energy and power into your circle. There is always power in a name.

When you cast a magick circle you should be keeping three things in balance: the call of the power of Divinity, the call to the power of yourself, and the call to the power of the local energy on which you are standing. In tune and working together, these energies become a pattern—the pattern of power.

The Permanent Power Matrix

Building a power matrix around your home is important for several reasons. First, it is a protective measure for your home and family. Second, it becomes a bridge of energy that you can tap at any time. Finally, it becomes a natural support system that allows your mundane and magickal life to run smoothly from day to day. The matrix itself takes time to build and its power depends on how determined you are and how often you wish to work on it. To begin, you should research your area regarding indigenous peoples and their legends. You also should visit senior citizen centers to discover any local legends that may be attached to your town or area. Check out libraries and newspaper archives. Often you will find unusual stories, both good and otherwise, that will help you understand the energy where you live.

Your next step is to localize and contact the energies of your area in a personal way. If there is a lake nearby, visit it and meditate by it. Who commands the lake there? Through vision questing and meditation, you should contact woods, streams, lakes, and other natural landmarks in your area. There is a wealth of energy there if you just reach out and touch it.

Concentrate on your home as well. Walk in your yard and call upon the energy source there. See, hear, feel, and touch with your mind what comes to you. Take your time and begin to build your association with these energies. They may come to you as animals, plants, elves, fairies, or Gods and Goddesses. Just remember that though they appear as separate entities they all come from the All, the Source of creation, which is neither male nor female, but a perfect balance of energy.

In ritual, then, you should begin to pull this energy into your circle over a period of several months. Start by sitting inside the circle and lacing your fingers together as you chant or meditate. Many magickal persons incorporate needlework in this power tapestry. With each stitch or knot, they envision pulling in and uniting with the local power sources. Others tie knots in cords or fashion latticework in wood, metal, or stone. This is how you build a powerful, positive energy matrix. This is how you dance the pattern of life.

Four Seasons Garden Charm
Designed by Silver RavenWolf

Herbs in the Pow-Wow Cupboard

Indigenous Herbs

The herbs listed here are indigenous to the south-central Pennsylvania area. These are herbs specifically mentioned by Pow-Wows or found in research material about the magickal system.

Angelica

Planet: Sun

Element: Fire

The folk name for this herb is archangel or masterwort, and it came only from Syria. The word "wort" means "herb," so this is the master herb with the basic function of protection and breaking hexes. It is part of the carrot and parsley family. The first Pow-Wows combined angelica with other herbs to make a drink, called carmelite water, to cure headaches, protect against poisons, break witches' spells, and ensure a long life. Angelica takes its name from the dream of a sixteenth-century monk. This man dreamed he met an angel who told him how to cure his people of the plague. He named this herb angelica, after the angel in his dream.

I scatter it at the four quarters of a magickal circle. Its function is to ward off any evil that may be lurking nearby. Then I envision a lion circling the magickal space in a clockwise direction to guard the barrier between the worlds.

Angelica is a perennial, and grows in fields and damp areas. You can see its greenish-white flowers from May to August. Parts of the plant used are the roots, herb, and seeds. Today, angelica is used to treat digestive difficulties as there are certain chemicals within the plant that have antibacterial functions. It may be of some assistance in treating colds. Asians use it for arthritis and Chinese studies report that it may increase red blood cell counts, perhaps being effective in anemia cases. It often brewed as an eye lotion and is said to increase the strength of the eye.

Assyfetida (Asafoetida)

Planet: Mars

Element: Fire

"Whenever I had a cold," explained one senior citizen from Mechanicsburg, Pennsylvania, "my mother would force me to wear a white muslin bag filled with assyfetida and garlic around my neck to school. What noxious stuff that was! Nobody ever laughed because their mothers made them do it, too. It literally made you smell like shit!"

Assyfetida also went by the folk name of "devil's dung." The idea of equating it with excrement is not a joke—it does smell like it. Although the herb's prime use appeared to be for warding off colds, fevers, and flus, it also played an important part in dispelling evil spirits. When a Pow-Wow brings out assyfetida, he or she is involved in a big-time banishment. The herb is burned in an earthen bowl for exorcism, purification, or protection. Just be sure there is plenty of ventilation and be warned that the house will smell like a dung heap. I picked up a bag of powdered asafoetida (notice this is a different spelling) for research purposes. It smelled so bad that I had to store it in its plastic bag in a Mason jar.

Bat's Wings (Holly)

Planet: Mars

Element: Fire

Holy water with a holly infusion is used externally only to baptize Wiccan or Christian babies. Holly is thought to be an anti-lightning plant, and an herb for protection and sweet dreams; again, it is only for external magicks. It is carried by men for good luck and planted around the homestead to ward off evil spirits, nasty sorcerers, and wild animals.

Beaver poison (Hemlock)

Planet: Saturn

Element: Water

Hemlock is a poison. Its magickal properties include the ability to make a man impotent. Poppets were rubbed or stuffed with hemlock to weaken a person who had hexed you. Hemlock is not to be taken internally for any reason.

Belladonna (Deadly nightshade)

Planet: Saturn

Element: Water

This is a poison also. At one point, belladonna was used as a treatment for rabid dog bites. It is highly toxic and all portions of the plant are poisonous. Because of so many accidental deaths, it is no longer offered on herbal markets.

In actuality, belladonna and deadly nightshade are two different plants that can bring about the same result. Deadly nightshade (often called garden nightshade) is found growing along walls, fences, and in gardens in many areas of the United States. It has small white or pale violet flowers that bloom in July and August. Some plants produce bright orange-red berries, which are poisonous. Deadly nightshade is not hard to find and grows all over the East Coast. The plants we found have red berries and very delicate purple flowers. We suggest using plastic gloves when handling the herb in case you forget and put your fingers in your mouth during the cultivation process.

Magickally, deadly nightshade is used to take care of the scum bunnies of the world. Leaves and berries are carefully crushed in poppets or conjuring bags to catch rapists, thieves, murderers, and control abusive personalities. Garden nightshade rambles as it grows. Magickally it seeks out and binds those energies that are negative in nature.

Boneset (Indian sage)

Planet: Saturn

Element: Water

Boneset is a member of the dandelion and marigold family and was the most used herb of the Native Americans. Boneset is put in the pocket before travel to bring forth its protective properties. I often hang some on the car rearview mirror before a long trip. The root is great in money spells in combination with five finger grass. Sprinkled around an orange candle, these two herbs assist in finding gainful employment, whether you wish a

job of short- or long-term duration. It also causes discord between two people if dipped in both their drinks or added to their food. To regain peace,
valerian was used in the same way. Overprotective Pow-Wow mothers often
snuck a pinch of boneset into the drinks of gentleman callers of whom they
didn't particularly approve.

In the medical world, boneset is not used to mend broken bones. Native
Americans introduced this herb to the colonists, indicating it was used to
break all fevers and to treat colds, indigestion, and constipation. Often used
in sweat lodges, it is now thought to be the best remedy for the flu. *Fresh
boneset is toxic.* Boneset grows all over the United States and likes low, moist,
and damp lands. Its medicinal parts are the tops and leaves.

Buckeye (Horse chestnut)

Planet: Jupiter

Element: Fire

Buckeye is poisonous. It is carried to attract money and success and to
ward off backaches, arthritis, chills, and rheumatism.

Chamomile

Planet: Sun

Element: Water

Chamomile is part of the daisy and marigold families. The flowers of the
chamomile plant are best known for their restful properties. The herb is also
used in money and good fortune conjuring bags. Taken as a tea or burned as
incense, it promotes sleep and relaxation. Grown around homes, its aroma,
sparked by the summer heat, brings heady daydreams, peace, and tranquil-
lity. It is said that the more one walks on it, the better it grows!

Medicinally, Germans have used this plant for centuries to treat digestive problems and to relieve menstrual cramps. Modern Germans feel this
plant can do practically anything. Although not available in the United
States, there is an extract of this plant that is used topically to treat wounds
and internally to treat ulcers. The herb is used in the United States as a tranquilizer, for arthritis relief, and to stimulate the immune system. It is one of
the nation's best-selling herbs.

In magickal practice it is used to calm a nervous client, prescribed for
insomnia, and brewed for rites of passage. A cup is often drunk by the Pow-
Wow student before power is passed or energy centers are opened. Students
have reported odd experiences when given a small cup of this herbal tea
mixed with honey before their dedication ceremonies. One of the strengths
of the Pow-Wow system is the mystery that surrounds it. Although there is

no medical foundation for hallucinations, when a Pow-Wow hands a student or client this brew, the mind of the recipient conjures up a supposed mystical essence. The person allow him or herself to be more receptive to the magickal and spiritual nature of the universe. This opening takes place without a word from the Pow-Wow artist. The student assumes that something special is about to happen—so it does. One student of mine reported that he saw fairy lights as he sat in my backyard, awaiting his dedication ceremony. I don't doubt his word.

Celandine

Planet: Sun

Element: Fire

Celandine is used magickally to get you out of fixes where you think there is no escape, either mental or physical. It is a must in legal matters to win favor, and brings joy and happiness to the wearer. It is used to banish depression, stop arguments, and overcome enemies. A marvelous talisman for victory in all matters.

If a Pow-Wow wondered about the fate of a person who was ill, the Pow-Wow would place a bit of this herb on the patient and ask him or her to sing. If the patient could only whisper or sing in a soft voice, chances were he or she might not recover. If the patient sang in a strong voice, his or her recovery was assured. Another test was to rub a piece of bread on a patient's teeth, then give it to a dog. If the dog refused to eat the bread, it was assumed that the sick person was battling something truly nasty and may not live.

Celandine was brought to the New World by the colonists. It is a perennial that grows wild along fences and roadsides. Medicinally, it has been found effective in topical applications for swelling, tuberculosis, and skin abrasions. However, this herb is poisonous in the wrong hands, and cannot be consumed by animals.

Cinnamon

Planet: Sun

Element: Fire

Cinnamon belongs to the same family as nutmeg and sassafras. It raises spiritual vibrations when used as an oil or infusion. Pow-Wows often set a pot of water with a mixture of cinnamon, cloves, and other herbs to simmer on a stove. This brings happiness and prosperity, as well as protection, into the home. Money is dressed with cinnamon oil, using various runic and magickal symbols to bring it back as soon as it is spent.

The twelfth-century German abbess and herbalist Hildegard of Bingen claimed cinnamon was the universal spice for sinuses and was to be used to treat infection. Today cinnamon is used to prevent infection, relieve pain, reduce blood pressure, and as a digestive aid. Cinnamon is not native to the United States and is not grown or harvested here. Most of our supply comes from Asia and the West Indies.

Cinnamon oil is used often in dressing candles and other magickal endeavors. Please be reminded that it can cause skin irritation. Be sure to keep it away from your eyes and wipe your fingers as soon as you use it. The oil is not to be taken internally as it can cause kidney failure at worst, and vomiting at the least. It should not be used under any circumstances to anoint the body. During a healing, one of my students grabbed the wrong bottle and anointed my forehead with cinnamon oil—ouch!

Cloves

Planet: Jupiter

Element: Fire

Cloves are a member of the myrtle and eucalyptus family. They are used to attract money, for purification, and to stop gossip. Used both as an oil and as an infusion, cloves drive away negative situations and people. Mixed in a conjuring bag with the petals of a red rose, it is believed to attract loving influences. Clove oil is often placed on windowsills and above doors to prevent evil from entering the house. Whenever one of my students moves to a new home or apartment, we fill a gift basket with clove oil, holy water, angelica, cinnamon oil, cinquefoil, rue, and vervain along with unbleached muslin swatches and red ribbon for conjuring bags.

Medicinally, cloves are very ancient indeed, having been tracked to 207 B.C. in China. They found their way to Europe by the fourth century A.D. The German abyss mentioned earlier used the herb in her anti-gout mixture. Cloves are considered a great anesthetic, antiseptic, and digestive aid. Dentists sometimes use clove oil to disinfect root canals. It is the active ingredient in Lavoris mouthwash. Clove is another herb that is not grown in the United States. Tanzania produces about 80 percent of the world's supply.

Coltsfoot (Coughwort)

Planet: Venus

Element: Water

Coltsfoot is one of those herbs that was used more for medicinal purposes rather than magickal ones. In magick it is added to love potions. Medicinally it was used to treat colds, flu, and congestion. American colonists soaked blankets in buckets of hot coltsfoot water and wrapped them around a sick person. It was also applied to external swellings.

Herbalists of today are divided on the use of coltsfoot. Some feel that it is a carcinogen, and are currently pushing the FDA to ban it. It has already been banned in Canada. An appropriate substitute is slippery elm.

Comfrey (Boneset, knitbone)

Planet: Saturn

Element: Water

Comfrey is another herb that was used more in medicinal situations than magickal ones, although its medical benefits are debatable. Used as a paste, it was wrapped around broken flesh and bones. Today it is used as a tea to heal wounds and aid in digestion. Comfrey contains a chemical called allantoin that is said to promote new cell growth. However, Canada has banned this herb, claiming that comfrey taken in large amounts causes liver damage. Magickally, it promotes safety while on a journey and prevents items from being lost or stolen while one travels. It is occasionally used in money spells.

Coxcomb (Amaranth)

Planet: Saturn

Element: Fire

A chaplet of coxcomb is placed about the head to magickally speed the healing process. The red heads were used to call forth the dead, and carried to cure minor bodily ailments and mend a broken heart. When mixed with other herbs, it was said to render a person invisible. A whole plant harvested during the Full Moon was placed in a conjuring bag sewn shut with red thread and worn against the heart to make one "shot"-proof. Coxcomb is a prime ingredient in Pow-Wow power oil. Other ingredients include orange trumpet flowers, large gold marigolds, and sunflower petals. Place the flowers together in a Mason jar, pour virgin olive oil over them, and cover the jar tightly. Shake every day for three days, then strain thoroughly. Repeat this process twice more, straining finally with cheesecloth. Place the oil in small glass bottles that are labeled and dated. The oil is used for career matters and in any situation in which you feel extra "oomph" is needed. The oil is not edible.

Fennel

Planet: Mercury

Element: Fire

Fennel is definitely an herb of protection and is used to ward (protect) people as well as material objects. It is native to southwestern Siberia. A basic protection mixture usually includes fennel, angelica, and rosemary. Medicinally, fennel has been around for a very long time and was known to the Greeks, Romans, and Germans. Our famed German abbess used it to make people happy, eliminate body odors, aid in digestion, and in cold and flu remedies. It is also a mosquito repellent. Colonists brought fennel to the New World. Today it is used primarily for treating indigestion. Fennel oil is another one of those mixtures you should use carefully. It may cause skin irritation and, if taken internally, it can cause vomiting or fatal seizures. So don't put fennel oil in your mouth!

Fenugreek

Planet: Mercury

Element: Air

Fenugreek is another herb that was brought to the New World by the European settlers. Its main magickal power is to bring money and prosperity to the bearer or into the home. Half filled crocks of fenugreek are left open in the main room of the house to attract money. Each day a pinch of five finger grass and fenugreek is added to the crock until it is full. It is then returned to the ground (in private ceremony) and the ritual begun again.

Fenugreek comes from the family that includes beans and peas. The part of the plant used was the seeds. Traditionally, fenugreek is used to control cholesterol, treat a sore throat, ease arthritis, and stimulate the uterus. Studies are underway to determine if it reduces glucose levels, but nothing conclusive has been found to date.

Frauenschlussel (Cowslip)

Planet: Venus

Element: Water

Cowslip is a wonderful herb; it can be magickally empowered to discourage visitors. It is placed under the front porch step or set near the front gate. It was also considered a "beauty herb" and worn to preserve youth as well as create an enchanting aura. It is best gathered, as one might guess, at the hour of Venus. Folk medicine pegs this one for colds and bronchitis. Its leaves are considered a source of vitamins and are used in teas and foods. Its homeopathic use includes treatments for eczema, fevers, migraines, and vertigo.

Five finger grass (Cinquefoil)

Planet: Jupiter

Element: Fire

   This plant is a "catch-all" for the Pow-Wow. It serves a variety of purposes, as each "finger" of the plant represents something different. The five points are love, money, health, power, and wisdom—all that the Pow-Wow desires to receive and to give. It is also a popular hex-breaking plant. Five finger grass is sometimes hard to find at herbal shops. It is common in the United States and grows by roadsides and meadowbanks. It grows like a strawberry plant, in that the roots join. It has bright yellow flowers that bloom from June to September. The herb is also used to process leather and in textiles and for dying cloth and leather red. Medicinal uses come from the roots.

Gag root (Lobeila)

Planet: Saturn

Element: Water and Fire

   This is a poisonous plant. Gag root is popular for stopping gossip and is often placed in poppets or thrown into a fire. It is used in storm magick by casting it before the winds in sacrifice to prevent what we call around here "a real thunder bumper." Native Americans gathered lobeila from July to mid-October, using the leaves and stems for medicinal purposes. Red lobeila was used to treat syphilis and destroy intestinal worms. This is another controversial herb and is sold with a tag indicating that it is poisonous, yet many experienced herbalists do use it as an ingredient in poison antidotes. Alone, lobeila is relatively useless; it must be mixed with other herbs.

Garlic

Planet: Mars

Element: Fire

   Many conjuring bags for healing contained garlic. Magickally, it absorbs disease and pain, and breaks a fever as well. It was also rubbed on the unhealthy portion of the body and thrown into the fire or held under running pump water. Garlic has a long history of magickal uses, including protection against real, surreal, and imagined foes. Cloves of garlic were hung on the headboard of the bed of a child to protect his or her dreams, and pots and pans were rubbed with garlic to remove any negativity that could be attached to them. Why, if you used a pot or pan every day, would negative energy collect there? The only reason I can imagine is if the wife brained the husband before she cooked the stew. Perhaps it was thought that the metal of the pot naturally drew both negative and positive vibrations to it. Of course, garlic was used to ward off psychic vampires as well as those of the physical variety. During the Second World War, Russian soldiers took garlic like the Americans took penicillin. Garlic was also used to scare away things of "the otherworld," such as ghosties and banshee-type things. One warning with this herb: never rub it on your lodestone, as the lodestone will lose its power.

The use of garlic for medicinal purposes dates back to 3000 B.C., when it was harvested by the Sumerians. Garlic is purported to be the most powerful antibiotic around. Garlic kills bacteria that causes tuberculosis, food poisoning, and bladder infections, and is also a flu remedy. Chopped, crushed, or chewed, it is used by modern herbalists to treat heart disease, stroke, diabetes, and to counteract lead poisoning; some researchers have found breakthroughs with it in treating AIDS patients.

According to modern researchers, AIDS patients taking one clove of garlic a day have shown significant increases in immune functions over a three-month period. It also helps to clear up sores and chronic diarrhea symptoms in these same patients. However, garlic should not be used by people with blood-clotting disorders. To eliminate garlic breath, chew some parsley or fenugreek.

I'm not one for believing in psychic attack, but there is one time when I used garlic and it solved the problem. My house is considered a "safe house" around here. If any of my students, friends, or relatives are in trouble, they are welcome to come by. They are also welcome to bring their friends. Often we get at least two new visitors a week. One soft summer evening I found myself entertaining a rather odd group of people. I guess there were two or three regulars and several "new" people. The new ones were interested in meeting a "real writer" and had come to visit merely out of curiosity. Normally I don't mind these visits. I get to meet fun and interesting people. Often they want to talk about their writing dreams and I encourage them to do so. During our conversation, I found that one of my guests was very much interested in vampirism and other unusual subjects. We got on the subject of personal energy shields. I made the mistake of mentioning that I try to keep myself as open as possible because I am an empath. I enjoy picking up things that are happening in the Universe. This was a mistake on my part.

That night I had the most horrendous dreams. They remained with me, clear as my crystal ball, when I awoke. This is unusual. I'm one of those busy-bee people, and I often stay up too late. When my head hits the pillow, I'm fast into pleasant dreams. During the day my dreams faded somewhat, but not like they normally would. The next night, the same thing happened. Hmmmm, I thought, I wonder if someone has the nuggets to try to pull my psychic chain. The third night I whipped out my trusty black candle, anointed it, and set it before the triple mirrors in my bedroom. I also dug in the refrigerator and pounced on the large store of garlic there. I smashed it up in a bowl. Whole cloves do not work; you must crush them for both medical and magickal purposes. (This is why there are still real vampires around, you know. Hanging a string of whole garlic on your door won't do any good—just kidding!) I put the bowl under my bed. As a result neither my husband nor my dog would sleep with me that night. However, I slept peacefully and haven't been bothered since—by the dreams, silly! Whether I was really under attack is debatable. The actions I performed gave me peaceful sleep. I don't care if the cure was mystical or psychological—it worked.

Henbane

Planet: Saturn

Element: Water

Like deadly nightshade (and part of that family), this plant is highly toxic and considered a powerful narcotic. Even its fumes can get you. Therefore, it is no longer marketed in herbal stores. Henbane was used to get rid of rabid or wild dogs and was said to break the silver cup that held it. Mixed with the blood of the first trapped rabbit and set out as bait, it would call to the other rabbits of the glen and force them to gather together so they could be taken easily. Because henbane is found growing in waste grounds of old settlements, graveyards, and around foundations of ruined and abandoned houses, it is excellent for banishing and removing unwanted circumstances in your life, as well as breaking hexes. The plant flowers from July to September, with leafy spikes of yellow.

Hexenmannchen (Mandrake)

Planet: Mercury

Element: Fire

In German, *hexenmannchen* means "Witch's mannikin." Another German word for it is *zauberwurzel,* meaning "sorcerer's root." Mandrake is a protective herb, and must be in your house for three days before you work with it. It is also used for protection, dreams, fertility, and prosperity and enchantment. Unlike simple empowerment or enchantment, the mandrake root needs to be activated by warm water overnight. The water is also used to ward windows and doors. Indigenous peoples of the United States used American mandrake to treat several disorders, including circulatory problems and urinary incontinence.

Horehound

Planet: Mercury

Element: Air

Horehound has always been used as a protection against sorcery and unethical magick. It is burned and scattered to exorcise evil spirits, or drunk as a tea to invite clarity of mind. Crushed, it is sprinkled around the sick bed to promote healing. As a medicinal herb, the use of horehound dates back about 2000 years. Its major function was for treatment of colds and the flu. Incidentally, the FDA banned it from cough medicines, indicating it was not effective. Herbalists have protested long and hard on this issue, feeling that the replacement ingredient now used isn't effective. Horehound grows on dry, sandy fields and around roadsides. Its flowers appear from June to September and should be gathered before they open.

Hound's tongue

Planet: Mars

Element: Fire

Hound's tongue, also called gypsy flower, was thought to silence dogs—wild, trained, or simple pet. Used in conjunction with the appropriate chant, the herb did the trick for the dog. In folk medicine it was used as a poultice; the leaves were bruised and applied to the bite of a mad dog. Native Americans used it to treat coughs and other lung disorders as well as diarrhea.

Ivy

Planet: Saturn

Element: Water

Planting ivy around your home provides protection for those on the property. We erected a fence along one edge of our property just so we could line our boundaries with ivy. It works marvelously for unwanted human contact, but not for animals. Neighbors thought we were having a sales meeting every Thursday night, when in fact we were holding healing circles for over a year. Ivy is also used in love charms and strewn on doorsteps to guard against "bad magick." We use it as a chaplet for both brides and initiates in magickal traditions. Indians used the bark and twigs as an astringent. Folk medicine often used it to treat dropsy (congestive heart failure) and bronchitis.

Laurel (Bay)

Planet: Sun

Element: Fire

Bay is often added to conjuring bags and infusions to promote wisdom and protection. It is another all-purpose herb that renders strength, brings love and protection into the home, scatters negativity, and guards against sickness. Magickal stones (especially lodestones) and pieces of paper with spells on them are wrapped in bay leaves to act as the catalyst in the operation. Native Americans often threw laurel leaves into the fire to divine the future as well as benefit from the herb's medicinal qualities. If the leaves burned brightly and loudly, the answer was said to be positive. If they did not burn or sputtered and died quickly, the answer was negative. Bay chaplets have been bestowed upon the heads of athletes, poets, and warriors since Roman times. Use bay in spells in which you wish to be a winner. For medicinal purposes, very low doses of bay infusions are used to ease stress and given topically to treat minor infections.

Marigold

Planet: Sun

Element: Fire

Marigolds are strung together on red thread and hung as garlands over doorways to keep evil from entering the home. They are at their full strength when picked at noon, and doubly so when harvested during the month of the Lion. Along with sunflowers, they are good in "to catch a thief" spells, to leave your reputation in good standing once you have left a room, and of course, to have the court and justice smile favorably upon you. If you wanted to know if your spouse had been cheating on you, an old Pow-Wow test included marigolds. Simply set them in the church before he or she enters, and if that person has been unfaithful, he or she will not be able to find a way out when the service is over.

A conjuring bag containing marigolds, bay leaves, gag root, and the tooth of a wolf is a strong talisman indeed. It prevents gossip and encourages only words of peace. If something is stolen from you, a conjuring bag containing marigolds and sunflowers is to be placed under your pillow at night. Dreams identifying the thief and where he or she is hiding the goods will remain with you until your valuables are returned.

Meadow cabbage (Skunk cabbage)

Planet: Saturn

Element: Water

This plant was basically used in legal matters and often mixed with bay leaves for prosperity. Skunk cabbage contains wax, starch, volatile oils and fats, salts of lime, silica, iron, manganese, and fixed oil. Its pollen draws bees like crazy.

Medicinally, it was used to treat asthma and tuberculosis, although today's herbalists choose safer herbs to reach the same end. This plant is definitely of more magickal than medicinal value.

Mistletoe

Planet: Sun

Element: Air

This is a poisonous plant; however, Europeans have used it for centuries to treat high blood pressure, cancer, and tumors. It is best when harvested at the Summer Solstice and not allowed to touch the ground (ever). It can also be gathered when the Moon is in its sixth day. This is another all-purpose plant with applications varying from protection, healing, love, fertility, and sweet dreams to casting out bad spirits. It is also used for luck in hunting and opening locks (along with the appropriate chant, of course). Mistletoe was used in divination to determine which path was the proper one to take.

The mistletoe legend comes straight from the Norse. Balder, the son of Odin and Frigga, was slain with an arrow made of mistletoe. When his parents restored him to life they gave the plant to a love goddess, hence anyone who passes under it is to exchange a kiss in fealty to the Goddess of Love.

Be careful with that mistletoe; although there have been no cases of adult poisoning on recent record, children have died from eating as little as two berries from this plant. Therefore, keep it out of reach of children!

Nettle

Planet: Mars

Element: Fire

Nettle is widely used for breaking hexes and sending them back from whence they came. Often it is stuffed in poppets or thrown into the fire to ward off evil. Another all-purpose herb, it is sprinkled on the comforter of a sick person to assist in healing, or used to banish ghosts or enhance lust in your mate. Nettle mixed with yarrow in conjuring bags is an old and interesting combination. Each herb acts upon the energies of the other, creating a twinning process between the plants. This doubles the power of the bag. Nettle and yarrow together are considered the best combination to ward off fear. In Germany, nettle was also used for weaving when cotton was in short supply. Therefore, to contact the Sisters of the Wyrrd, one would weave nettle.

Native Americans drank nettle tea to strengthen their babies and provide a smooth delivery. Early colonists thought that drinking nettle tea would increase their milk quantity. Medicinally, the nettle juice helps to reduce high blood pressure, hay fever, and PMS symptoms. Studies are underway to determine if the juice may be helpful in cases of noncancerous prostate enlargement. The leaves are excellent for slowing the flow of blood. Powdered root or crushed leaves of this plant can be applied topically to immediately staunch blood.

Pennyroyal

Planet: Mars

Element: Fire

There are two types of pennyroyal: the American plant and a European plant. If you were a beekeeper, then this was the herb for you, because it ensured that the bees would never leave the hive. It is the plant of peace and is used in conjuring bags to stop marital spats and protect the wearer from the evil eye. The plant is common in many areas of the United States.

Native Americans used pennyroyal to treat colds, dress wounds, and as an insect repellent. Today, an infusion of pennyroyal in small does for colds, flu, upset stomach, and menstruation promotion is recommended. However, as with other essential oils previously mentioned, the oil of pennyroyal is definitely poisonous and should not be used to terminate a pregnancy.

Pennyroyal as a topical treatment is a terrific herbal flea collar. Crushed fresh on the skin with a little oil or body lotion, it repels insects.

Plantain

Planet: Venus

Element: Earth

Crushed plantain is the best remedy for a bee sting. Place it directly on the swollen area to reduce pain and swelling in under 10 minutes. Its folk name was snakeweed or ripple grass. Other uses were placing it upon the head to rid oneself of headaches or weariness, and to banish snakes.

There are over 200 species of plantain in the United States. The leaves are dark green in color and usually very wide. It grows low to the ground and you can find it in just about any backyard, baseball field, or meadow. If you use plantain on bee stings, you will become the most popular person on the ball field. Kids eye you with skepticism if you say, "Just a moment. I've got something that will take the sting right out," and promptly begin scouring the grass for this wonderful plant. Their eyes open wide as you crush it and place it on the sting. They are so busy watching you that they lose their fear of the injury and later say, "It does work! I'm going to tell my mom about this!"

Rose

Planet: Venus

Element: Water

Roses, especially the red ones (mixed with honey), are most known for their love-bringing properties. White roses are often used for purity and healing. Red and white roses should be placed upon your altar when accepting the system of Pow-Wow into your everyday life. York, Pennsylvania, is the City of the White Rose, and Lancaster is still known as the City of the Red Rose. I have often thought there is a magickal reason behind the naming of these two cities.

As much as roses are said to be a loving and nurturing flower, they are often used for stronger pursuits. Hanging the kernel of a rose and mustard together on a fruit-bearing tree kept it from bearing fruit. Mixed with a few other ingredients, it could set a house aflame when the sun rose. Thorns of the rose are used in spells when rusty nails are not available.

Medicinally, only the "hips" of the plant are used. Germans used them for just about everything. Unfortunately, the drying process of rose hips kills most of their Vitamin C content.

Rosemary

Planet: Sun

Element: Fire

Rosemary is another all-purpose herb and is often burned to cleanse the home or a sacred space prior to a magickal working that is going to take some real effort. Frankincense was not easily obtained in the early days of Pow-Wow, and rosemary was the preferred herb to use in its place. Its powers include protection, healing, restful sleep, mental agility, and the ability to attract either romantic or lustful love. When mixed with lavender, it is said to aid in conjuring the ghosts of loved ones.

Rosemary is still placed around the coffin of a deceased loved one in remembrance of shared joy and happiness, and given as a bouquet on New Year's Day.

Medicinally, rosemary sprinkled on potato salad or other perishables taken out into the summer heat will help guard against food poisoning, as it is a good preserver. It can also be used as a digestive aid. However, pregnant woman should not drink infusions of this herb as it is thought to cause adverse effects. Rosemary is part of the mint family.

Rue (Meadow rue)

Planet: Mars

Element: Fire

Rue is a great herb to aid both prevention of and recuperation from ailments. It is another herb (along with eyebright) that was used to bring clear thinking and quick, logical thoughts. Rue is a major hex-breaking herb, a good protection agent against werewolves (should you happen upon one), and can be worn to protect oneself from the evil eye. Of course, not all predatory wolves are werewolves, and therefore it is used to ward off unwanted advances from both males and females, should you find yourself in that delicate predicament. The only major drawback to rue is that some magickal people feel that it can cause obsession and force you to deal with the problem on a one-to-one level, rather than permitting you to shut your eyes and believe the problem is not there. Rue is an excellent flea repellent and disinfectant.

A bit of rue, a piece of bread, a pinch of salt, and three seeds of cumin were placed in a white conjuring bag and tied with red thread. As the bag was being filled, the following rhyme was said:

This bag I sew for luck to me
And also to my family
That it may keep by night and day
Troubles and illness far away.

Sage

Planet: Jupiter

Element: Air

Sage was burned to cleanse everything from the room to your body and mind. Worn, it guarded against the evil eye. It promotes wisdom and long life, and makes wishes come true. It was thought that sage could be conjured into a black bird. If you could get the bird to fly into your hearthfire, you could create a gorgeous rainbow with horrible thunder.

Sage is another herb that was introduced to the New World by the colonists. The Germanic peoples used it to treat headaches, colds, measles, insomnia, epilepsy, seasickness, and intestinal worms. It was grown in just about every garden to ward off untimely death.

Today's herbalists recommend sage for topically treating wounds and bites. As a tea it is used for sore throats, bleeding gums, upset stomachs, and to reduce perspiration. Like rosemary, it is also a preservative. Also like rosemary, this is an herb that pregnant women should avoid.

Saint John's grass (Mugwort)

Planet: Venus

Element: Earth/Air

Mugwort is also known as St. Peter's root, St. Peter's plant or *artemis vulgaris*. Other common names are artemisia, felon herb, moxa, Salor's tobacco, and witch herb. This should not to be confused with St. John's wort, which is a totally different plant. St. John's grass is used to aid prophetic dreams, healing, astral protection, and psychic prowess. The infusion is used to cleanse magickal tools (such as the magick mirror), but is not to be taken internally. It is often used to ward off the evil eye. Mugwort grows wild in the United States and can be found in hedges and waste places. Native Americans used it topically to ease wounds; the juice was used to treat poison oak.

The parts of the plant used are the rootstock and the herb itself. The rootstock is harvested in the fall, while the herb should be harvested when in flower. This herb is used magickally to increase the powers of others herbs and to influence worldly events (some information supplied by Pete Heinz from Illinois).

St. Joseph's wort (Basil or Witches' herb)

Planet: Mars

Element: Fire

Here is another herb that was used as often in the kitchen as it was in magick. In magickal applications it is a protective herb, but is well known for causing sympathy between two people. A pot of basil surreptitiously boiled on the stove by one of my students while her nephew and his wife were arguing worked well to calm the atmosphere and make them both more open to each other's ideas. Basil is an all-purpose Witches' herb, used in love divinations and to make sure a lover remains true. It is also used in the good luck and success department.

Medicinally, basil has been used for centuries to treat intestinal parasites and skin infections. It was considered a great bacteria killer. Although many other cultures use basil in healing, using the herb for this purpose never quite took off in the New World.

Slippery elm

Planet: Saturn

Element: Air

This is another herb that appears to have had more medicinal value than magickal, although when mixed with gag root, it was a great gossip stopper. Native Americans introduced slippery elm to the settlers in the New World.

They used it for a variety of purposes, including topically for wounds and as infusions for sore throats and coughs. Peeled elm sticks were used to break the water of a pregnant woman to induce labor.

Slippery elm is still used to treat wounds, coughs, and sore throats; it is also one of the few herbals (the bark is used) that is considered safe for most pregnant women. However, a physician should be consulted before it is used.

Solomon's seal

Planet: Saturn

Element: Water

This herb is basically used to break hexes and banish ghosts and other assorted nasties, as well as provide an atmosphere of protection. It is considered more of a magickal herb than a medicinal one. Often used in ritual healings, it is placed at the four quarters of the healing room or mixed with other herbs to cast a magick circle. To country folk, a salt circle was considered suspicious in nature to outsiders, therefore Pow-Wows mixed angelica, Solomon's seal, and vervain to create an area of protection inside a room. It could be swept away easily without raising any undue attention. "Oh my goodness, lookie there! I was preparing the roast and spilled the herbs. I'll just sweep that up in a second!"

Solomon's seal is native to moist, shady woodland. Externally, it was used to fade freckles or other skin discolorations. It was also used by colonists as a drink to assist in mending broken bones.

Sunflower

Planet: Sun

Element: Fire

Although sunflowers have many magickal uses, their prime use lies in catching thieves and discerning the truth of all matters. If you see a field of corn in Pennsylvania ringed by sunflowers, you know that farmer is part of the "old school," for sunflowers planted in the garden or with the crop are said to stand guard against both physical and astral pests.

Sunflower seeds are nutritious. Native Americans used the roots in combination with other herbs to cure snake bites. The flower heads were boiled to extract oil, which was used as a hair tonic.

Valerian

Planet: Venus

Element: Water

Both magickally and medically, valerian is known as the sleep inducer. Many of my students have made valerian sachets to place under a pillow to bring sweet dreams. It is also used to protect and purify the home and to guard against lightning. Mixed with basil and boiled, the steam stops an argument immediately. When valerian is used in a conjuring bag for love, men (or women) hopefully will follow you anywhere. It is also used to enchant animals, including rats and cats.

Germanic tribes used valerian as a tranquilizer to bring about restful sleep. It was also used in the treatment of the plague. Native Americans were working with it as a topical wound treatment before the colonists arrived. Valerian was to be gathered by the left hand as Sirius was rising in the heavens, after the Sun set but before the Moon rose high in the heavens, or when the Moon could not cast her silvery gaze upon the herb (meaning during a New Moon). Honey is to be left as an offering once the plant is harvested.

Mixed with rosemary, fennel, lavender, sage, mint, basil, hyssop (if all plants were gathered on the day of Mercury in the planetary hour of Mercury under a Waxing Moon), and a good quantity of holy water, all evils and odd elementals would be banished.

Valerian was a favorite among Pow-Wow artists. The following (from *Mastering Herbalism* by Paul Huson) is a conjuration for this herb:

> *I conjure thee herb that are called valerian, for thou art worthy for all things in the world. In pleasance, in Court before Kings, Rulers, and Judges thou makest friendship so great that they bare thee his will, for thou doest great miracles. The ghosts of Hell do bow to thee and obey thee. For whosoever hath thee, whatsoever he desireth, he shall have in the name of the Father, of the Son, and of the Holy Ghost. Amen.*

Modern herbalists use valerian as a sleep aid and stress reducer in tea form. It is considered an excellent sedative. Tests of valerian have indicated that it may lower blood pressure, but if your blood pressure is high, seek the advice of a physician. Valerian is found in low meadows and woods as well as along river and stream banks, marshy and swampy places. Both the Native Americans and colonists used it as a medicinal preservative.

Vervain

Planet: Venus
Element: Earth

It took me a long time to figure out that vervain and verbena are magickally considered the same thing. This is definitely an all-purpose herb and a necessity in the Pow-Wow's cupboard. Its powers include inducing love, protection, purity, chastity, and healing as well as bringing money, peace, and sleep. It was to be gathered during the month of the Ram (which would be March) when Sirius is rising on the horizon. The Druids mixed vervain in their holy water. It was also believed that you could make the sun turn blue with the use of this herb—sorry, no explanation is given on this one. Vervain was used to call doves to bring fine weather and is used to "make spells go," enchantment being its prime operative.

The word "vervain" is actually Celtic in origin, meaning "to drive away a stone." It was used as an infusion to rid oneself of kidney stones. Druids were said to have used it extensively, hence it was called the "enchanter's herb." Medicinally, German researchers have found the effects of vervain to be like aspirin, bringing simple relief from pain and reducing inflammation. Topically it has been applied to wounds, and was even used for this purpose in the Civil War. Vervain is said to suppress the heart rate, so as with all herbs, check with your physician before using.

Yarrow

Planet: Venus

Element: Water

To hold yarrow in one's hand is to instill calmness and courage. It is used to banish negativity, break hexes, and bring lovers and relatives back to you. Yarrow was believed to be an herb of snake charming and conjuring and a favorite in love potions. If a woman wanted to dream of a future husband or lover she would cut a stalk of yarrow from a young dead man's grave and intone the following:

> *Yarrow, sweet yarrow, the first that I have found*
> *In the name of Jesus Christ, I pluck it from the ground*
> *As Jesus loved sweet Mary, and took her for his dear*
> *So in my dream this night, I hope my next lover will appear.*

Colonists brought yarrow to the New World where the indigenous peoples adopted it readily. It was used topically to treat wounds and burns. As an infusion it was taken to ease colds, sore throats, and indigestion. It is a perennial plant that blooms from May to October and was used in a variety of applications, including treatments for colds, measles, fevers, chickenpox, and smallpox.

Fresh yarrow leaves are still used today to treat wounds; the infusion is used as a mild sedative, a digestive aid, and to ease menstrual cramps. Yarrow may also protect the liver from toxic chemical damage.

If you examine the previous list closely, you will see that 24 of the above listed herbs have fire properties, 14 correspond with the water element, 5 with air, and 3 with earth. I did not do this on purpose. Data collected indicates the Pow-Wows primarily worked with the elements of fire and water. This leads back once again to the lore of fire and ice of the Norse, and fire and water of the early Germanic peoples.

Planetary correspondences were more evenly split. Mars is equated with ten of the listed herbs; Saturn corresponds with ten, the Sun with nine, Venus with eight, Jupiter with four, and Mercury with four herbs. All these herbs reflect a patriarchal system more than a matriarchal one. The above listed herbs are by no means the only herbs used by Pow-Wow practitioners, nor did all practitioners use all the herbs on this list. However, the herbs given are a good starting point for your own experimentation and are those that were most often cited in research material or in interviews.

The best way to learn herbal magick is to begin with the plants that grow in your own backyard or are indigenous to a 100-mile radius around where you do your magickal work. If you don't know where to begin, contact your nearest college or agricultural informational outlet and ask for a list of plants that are indigenous to your area.

Where to Get Herbs and How to Use Them

The modern Pow-Wow has three outlets for procuring his or her own herbs: grow them, purchase them loose at an herb store or mail-order outlet, or buy them packaged in a specialty or grocery store. At our home, my father and I grow several herbs to run experiments. Those we do not grow, we normally buy in bulk at an herbal store. We don't buy them pre-packaged because we have found that even for medicinal purposes, those herbs do not work as well. My father is the herbalist of the family; I work the experiments on the magickal properties.

For example, on New Year's Eve 1992, my husband and I were invited out to dinner by a couple of friends. During the evening, our hostess indicated that she had not been sleeping well at night. She had seen a doctor, but his efforts were not helping. We mentioned the use of herbs and she explained that they didn't help, either. A friend had recommended that she drink chamomile tea, which she tried, but admitted it had done her no good.

When we got home, I asked my father what else we could recommend for her. We talked about it for awhile and then he said, "You know, I don't understand why the chamomile didn't help her, unless she was trying that packaged, store-bought stuff. That never works for me, either. What she should do is buy it from the herbalist. In the evening, after her kids have gone to bed, she should run a nice warm bath and add the chamomile to the water. She should brew a cup of chamomile tea, and drink it while relaxing in the tub. If she is really stressed out, tell her to bathe by candlelight."

I decided to run my own experiment with store-bought tea versus the loose herb from the shop in town. I waited until a particularly stressful time, which happened to be two weeks later. I enchanted and drank the packaged tea. It didn't help a bit. The following evening I was up very late, still unable to sleep. I enchanted the herb and made myself two cups of chamomile tea from the loose flowers I'd picked up at the herbal shop. During the first cup I could literally feel the stress draining away. After the second cup, I fell into a restful sleep and awoke the next morning feeling very well.

Later that month I gave another friend the loose enchanted tea, instructions for its use, and some stress meditation tapes. She reported good results. Now, when I've had a particularly stressful day, I'll brew some chamomile tea. If my children are having a tough time sleeping or are overly anxious about a test or other situation in their lives, I'll brew some chamomile and put on a relaxation tape. Works every time. Granted, a cup of tea and a cassette tape aren't going to solve all your problems, but they are steps of improvement toward your overall well-being. To be able to sit and relax and consider your options is a far better way to solve a problem than being so concentrated on the stress you can't think straight. It is amazing that something so simple as a cup of tea can make so much difference.

Herbal Supplies

The herbal supplies of the Pow-Wow were simple. Remember, you are dealing with a time when people didn't have much in the way of luxuries or an overabundance of materials. Dried herbs were crushed in a wooden or earthenware bowl with a smooth wooden spoon or stick and kept in glass bottles and canning jars. Herbs were boiled in spring water in small pots and strained either through cheesecloth or a wire strainer. Most herbalists of today do not approve of metal utensils, so you may wish to use glass pots and a plastic strainer.

Conjuring bags are fashioned from unbleached muslin. Some are hand-sewn into bags, using the time spent sewing to empower them. If you aren't a whiz with a needle and thread, just gather a small square of the cloth by the four corners to form a pouch. The bags are tied together with red yarn or ribbon, keeping the ends long enough to tie around the neck of the patient. In most cases, the bags remained undecorated and were buried when they were no longer needed. Occasionally, a woman would embroider crosses or geometric patterns on the conjuring bag in red thread.

Dream pillows were popular during the 1800s. Much like the conjuring bag, they were made of unbleached muslin, sewn on three sides with red thread, stuffed with various herbs, and then stitched together on the fourth side. The pillows were used to induce clairvoyant and telepathic dreams.

It takes time to learn the properties and medicinal qualities of herbs. Filling your own cupboard is a rewarding experience, and the time you invest in herbal knowledge will serve you well throughout your lifetime. Always remember to check with your physician first before ingesting herbals and follow specific directions for doses.

Herbs and Life Force

It is important for us all to remember that plants, herbs, trees, and flowers are living entities and therefore should be treated with respect. Part of herbal enchantment is talking to the herb during its growth cycle and harvesting. They do have personalities that are capable of responding to our thoughts, feelings, and voice intonations. Through the Backster experiments in the 1960s, Cleve Backster discovered that when plants were hooked up to a polygraph, they did not respond to physical actions performed upon them but did respond to the thoughts of the people around them. Therefore, it is necessary to align the living plant with your intention *before* it is harvested in order for it to work best.

The following poem (from *Mastering Herbalism* by Paul Huson), dating back to a Saxon herbal known as *The Lacnunga*, contains a collection of spells for enchanting nine herbs. The appropriate portion of the poem was said over its corresponding herb.

The Nine Herbs Charm

> Forget me not, mugwort, what thou disdst reveal
> What thou didst prepare at Regenmeld.
> Thou has strength against three and against thirty
> Thou hast strength against poison and against infection
> Thou hast strength against the foe who fares through the land!
>
> And thou plantain, Mother of herbs
> Open from the East, mighty within
> Over three chariots creaked, over three queens rode
> Over three brides made outcry
> Over three bulls gnashed their teeth.
> All these thou didst withstand and resist
> So mayest thou withstand poison and infection
> And the foe who fares through the land!

Herbs in the Pow-Wow Cupboard

This herb is called watercress and it grew on a stone
It resists poison, it fights pain
It is called harsh, it fights against poison
This is the herb that strove the snake
This has strength against poison
This has strength against infection
This has strength against the foes who fare through the land!

Now, garlic, conquer the great poisons, though thou are the lesser
Thou, the mightier, vanquish the lesser until he is cured of both!

Remember, chamomile, what thou didst reveal
What thou didst bring to pass at Alford:
That he never yielded his life because of infection
After chamomile was dressed for his food!

This is the herb which is called nettle
The seal sent this over the back of the ocean
To heal the hurt of other poison!

These nine sprouts against nine poisons
A snake came crawling, it bit a man
Then Woden took nine glory-twigs
Smote the serpent so that it flew into nine parts.
There the apple brought this to pass against poison
That she nevermore would enter her house!

Thyme and fennel, a pair of great power
Woden, holy in heaven
Wrought these herbs while he hung on the tree
He placed and put them in the seven worlds to aid all, the poor and rich.

It stands against pain, resists the venom
It has power against three and against thirty
Against a fiend's hand and against sudden trick
Against Witchcraft of vile creatures!

Now these nine herbs avail against nine evil spirits
Against nine poisons and against nine infectious diseases
Against the red poison, against the running poison
Against the yellow poison, against the green poison
Against the black poison, against the dark poison

Against snake blister, against water blister
Against thorn blister, against thistle blister
Against ice blister and against poison blister
If any poison comes flying from the east or any comes from the north
Or any from the west or south upon the people.

Magickal Quick Reference Herbal

Healing
Angelica
Asafoetida
Boneset
Buckeye
Chamomile
Coxcomb
Cinquefoil
Garlic
Horehound
Laurel (Bay)
Mistletoe
Nettle
Rue
Sage
Mugwort
Vervain

Love
Basil
Cowslip (reverse)
Cinquefoil
Coltsfoot
Ivy
Mistletoe
Pennyroyal
Rose
Rosemary
Vervain
Yarrow

Protection
Angelica
Asafoetida
Basil
Boneset
Cinnamon
Cloves
Comfrey
Coxcomb
Fennel
Garlic
Holly
Horehound
Hound's tongue
Ivy
Laurel (Bay)
Mandrake
Marigold
Mistletoe
Nettle
Rosemary
Rue
Sage
St. John's grass
Slippery elm
Solomon's seal
Sunflower
Vervain
Yarrow

Wealth and Success
Boneset
Buckeye
Chamomile
Celandine
Cinnamon
Cinquefoil
Comfrey
Fenugreek
Gag root
Mandrake
Meadow cabbage
Sage
Vervain

Breaking Hexes
Angelica
Hemlock
Henbane
Horehound
Nettle
Rue
Solomon's seal
Yarrow

Magickal Record Keeping

One of the most important aspects in the performance of magick is record keeping. Books are great and can be used for reference. It is true they can catapult your mind. Sooner or later, however, you are going to have to fly on your own. You will find your personal records invaluable for years to come.

These days, computers are the information storehouses and many individuals prefer to keep their personal diaries and notes on their home computer. This is great; just don't forget to back it up frequently. Give a copy of your notes on disk to a close friend or family member. If that idea doesn't sit comfortably with you, rent a safe-deposit box and put your disks there.

Keep a hard copy somewhere around the house. People often call me out of the blue to ask various questions about magick and healing. My days are pretty busy and I often can't give a full answer without a little thought and my Book of Shadows (a name modern Witches have coined for their magickal records).

All my students begin with a notebook, plenty of paper, and some type of dividing or filing system. The front of my book contains theory, philosophy, definitions, etc. The second half of the book contains hands-on spells, rituals, charms—that sort of thing. Often you may find a spell or charm, copy it into your book, and not use it for at least a year or more. When your book becomes quite full, you may not remember if you have ever used the charm or not, and if you did, if it was successful. To handle this problem, you have two options: Either make enough room on the page to write such information, or keep a separate notebook, much like a magickal diary.

I prefer the magickal diary format because it enables you to properly plan each individual working. A money spell for paying a particular bill and a money spell for extra cash in your pocket are two entirely different procedures that may use the same chant. If you use the diary format, you will be able to remember these distinguishing factors, when your magick was performed, and if it indeed was successful—even to what degree.

Granted, you don't always have time to sit down and plan out a magickal procedure and there will be times when using such a format will not be feasible. When you do have the time to use it, you will find a higher success rate in your practices. A plan well thought out is a plan that usually brings success. At the end of this chapter you will find a sample form I designed for diary purposes. Llewellyn also offers a magickal diary, designed by Donald Michael Kraig.

HexCraft

Type of Working: _____

Date: _____ Severity: _____

Outline of Situation: _____

_____

_____

_____

_____

Peformance: _____

_____

Best Moon Phase: _____ Best Day: _____ Best Hour: _____

Desired Outcome: _____

_____

Outline Solution: _____

_____

_____

Conjuring Bag: _____ Herbs and Properties: _____

_____

Runes: _____ Rune Symbolism: _____

_____

Bind Rune: _____ Other Ingredients: _____

_____

Charm: _____

_____

Herbs in the Pow-Wow Cupboard

Type of Working: _____

Date: _____ Severity: _____

Outline of Situation: _____

_____

_____

_____

_____

Peformance: _____

_____

Best Moon Phase: _____ Best Day: _____ Best Hour: _____

Desired Outcome: _____

_____

_____

Outline Solution: _____

_____

_____

Conjuring Bag: _____ Herbs and Properties: _____

_____

Runes: _____ Rune Symbolism: _____

_____

Bind Rune: _____ Other Ingredients: _____

_____

Charm: _____

_____

HexCraft

Type of Working: _____

Date: _____ Severity: _____

Outline of Situation: _____

_____

_____

_____

_____

Peformance: _____

_____

Best Moon Phase: _____ Best Day: _____ Best Hour: _____

Desired Outcome: _____

_____

_____

Outline Solution: _____

_____

_____

_____

Conjuring Bag: _____ Herbs and Properties: _____

_____

_____

Runes: _____ Rune Symbolism: _____

_____

Bind Rune: _____ Other Ingredients: _____

_____

_____

Charm: _____

_____

Herbs in the Pow-Wow Cupboard

Type of Working: _____

Date: _____ Severity: _____

Outline of Situation: _____

_____

_____

_____

_____

Peformance: _____

_____

Best Moon Phase: _____ Best Day: _____ Best Hour: _____

Desired Outcome: _____

_____

_____

Outline Solution: _____

_____

_____

Conjuring Bag: _____ Herbs and Properties: _____

_____

Runes: _____ Rune Symbolism: _____

_____

Bind Rune: _____ Other Ingredients: _____

_____

Charm: _____

_____

Witches' Abundance and Good Will
Designed by Silver RavenWolf

The Fine Art of Warding and General Magick

Resistance is the secret of joy.

—Alice Walker,
Possessing the Secret of Joy, 1993

Protection (Warding) Magick

Protection magick was important during the reign of the Pow-Wow artist. It was necessary to protect your health, family, and home from sickness and other negative circumstances. These concerns are still with us today. All of us want the best for our families and seek safe and secure lives. Protection magick is a psychologically sound move. It also works.

There are those people who feel that to concentrate on protection magick is to draw negative circumstances into their lives. To "protect" yourself, they say, implies that you must be afraid of something in the first place. This would be true if you constantly worry that "something" is going to go wrong in your life, or the lives of your loved ones. Negative thinking does draw negative situations to you. If the idea of this sort of protection magick disturbs you (it does me), then it is time to rethink the meaning of the word "protection." If the idea of protection links to thoughts of fear and worry, you will need to revise the definition for yourself, or choose another word entirely.

Protection magick is like preventative medicine. You are actively manifesting positive energy to deflect or strengthen your circumstances. The idea here is to keep the essence of what is positive in your mind. You need to view your activities in the right perspective, that of taking control of your life and the situations that evolve both from it and around it. One must learn to travel through life without fear of what may happen at any given moment. For example, if before you left the house every morning you filled pocket and purse with a variety of charms to ward off evil, splashed holy water all over your body, and recited a litany of verses just to make it to the car, you've got a problem. The fear is taking control.

Taking on the thought form of "us against them" is also heading for trouble. Remember that the universal connection is a reality, and there simply is no such animal as "usandthem." What others do affects you and what you do influences others, whether it is a conscious act or not. There are some people who have no trouble with "protection" of both themselves and their loved ones, including in the mundane sense. Then there are those of us (me included) who can delicately rip the face off an opponent who has harmed a loved one or a friend, or even take on a group of people they do not know, but are lousy at personal verbal defense. Positive magickal people, Witches and Pow-Wows included, get very balled up on ethics under personal circumstances. To do, or not to do—that is the Crafty question.

Perhaps if we thought of it not as "protection" magick but as "warding" (being responsible for oneself, as in being a "ward" to a child), we could jump over that little psychological speed bump on the path to controlling our own destiny. The charms and spells in this chapter are designed to give you different methods to ease your way along that path of destiny. They allow you to take active control of your personal circumstances and surroundings. A Pow-Wow is a victor, not a victim.

Even before I became a Llewellyn author I was an avid reader of the *Llewellyn New Times,* now called *Llewellyn's New Worlds of Mind and Spirit.* The magazine frequently prints letters from readers. One particular letter (and forgive me because I have no idea in which issue it appeared) really stuck in my mind. It was from a discouraged reader of occult/New Age material. The reader inferred that the only people who became successful and lived secure lives from the practice of the occult were people who wrote books on the subject. The letter writer felt that magickal information was hogwash because it had never worked for him or her, and that all occult writers were more interested in a quick buck than in the lives of the readers.

Interesting point, but not true.

First, writing a book does not make you instantly rich, or famous, or successful. I realize this is the Great American Dream, but if you think most writers of occult how-to books are living on easy street—think again. This goes for all writers, not just the occult ones. Writing a book and becoming one of the rich and famous does not happen to many occult writers. Most people write because they love to do it, not because they expect to plug their book on a late-night television show. On the other hand, you could write 10 books and be rich and famous, but that doesn't mean you are successful in your personal life. In essence, you have to use the information you write (or read) about to guide your destiny—which may not have much to do with the marketplace. One of the major lessons that my students learn in my home has to do with self-confidence. This is obviously something the letter writer missed.

As I tell my students, magickal people are very special. Unlike their friends and neighbors, they have the ability to change the circumstances in which they live and work. More importantly, they have the knowledge that they can actually do it. They are also unique in the fact that they can plan ahead to avoid major difficulties. One doesn't need to wait until the proverbial "other shoe" drops.

For example, many people go to work and hate it. They either hate what they are doing or the people with whom they are doing it. Despite this unhappiness, they keep going to work because they need the money. The media of today has managed to convince people that stress is necessary to make money. The person's life will eventually go one of three ways: he or she will either get sick, get even, or get fired—maybe all three.

Magickal people, on the other hand, have more choices at their disposal. They will not allow the matter to make them sick. They will do warding (protective) magick, including protecting their mental and physical selves, as well as their property and reputation. They will use stress-reducing mediums, such as herbal teas and meditation. They will not get even because they follow the rule of three. They will, however, turn back any negativity that is sent to them. They also will chill out long enough to consider logically the root of the problem and work out the best solution by using divination tools. If the best course to take is getting another job, they will work magick to bring the best job to them.

In essence, a magickal person doesn't have to put up with crap from any person or group of persons, if he or she subconsciously doesn't want to. The only prerequisite is that you believe in yourself and Divinity. This, in itself, breeds self-confidence. Should you choose to stand and fight for what you believe, you do it with the confidence that you are fulfilling your destiny, regardless of the outcome. Self-confidence and warding magick go together. By working on warding yourself, your loved ones, and your possessions, you take a step forward in self-confidence. Your self-esteem rises. No longer are you a victim of circumstances—you are the controller of your destiny.

On Failure

Failing in an act of magick (or anything else, for that matter) is not a bad thing. Failure is a teacher and her subjects are required learning along the path of life. Instead of seeing her as something to be ashamed of, envision her as a beautiful instructor and mentor, dressed in the long white gown of knowledge. She exists to encourage us to go beyond our normal, lazy selves— to try harder, to see farther, and to reach for the stars, one step at a time. Through failure, we can see where we have made our mistakes, and if we are smart, steer away from repetition of them. Sometimes our reason for being with failure is not readily apparent. Perhaps we are subconsciously bucking our true destiny or fiddling with someone else's by accident.

Our failures can be corrected. Albert Einstein once said, "In the middle of every difficulty lies opportunity." Perhaps you were not focused on the issue, or were simply moving in the wrong direction. Correct your travel plans and move toward a more positive path to your goal. There will be days, sometimes even weeks, when you are not capable of producing one little magickal sparkle. This is a growth process, not an indication that you have "lost your power." If this happens, sit back, relax, and find enjoyable mundane activities to keep you busy. Your sparkle will come back—better than before. It may simply be a signal that you need some rest and relaxation.

Incidents can also dampen magickal abilities. Right before the Christmas/Yule season in 1992 I was in a major hurry. I had a guest stopping by who was traveling from Virginia to New York, and I was anxious to see him. As fate would have it, I also had to attend a children's Christmas party in the morning and do grocery shopping—there was nothing in the house to feed the kids or my guest for lunch. I knew the store would be crowded, but wasn't worried because my parking spell always works. Ahem.

Just like the scene in the movie *Fried Green Tomatoes,* I found a good space and waited until the lady with the big boat of a car maneuvered out of it. This took her a total of seven minutes to do. I had to wait until she drove past me to get into the space. By this time, I was drumming my fingers on the steering wheel. Everyone in the parking lot was at a standstill until that big green Impala lumbered toward the exit. As I moved forward, an older man in a white pick-up careened around the corner at the opposite end of the parking lane and flew into the space. Needless to say, I was livid. He had seen me sitting there, waiting for the spot, and ignored me.

Now, you have to imagine the hysterical note of this scene. I was dressed like an elf. (Well, I said it was near Christmas, didn't I?) I weigh 113 pounds—not the ideal wrestler type. I promptly parked in front of his truck, leapt out of my car, and proceeded to tell him exactly what I thought of him. (Just because I'm skinny doesn't mean I don't have a big mouth!) I will never forget him. He was five foot five or six, thick around the middle, but small in overall build—grey hair and not particularly handsome. A typical Pennsylvania good-old-boy in his sixties.

In response he smugly insulted me; I watched him in absolute fury as he walked slowly across the parking lot toward the store—and so did everybody else who now stood gaping around me. "He's got some Christmas spirit," mumbled one lady as she shook her head and maneuvered her cart around my car.

There were many things going through my mind, including my screaming, "May the hounds of hell visit thee on Christmas night!" on the lines of a Scrooge story—but I didn't. I knew I was mad enough to really hurt him, and magick in anger is not the avenue to take. After all, he only took my parking space—not a major crime. Instead, I got back in my car and left the parking lot, asking the universe to melt that cold man's heart. I chose to go to a different store, found a place immediately, and got my groceries in record time. Unfortunately, I still missed my guest from New York, who had a schedule to keep and couldn't wait around for me.

For two weeks after that incident, my parking lot spell didn't work at all. I would drive around for ages, looking for a spot. I began to take my oldest daughter with me and let her do the spell for me, while I tried to figure out why mine wasn't working. Mentally reviewing my failure, I realized that I was condemning myself for getting angry at the man. I was also appalled at my own thoughts of violence over an issue as stupid as a parking space. Part of me was glad I drove away, not out of fear, but out of protecting the man. A different part of me was mad at myself, because I didn't continue to confront him until I had won the battle. I felt I should have been able to either magickally or mundanely resolve the problem without letting that old you-know-what get the better of me! Finally, I realized that my spell was not working because I had attached the negative incident to it. Every time I performed the spell, I inadvertently thought of the idiot who took my space.

With these thoughts neatly set out, the solution was to change the spell. The wording needed to be somehow different so it still worked for me, yet should be altered enough to control the memory of the incident. This would prevent the situation from happening again. After much trial and error, I decided to leave the original spell intact, then added a ward spell to the back of it to protect the parking space once I had found it. It worked perfectly. The moral of this story is this: You must allow your magick to grow with you and change to handle new circumstances in your quickly moving and sometimes volatile world. It is important to analyze your reactions to the world around you and consider your best course, both at the time and after the fact, should a difficulty arise. The act of warding is often just the ticket.

As for the nasty man? I'm confident that the rule of three will apply itself to his actions, if it hasn't already.

A Simple Charm to Carry

Write the following on a piece of plain white paper along with your full name and pin it to your skirt or suit coat:

Awnania
Azaria
Misael

Blessed be Hecate, the Goddess of Wisdom, for she has regenerated us from the Underworld, and has saved us from spiritual death, and She has preserved us even in the midst of the fire and ice. In the same manner may it please Him, the God, that there be no fire or danger to me in any way. In the name of the Lord, the Lady, and the All. So Mote It Be.

A Protection Against Cross Dogs

My daughter uses this charm every night as we walk our sheltie. We live in town of dog lovers and just about every neighbor has at least one. On a summer night, there are dogs who run at breakneck speed to their fences or gates as we pass by. One particular dog paddles furiously at the plate glass window when it sees us—or rather, when he sees our Cujo. (Got a good laugh out of that name, didn't you? Well, I didn't name him, the breeder did!)

Dog hold thy nose to the ground
Goddess has made thee, me and hound
In the name of the Maiden, Mother, and Crone.

The Christian version, of course would be:

Dog hold thy nose to the ground
God has made thee, me and hound
In the name of the Father, Son, and Holy Ghost.

If you are a movie fan, you may have caught the scene in *Hex* where the Pow-Wow stilled an angry dog with this little chant. It does work, though in the screen version the Pow-Wow confronts the dog, face to muzzle. The charm should be recited three times *before* you get near enough for the dogs to hear you. Make either the sign of the equal-armed cross three times on the ground (as in the movie version), or three pentacles in the air. However, my daughter usually forgoes the signage and we still manage to walk quietly down the street. The trick is to calm yourself first, center your energy, then move that calm before you and into the dog (if necessary). We have found it isn't necessary to move into the psyche of the dog if we remember to place the calm before us (almost like a flashlight beam) as we walk down the street.

Many warding Pow-Wow spells took on the form of benedictions. Although they may have sounded lovely for the era, I cannot imagine intoning spells such as the following three times every morning. This benediction is from *The Guide to Health or Household Instructor,* which is no longer in print. Thanks to the Cumberland County Historical Society, we are able to print it here.

> *The cross of Christ be with me, the cross of Christ overcome all waters and every fire, the cross of Christ overcome all weapons, the cross of Christ is a perfect sign and blessing to every soul. May Christ be with me and my body during all my life, at day and night. Now I pray to God the Father for the soul's sake, and I pray to God the Holy Ghost for the Father and the Son's sake, that the holy corpse of God may bless me against all evil things, words and works. The cross of Christ open unto me; furthermore, blessed cross of Christ be with me, above me, before me, behind me, beneath me, and everywhere before all my enemies, visible and invisible. These all flee from me as soon as they know or hear Enoch and Elias, the two prophets who were never imprisoned nor bound or beaten, and who never came out of their power, thus no one of my enemies can injure me, or attach my body, or take my life, in the name of God: the Father, the Son, and Holy Ghost.*

Whew! On the surface this is a Christian prayer, but look again. Notice the part that speaks of the cross above, below, behind, etc. In ceremonial magick there is a beautiful benediction called the Lesser Banishing Ritual, wherein the following is said:

> *Before me, Raphael*
> *Behind me, Gabriel*
> *On my right is Michael*
> *On my left is Auriel*
> *Before me flames the Pentagram*
> *And above me shines the six-rayed star.*

Although the words are different, the magickal intent remains the same.

How to Walk Without Fear

Name me one person who has gone through his or her entire life unafraid. There are times when we find ourselves in circumstances we had not anticipated. It may be when our car breaks down on a country road after midnight, or when we are sitting in a mall parking lot waiting for a friend and a really greasy-type person circles the car once too often. Regardless of the circumstances, the following chant will be very useful to calm your nerves and place a protective aura around you.

Aradia walketh with me, she is my head
And I am Her limb.
Therefore walketh Aradia with (state your name).
In the name of Universal Love.

I know you will find this amusing, but I am a school-crossing guard and take my job very seriously. I've also come close to death on more than one occasion from foolish drivers who are in a hurry to get to work in the morning and don't care if they run over a kid or a crossing guard. I have also intoned this chant of protection before stepping out into traffic. One day I felt so brave after doing it that when a red truck tried to run me down I turned around and hit it with my stop sign. Luckily for me, no one was hurt and the guy didn't sue me. However, the message that the crossing guard with the high-heeled boots just did battle with a pick-up truck went out over every CB and scanner in the area. Traffic on my street that day was slow as pie. How about that!

Getting Rid of Nasty House Spirits

I have lots of things (both human and not) that bump around my house. Normally, all are welcome. I did have one instance, however, when something unwanted decided to take up residence in the children's room. At the time, all four kids were sharing the same room because we were repainting the girls' bedroom. With all this bubbling child energy, something was bound to happen. I thought it would be a few tears or several trips to the bathroom; possibly poltergeist activity at the worst. What I did not expect was a ghost.

It was my oldest son, then five, who told me (complete with wide eyes and lowered voice) that a lady ghost had come to visit the night before in the children's room. Thinking that he watched too much television, I listened patiently to his story, but busied myself getting ready for work. I promptly forgot as the babysitter blew in and I charged out. The subject was forgotten until the following morning, when I was again told about the lady ghost in the children's room. This time my youngest son was the informant. Thinking he picked up the story from his older brother (they do chat among themselves, you know), I figured ghosts had become the new fad in the house and zipped off to work.

On the third morning, I was again confronted by my oldest son, along with his seven-year-old sister. I put on my best Mommy smile and said, "Well, what did she want?"

"We don't know," said my daughter. "She just stood there for a few minutes and melted away."

My oldest daughter did not think any of this was amusing and made a point to let the rest of us know. "Well, Mother, I told you not to let them watch too much television!" (Just wait until she has kids!)

"Look," I said, reasonably looking at my watch. I was already ten minutes late and knew I was going to catch hell for it. "If she visits tonight, either ask her what she wants or come and get me." Everyone was filled with smiles (except my oldest daughter—she rolled her eyes in disgust and complained vehemently about not being able to sleep in her own room) as I flounced out the door. Mommy would do battle with the ghost, should it be dumb enough to appear.

That night, my oldest daughter (the unbeliever) jostled me awake. "Mother," she said oh-so-primly but with megaphone ability, "we all saw the ghost this time." I opened my left eye. There were four children lined up neatly, from largest to smallest, at the foot of my bed.

"Is she still there?" I mumbled. My right eye remained watching my dreams.

"Oh no, Mommy," piped my youngest son. "She came into your room!"

My right eye snapped to attention. I scanned the room—four kids, one snoring husband, and a fish who looked angry because of the commotion. "Well, she's gone now. Go back to sleep and we'll talk about it in the morning." I said. Four pairs of eyes stared at me in disbelief. I, their mother, was going to send them back into that room without an escort. How could I do this to them? The fact that their room was one step from mine did not make the least bit of difference. After all, I am a Witch and for all intents and purposes should be familiar with ghosts. This one was on my turf and my children expected me to do something about it.

"Okay, okay, I give," I said, and threw back the covers. My side of the bed is against the wall. This means I have to do an acrobatic routine to get over my husband to get out of bed. "Stand back, I'm coming through," I muttered. "Damn ghost, anyway."

Once I was in the room, the story of the ghost visit poured from four different mouths. Apparently she came through the wall, looked lost, and was calling for someone. She was dressed in white. She had dark hair. She wasn't ugly, but not overly attractive, either. Well, at least she didn't have worms pouring out of her eye sockets. Who this woman was and where she came from was a mystery to me. We had lived in our house for several years without so much as a rattle or bump. I did not know that this experience would herald many odd and unusual happenings to come. None, however, have been as graphic as this one. That night I slept on the floor. The children were delighted. I was not particularly thrilled.

At sunrise (hey, you try sleeping on a hardwood floor and see if you snooze till noon) I dragged myself out to the kitchen, put on a pot of coffee, and considered my problem. It was Saturday, so I didn't have to worry about crawling bleary-eyed to the office. I figured, first things first. The room had to be banished. Armed with holy water, salt, incense, and a candle, I banished the room (with a troop of children following behind me), then did the rest of the house for good measure. Then I drew protective pentacles on all the doors and windows with clove oil. If she was coming in from the outside, she could forget it. Remember, I hadn't seen her. For all I knew it could have been someone trying to scare the kids or their overactive group mind.

On the fifth night, she came again. This time the eldest child followed her into my room. The ghost stood over my bed and began weeping, according to her account. At no time did she try to harm any of the children. Even so, she was greatly upsetting my household. At a 3:00 AM kitchen table discussion, the four children agreed that the ghost always came through the wall at the same place; therefore, the veil between the worlds must, for some reason, be thin there. Call it a portal or door, I didn't want it in the kids' room. Who knew what the heck else might get curious and wander through? Our lady ghost could have some undesirable friends.

To solve the problem I dug out my Pow-Wow material on unwanted ghosts. First, I designed an equal-armed cross out of wood. I painted it black, then added seven silver pentacles. I cleansed and consecrated it with holy water and crushed nettle, then asked the universe for protective energy to flow through and emanate from the cross. That evening I again banished the room, cast a circle, and closed the astral door with my hands. At that point I uttered a prayer that the unhappy ghost would find peace and light, then hung the cross over the closed astral door. At midnight, I rubbed the cross with angelica, dragon's blood, St. John's wort, and horehound. We haven't heard from that odd lady since.

A Charm Against Guns

It is said that if this charm is spoken three times, the gun cannot fire.

*Three moonbeams cross the heavens from the heart of the Goddess
Three rays of sun greet Her as a gift from the God
As sure as the love of the two are pure
So sure shall no fire or smoke or bullet pass from the barrel of any gun
It shalt not give fire, nor flame, nor bullet, nor heat.
I walk in safety as Raphael is before me
Gabriel behind me
and Michael and Auriel are to the right and left of me.*

In the name of the All and the Love of the Universe.
So mote it be.

I wouldn't do a test run on this one to see if it works; however, it is a good charm to put in a sachet for those involved in law enforcement, the armed services (and do not carry a gun), or you favorite hubby/honey hunter.

A Warding Charm for Deer Hunters

Mighty Stag
Child of Diana
I call you forth
Encircle my body with your aura of strength.

This charm is said to prevent the hunter from doing injury to himself with his own gun and to guard him against all types of bad luck.

To Prevent Wounds

Meadow rue (also known as German rue) gathered during the month of September in the sign of Virgo was said to prevent wounds when carried on one's person. Meadow rue was also hung on doors and rubbed into floorboards to break hexes.

Warding Against Injuries

This original talisman was rather gruesome as it called for an actual wolf's eyeball. Yuck! You can fashion your own talisman without harming the animal. Simply sit in a quiet place and call on the collective spirit of the wolf. State your purpose and ask for its protection. Be sure to thank the spirit after your conversation. In this day and age, designs of wolves appear on everything from tee-shirts to rubber stamps. You could design your own patch to sew on a jacket or create a nice wall covering or banner for your home or apartment. You can load the protective energy given to you by the wolf into your own handicraft, thereby making it twice as protective. Another popular wolf charm was to take the seed of a sunflower gathered in the astrological sign of Leo and wrap it up with the tooth of a wolf in a laurel leaf. This talisman was to keep people from yelling at you. If something was stolen from you, the talisman was to be placed under your pillow at night to bring a dream vision of the thief.

General Protection Spell

This spell covers freedom from the danger of fire, lightning, enchantment, and evil spirits.

> *Welcome thou fiery fiend! Do not extend further than thou already hast.*
> *This I count unto thee as a repentant act.*
> *In the name of the Maiden, Mother, and Crone I command unto thee,*
> *O fire, by the power of the Goddess who careth and worketh everything,*
> *that thou now do cease, and not extend thyself.*
> *This I count unto thee as a repentant act.*
> *I command thee to abate thy flames and cease they wrath*
> *This I count unto thee as a repentant act.*

To Stop a House Fire

Take a cloth soaked in menstrual blood and throw it on the fire. Nothing need be said.

Although this may appear disgusting at first, remember that the Blood of the Moon (a woman's menstrual blood) is highly magickal in content as it is secreted at her most powerful time. It was used in a variety of ancient spells. The herb dragon's blood may be a substitute for the original menstrual blood due to the dictates of society.

To Protect Your House from Fire

You will need:

Black chicken feathers	1 block paraffin
1 egg	1 teaspoon rosemary
1 teaspoon dragon's blood	

Melt all ingredients in a pot and pour into a greased pan. When almost cool, inscribe the rune Algiz (see Chapter 14) on the block. When completely cool, take it out of the pan, load it with your protection intent, and bury it as close to the front doorstep as possible. It is said that as long as a stick of your house is standing, it will never burn.

To Put Out a Fire

Walk widdershins (counterclockwise) around the fire and say:

> *Our dear Brigid journeyed through the land*
> *Having a fiery brand in her hand*

The brand heats
The brand sweats
Fiery brand stop your heat
Fiery brand stop your sweat

Notice this one is very close to one of the Triple Charms for healing.

To Put Out a Fire when You Haven't any Water

Write the following words on each side of a plate, then throw it into the fire.

S A T O R
A R E P O
T E N E T
O P E R A
R O T A S

This spell has been recorded and used since medieval times. Its magical application is derived more from the arrangement of the letters and their numerical correspondences rather than the translated meanings of the words themselves. It is found on the second pentacle of Saturn and was valued against great adversities. Its act was one of repression, whether it be of fire or spirits. The numerical evaluation of the square adds up to IHVH, the name of God. It may mean something like this:

Creator! Stop! Exert! Hold! Turn!

or

Creator! Stop! Exert! Defend! Resolve!

Therefore, it is an excellent chant for many different circumstances including scaring away unwanted ghosties and ghoulies.

Llewellyn author Donald Tyson has this to say about the SATOR magick square. "Storms says it translates 'The sower shall keep the work of his hands' and he suggests that it is based upon the letters of PATER NOSTER written twice (vertically and horizontally) in the form of a cross, with A (Alpha) and O (Omega) repeated twice in the corners. (See Storms, *Anglo-Saxon Magic*, Martinus Nijhoff: The Hague, 1948, pp. 281-2.)"

To Prevent Mishaps and Dangers in the House

Write the following on a piece of white paper and place above your mantle or front door along with a basil leaf:

> *Sanct Matheus, Sanct Marcus, Sanct Lucas, Sanct Johannis*
> *Protection of One's House and Hearth*
> *Beneath thy guardianship I am safe against all tempests and enemies.*
> *Aradia Aradia Aradia*

To Keep Back Men and Animals

This is another good one for soldiers or law enforcement officers. None of us like the thought of violence or war and most magickal people steer absolutely clear of it. However, this day and age requires a police force, drug enforcement agents, etc., and if one of those people were a loved one of mine, I would certainly make sure he or she carried this charm.

> *In the name of the God and the Goddess*
> *I make the defense*
> *May it please my Goddess to assist me.*
> *Upon the assistance of God and Goddess I depend entirely*
> *Upon the holy assistance of the All and my gun*
> *I rely very truly*
> *Blessed be.*

A great many Pow-Wow artists made an everyday practice of "conjuring" things. They conjured knifes, pots, animals, people, angels, and (ahem) a few disrespectful creatures on occasion. A dictionary tells us that "to conjure" means either 1) To charge or to entreat solemnly, or 2) to summon by invocation or incantation and to affect or effect by magick. In other words, to practice the magickal arts. I find it most interesting that if you say the word "magick" to a Pow-Wow artist, nine times out of ten you would be reprimanded for going against the Bible, but to say the word "conjure" is absolutely acceptable.

This next spell is to conjure (or magickally affect) weapons that are being used against you.

> *I, (give your name), conjure thee, sword or knife, gun or weapon, by the*
> *spear of Lugh and the sword of Nuada, that I am kept from injury as*
> *one of the children of the Goddess. Amen.*

Because I often look at other people's material things as "their stuff," not "my stuff," I had never thought of influencing property or items belonging to someone else. Ethically, unless someone has asked you for help, you shouldn't touch what belongs to them. Of course, if some idiot is leveling a gun at my head, I'm sure I would sidestep ethics and consider survival.

To Protect Your Home from Lightning

Scatter ashes on the roof or hang St. John's wort underneath the highest step in your house.

To Keep a Hunter from Killing Game

With all the controversy about animal rights activism, it wouldn't be fair to not include a spell for animal protection.

> *(Say the person's name)*
> *Shoot whatever you please*
> *Shoot but hair and feathers*
> *Because all you can shoot is the breeze.*
> *Shoot but air and earth*
> *With what you give to the poor.*

Warding Your Stove or Fireplace

If you are lucky enough to have a home with a fireplace, you can use this little formula to bless the hearth. The hearth was usually considered the survival point of the home. It was used for cooking meals, warming the house, and of course, preparing magickal potions and brews for protection and health.

To consecrate and bless the hearth, dragon's blood, Solomon's seal, St. John's wort, vervain, and frankincense were mixed together on a plate of oak leaves. After these items had been reduced to ashes, half was placed in a white bag and hung above the hearth; the other half was sprinkled in the hearth, then overlaid with a thin sprinkling of salt.

When stoves made their debut, the entire mixture was hung on the wall above the appliance and renewed once a year. If you don't have a hearth, don't despair. Our "hearth" consists of several flagstones set around my altar in a half circle. It really doesn't take up much space. The stones help to ground you and pull up the power of earth energy as well. After you clean them up and set them on the floor, cleanse and consecrate them with the four elements, then draw pentacles in oil, water, and wine on each stone and dab each corner of the stones in the same process. Our stones are wide enough to place a large cauldron on either side of the set-up, giving the feeling of a hearth as items burn within. After you have designed your hearth, burn the formula in your cauldron.

Magic Mirrors

Although scrying wasn't talked about much, it was indeed used by many Pow-Wow artists who had not been totally Christianized. The instructions were simple. Obtain a piece of clear glass (your choice on size) that is framed on only three sides. The left side is to be unframed. Slide the glass out of the frame. Cleanse and consecrate the glass. Paint it with a steeped solution of eyebright, dragon's blood, and chamomile. Let it dry, then paint the same surface with black paint. When it is dry, return the glass to the frame with the black side touching the back of the frame, leaving the unpainted glass side facing you. The mirror is to be held in the physical direction of what or whom you want to see. If your enemy lived in the east, you would turn the glass toward the east, etc. Sometimes angels or spirits were called for guidance through the mirror; in other instances, no intermediary was used. I believe this depended upon the talent of the seer and the age of the mirror, whether or not it had been handed down from a previous seer, etc. It is claimed the magic mirror was used during the "thirty-years war."

Another formula for the magic mirror was a little more complicated. Buy a mirror and inscribe the following in your own blood on the back of it:

S. Solam S. Tattler S. Echogardner Gematar

Bury it at a crossroads (or paths) during an uneven hour. On the third day, dig it up. The warning here is that you are not to be the first person to look into the mirror; you should let your familiar do it.

Protection Against the Evil Eye

Cultures all over the world have believed in the evil eye for centuries. Basically it goes along with the old adage "if looks could kill"—with the belief that looks actually can, or at least make you very sick or unhappy. Somewhere along the line it was determined that not only are the eyes the "window of the soul" but they also can assail the unsuspecting person with both negative and positive energy rays. From the Celts to Voudon to the Pow-Wow, the fame of the evil eye has certainly gotten around.

The evil eye is supposed to manifest through negative emotions rising up from the center of power and magnified by the lenses in the eyes, much like catching a ray of sunlight with a magnifying glass and burning a piece of paper. It is said that many times the recipient of the evil eye is not even aware of it and does not realize that the sickness, injury, or unhappiness he or she experiences a day or so later has anything to do with that nasty look the person got during an argument with a coworker or neighbor. It also appears that

Protection of Clan
Protected Family Environment
"Safe House"
Designed by Silver RavenWolf

many people do not know they possess the ability to generate such difficulties in another's life (let's thank our lucky stars and garters for that one).

To believe this entirely leaves one fairly open to rampant superstition, but to totally discard the notion is not the wisest avenue to take, either. During the research for this book, I was holding Thursday night healing sessions. All of these individuals in this group use magick of some type, whether it be in prayer form or raising energy through their own belief system. I asked everyone for their opinion of the evil eye. The answers varied, but it appeared that most of the individuals either didn't put much stock in it or had simply not considered it before.

In these stressful and paranoid times, perhaps it is good that we have forgotten about such things as the evil eye. On the other hand, perhaps it is something we should consider without losing our heads. I have noticed that a discussion between magickal people becomes uncomfortable when issues such as psychic attack or black magick are mentioned as possible causes for misfortune. It is as if they are torn between the educational battering of the issue as nonsense and the paranoia that ensues when there may be such a possibility.

Once logical thought gives way and the idea of evil being manifested on purpose is considered, absolute fear takes over. Our voices are higher and faster. It is as if when we delve into the primal mind to accept the reality we are unable to bounce back to the logical. Fear automatically kicks in and brings on a panic attack. Often positive magickal people poo-poo the idea of the performance of negative magick by rationalizing the situation to death; that way they don't have to deal with the possibility that someone has it in for them through the use of magick. Is this wise?

Other people, like the Fundamentalists, go in the reverse—running around like Chicken Little, proclaiming that negative magick is constantly used, etc. etc. There has got to be a middle ground somewhere. We need to be rational, but not so closed that we cannot see out of the box in which we are living.

Most Pow-Wows used some type of charm or talisman on their own bodies to ward off the evil eye. Unlike those used by most magickal people, the Pow-Wow's charm was unobtrusive, often worn next to the skin where it could not be detected. Sometimes the charms were placed in conjuring bags or sewn to their clothes. One unique little trick was to empower a safety pin and pin it to the left shirt or dress sleeve. Another was to take two small bones, tie them together with black thread in the shape of a solar cross (a cross with equal arms), and wear it close to the heart.

Finally, the best advice against psychic attack comes from a ceremonial magician friend of mine. "Play country music," she says with a laugh. "It is so grounded, nothing can get through!"

Graveyard Dirt

Many Pow-Wow charms call for graveyard dirt. Although this sounds very mysterious and certainly instills a unique aura to the charm, the idea of snooping around a graveyard to gather dirt is an interesting one. In order to dispel rumors about visiting graveyards, one Pow-Wow family tradition found an interesting alternative. Each spring they would visit the graves of their loved ones and bring several pots of geraniums to place upon them. While paying their respects, they would add some of the dirt off the graves to the dirt in the pots, acting as if they were worried to leave the plants there without adequate soil. They would leave the pots at the grave site until the fall, then collect the flowers, dump out the geraniums, and use the dirt in the pots for their charms. No one in the town suspected them of unusual practices. They simply assumed the family was diligent in honoring their loved ones.

What was graveyard dirt used for? Plenty! Charms for catching thieves, stopping gossip, binding abusive family members, stopping a person from meddling in your private affairs, and uncrossings.

Fertilizer Magick

In magick you will find that not everything works at the snap of your fingers. Often charms made at the Full Moon come to form on the following New Moon and vice versa. There are other times when a working takes a Full Moon cycle—from Full to Full. Some spells need time to grow and nurture before they mature. To symbolize this, one particular family in Bucks County made fertilizer out of their charms!

Each spring, all the relatives would get together and pool their herbal resources and their cake pans. They would mix fertilizer and specific herbs in each pan. For instance, one pan would be for warding, another for stopping gossip, another for prosperity, etc. After the contents of the pans were tightly packed, the mixture would be empowered and cut into small squares. On each square a rune of purpose would be carved. The magick cubes would be split equally among the relatives.

As the planting season began, the magick cubes were used in the garden. For instance, for prosperity, they would be placed among a patch of mint; for protection, under rosemary and basil, etc. The cubes were also used for single purposes. If you were being slandered, a night-blooming flower was planted in a pot along with a magickal cube to stop it, along with the person's name (if you knew it) who could not keep his or her evil tongue still.

The Egg

The farmers and country people practiced *braucherei,* meaning "using." They used magick to help (or sometimes hinder) people and animals. They also "used" common items, such as the egg, in their practices. The egg was employed as the symbol of the threefold Goddess—Maiden, Mother, and Crone. The shell stood for the wisdom and protection of the Crone, the white of the egg stood for the Mother and her life-giving energy and nurturing qualities, and the yolk for the Maiden, for things yet to grow and the innocence of purity.

In healings, a raw egg was passed over the body, then broken in a bowl. If there was no blood, the patient was not under any evil influences. In general workings, the egg was empowered in the hands of the Pow-Wow then thrown into the hearth or wood stove fire. As the egg broke, the spell cast would begin its manifestation (or birth) into the earth plane.

"I never could see what he was doing," explained one woman about her trip to an old Pow-Wow. "But he would say, 'Now, I'll do my part, and you must go home and do yours.' He would turn around, hold the egg in both hands, then cast it into the cookstove fire—smack, just like that!"

To restore one's manhood, a fresh egg was to be dunked in fish oil, then boiled in water. The fish oil was to be discarded in a fast-running stream. The egg was then to be transported to a forest with fir trees and placed, slightly opened, on top of a red ant hill. As the ants fed on the egg, strength and potency would be returned to he who ailed.

Eggs were even inscribed with ink or one's own blood, then buried, broken, or eaten, depending upon the spell.

To Keep Thieves from Entering Your House

Take a white conjuring bag and fill it with jalop root, garlic, basil, mandrake root, lemon verbena, oak leaves, and rosemary. Write the following on a piece of white paper:

S A T O R
A R E P O
T E N E T
O P E R A
R O T A S

Sew up the bag, empower it, and hang it on your front door.

A Conjuring Bag for Warding

You will need a white sachet bag (about two inches wide by three inches long) that can be tied or sewn shut, a teaspoon of rosemary, and a piece of white paper. Write the following on the paper:

Goddess bless me here in this time, and there in eternity.

Write your full name below this. Empower the rosemary and put it in the bag along with the piece of paper with the verse. Sew or tie the sachet shut. It can be worn around the neck or pinned to the lining of your clothes. The Christian version of this charm designates that you write the following on the paper:

I

N I R

I

SANCTUS SPIRITUS

I

N I R

I

And this be guarded here in time
and there in eternity.

"Sanctus Spiritus" means sacred breath, pure energy, or Holy Ghost. There is also a rider with this charm. You are not to let anyone borrow anything from you or your household for nine days, and you are to protect your property so that nothing is stolen.

A Conjuring Bag to Stop Gossip

You will need a white cloth bag, a piece of John the Conqueror root (also known as jalop), a teaspoon of slippery elm, a half teaspoon of gag root (also known as lobeila), a half teaspoon of angelica, a quarter teaspoon of mandrake, a red thread and needle, a piece of paper, a pen, and one red candle.

Take a few pieces of your own hair and tie them around the jalop. Put all herbs and the jalop in the bag. Draw a human face on the piece of paper. Sew up the mouth on your drawing with the red thread. As you are doing this, you must think of curtailing any rumors about you and say:

Slanderous blabbering doth go away
I sew you tight this very day
You will not cause me any harm
Or raise about me any alarm.

Put the picture in the bag, and sew up the bag. Next, light the red candle and say the following:

Holy Mary Mother of God
Protect me now by staff and rod
Vanishing enemies I now see
Gag root is now with me.
Slippery elm and root of gag
Help shut the mouths that brag
Gossip is gone this very day
No harm to me in any way.

Let the candle burn until it is consumed. You can wear the charm bag, carry it in your pocket, or place it on your bed post.

Runes

The ancient runic alphabet of the Norse peoples played an important part in the magick of the elite German Pow-Wow. This grouping of magickal letters is really a system of secrets. Combined (called bind runes), I can honestly say they are just about the most powerful tool for practicing magickal peoples of today.

Runes were carved on candles, drawn on paper, sewn into clothes, placed in decorative art, inscribed in the dirt, and traced in the air. Their uses and their positive magicks are limited only by human thought. There are 24 runes, each representing a particular thought form (see Chapter 14). I encourage all my students who study at my home to learn them during the first 13 introductory lessons to Pow-Wow and the Craft. There are many excellent books on the market that explain the history and uses of runes. They are a versatile system that can be used in magick as well as divination. Runes were used for warding, increasing prosperity and fertility, hallowing, and other practices.

You can make your own runes by collecting 24 small creek stones and painting a rune on each one. You can also make them out of wood, or cut ceramic greenware in tiles and fire them or use a self-hardening clay. I made a set of bind runes out of ceramic discs and glazed them so they can be used repeatedly. I have also lent those discs to trusted friends on occasion, and they have returned them with comments about their wonderful success.

Protection in Court

One is always concerned that justice be done in his or her favor when entering a court room. Provided you are in the "right," the following talisman should be made and carried with you in a small conjuring bag.

Take a small portion of skunk cabbage that has been gathered during the month of August during the reign of Leo. Add to this one bay leaf and a dandelion. Empower the plants and place them in the bag. Carry it with you into the courtroom and you will receive great reward.

To Protect Yourself from an Attack

Say the following three times:

> *Two wicked eyes have overshadowed me*
> *But three other eyes overshadow them*
> *Maiden, Mother, Crone*
> *They watch my flesh, my blood, my bone.*

Conjuring the Driver or Footman for Protection

This is an interesting spell because it comes in two parts: one to stave and conjure, and the other to dismiss. The original spell was so Christianized that it has lost its true meaning, so here is a better version for you.

To call:

> *Ye driver and footman I conjure thee now*
> *Thy evil and weapons against me are bound*
> *My flesh is protected, my spirit is shielded*
> *All mine enemies are now fielded.*

To dismiss:

> *Ye driver and footman I now release*
> *Henceforth will you walk only in peace.*

A Simple Charm for Release from Locks, Bonds, Etc.

> *Moses travelled through the sea*
> *And beheld the land*
> *Hence must break all locks, fetters, and bands.*

Oh, by the way—this one called for frog guts. I guess it was to help grease the lock.

For Money and Love

Although Pow-Wows were best known for healing, protection, and hexing, they did do a bit of money and love work. Conjuring bags were very popular for these issues, with vervain (verbena) popular for love charms, and cinquefoil (five finger grass) the all-time favorite for money and success issues. Red candles were burned for both.

Three sisters rode across the land
Each had pieces of gold in their hands
The first one said, "She needs one"
The second said, "She gets some"
The third said, "She has plenty, just as she wished
Plenty of gold to fill her dish!"

This is a Triple Charm Spell invoking the Sisters of the Wyrrd. I "shotgunned" this one in the presence of one of my students. My husband was fretting that someone hadn't paid him for work he had done on her house. It wasn't an issue that the client didn't want to pay up, more of a problem of timing between the two of them. "I wish she would pay me tonight," he mumbled as he walked out the front door.

In a small dish I sprinkled cinquefoil (for money) and vervain (enchantment to make things move). I wrote on a piece of paper exactly what my husband wanted (for the client to pay him that night), called the element of fire to move things along, burned the paper and herbs in the dish, then placed it on the pentacle on my altar. Satisfied, I smiled cockily at my student and said, "No problem."

My husband came home without the money. He didn't see the client; she wasn't home. I thought I had failed.

Wrong—I wasn't specific.

Later in the week I discovered that the client had indeed written my husband a check (the cinquefoil) that very night. However, fearing that she might miss him (the vervain), she put it in the mail to be sure he would receive it. The cinquefoil worked perfectly, the vervain worked like a champ; my wording was not specific enough. Lesson one hundred thousand in spell casting.

Here is another prosperity spell.

The Lord and the Lady came from the East
Bringing gifts in order to please
He said, "She has none"
She said, "She has some"
Together they said "She has plenty to spare!"
Now your cupboards are no longer bare.

I don't know how ethical Pow-Wows were in attracting love interests, but Witches never enchant someone by name. This is considered highly unethical. The following love charm should be used without mentioning a person by name. Instead, you should concentrate on bring the best love interest toward yourself. You will need a red candle, rose petals (red), basil, vervain, a small bowl, a red construction paper heart, and a piece of red yarn.

Mix the rose petals (for love), basil (for sympathy), and vervain (for enchantment and to make it go) in a bowl. Enchant the herbs while you are gently mixing them together. Light the construction paper heart and place it on the herbs; move a few of the herbs onto the burning heart. This is the heat of desire, and the fire is the flame of passion. Pick up the yarn and repeat the following chant:

Three sisters danced over the land
The first called him (her)
The second brought him (her)
The third bound them together!

As you repeat the chant, tie a knot for each sister's statement. The chant is repeated three times so you will end up with nine knots on the strand of yarn. Pass the yarn over the smoke of the herbs, then carry it with you.

Summary

The use of ward (protective) magick allows you to control thousands of life situations. From minor circumstances to major problems, you can anticipate or control the outcome for your well-being. People often create their own problems out of simple boredom. Working protective magick keeps you on your toes and alert to the world around you. This stops that bored feeling and occupies the mind. It also allows you to feel at ease with your surroundings. So many magickal and mundane people forget that living in wisdom means living in peace—don't you forget.

Cursing, Banishing, and Dealing with Difficult People

Cursing

Cursing appears frequently throughout Pow-Wow material. It is one of the few forms of the original Craft that hung around, both in the belief and the practice. More amusing is the fact that few self-respecting Witches (or anyone else, for that matter) of today will admit that cursing exists. True, it is used infrequently, if at all, but to tell you there is (or was) no such activity would not be true. To tell you "no self-respecting Pow-Wow artist ever cursed" also would be a misrepresentation of the facts; however, to tell you that no Christian, Hindu, or Jewish person has ever uttered a curse is also a fib. I have been present at church meetings where the pastor has led the congregation to pray for the demise of a person, persons, or even a way of life that does not agree with his or her own thoughts on how the world should be run. Not because the person or issue in question was bad, but rather that the person simply did not conform to the standards of the particular sect, tradition, or religion.

With this in mind, I can't understand why everyone starts pointing fingers when the subject of cursing hits the floor after rounds of "why my religion is better than yours" debate. You can't hang the act of cursing on a particular religion, cult, or group. Big business curses people with high-tech marketing skills. The government avidly curses people and opportunity—just look at the emotional litter on the political campaign trail. The American public constantly curses people or situations by "declaring war" on them. Excuse me—to declare war is to curse something.

Therefore, why is it whenever someone finds out I'm Wiccan and practice Pow-Wow, one of the first questions they want to know is if I have ever cursed anything, and naturally, anybody. I often find myself at the brunt of well-meaning jokes about my ability to jinx or curse someone. I actually know people who surreptitiously check the cream in their coffee to see if it has curdled whenever I am around.

Gee, I didn't know I was so powerful.

There is the key—power. People believe that you are not very powerful as a magickal person if you cannot harm someone or something or have absolute control over it. This is not singling out the American culture, but the general human culture that teaches us to use money, sex, or violence as weapons to hurt, maim, and kill the human body and mind to gain the upper hand in any given situation. This, to me, is ludicrous.

There is truth however, in the statement that "a Witch cannot heal if (s)he cannot harm." The meaning of this is not that you are supposed to go out and intentionally hurt someone so you can cure an illness. It means the energies raised in anger and hatred are far easier to create than those used in healing. Why? Anger will lead you to an outburst of energy and emotion, where feelings of unconditional love (due to the nature of our society) are much more difficult to cultivate (barring puberty, of course). Simply put, if you can't get your energy moving when you are angry, you certainly won't be able to cultivate the loving emotions you need to heal. Harming someone is not a prerequisite to healing, but the raising of controlled energy is.

When Pow-Wow was at its height there were no police officers, not much of a court system, and certainly little "justice" on small matters (like stealing a pig or pop's best ladder). There were no sophisticated techniques to catch criminals—no fingerprinting system or television shows like *America's Most Wanted* to bring in the culprit. If you wanted your stuff back or the thief caught, you went to the Pow-Wow to find out what to do. Usually, it involved either putting a curse on the criminal or taking one off the victim. Often the Pow-Wow artist would instruct the victim on how to perform his or her own magick, hence the watering down of many of the chants, spells, and rituals. In this way, the Christian religion was used as an acceptable backdrop. Also, the Pow-Wow would not be directly responsible for the curse, should it take effect.

When you mistakenly hurt someone with magick, the universe considers your stupidity and usually makes allowances. If you hurt someone on purpose, whether it is through magick or everyday nastiness, the universe rights the situation. Sometimes it may take years to manifest, but I have always found that those who create flagrant injustices on purpose are well taken care of by the Goddess and the God somewhere down the road. Once you have the knowledge, the universe considers you responsible for it, regardless of your own opinion. The real power in magick is much like those words in the song "The Gambler"—You've got to know when to hold it, know when to use it, know when to walk away, and to know when to be smart enough to run like hell. Magick works on three levels, but begins on the spiritual plane. If your intent is not pure from the get-go, you might as well pack it up and head for other theological pastures.

Some of the information you will find in this chapter may not be to your liking, or you may feel that the information is borderline and should not be printed at all. Most Wiccans (those of the Craft) would not even entertain the thought of using them. Again, I feel it would be a total disservice to the research done on the material not to include this information.

When some type of negativity affected the body of a client, the Pow-Wow would create a cure on the spot, plus give the victim something to do as well. If the matter involved stolen property or other criminal activity, the Pow-Wow would give specific instructions to the owner/victim on how to correct the injustice. In this way, the Pow-Wow felt he or she was not responsible in case something bad should occur, either on purpose or by mistake.

Many of the old chants and spells bastardized to suit Christianity are simply not appropriate for the modern magickal practitioner. For example, to heal a snake bite one was to curse the snake. Therefore, the snake would die and the patient be cured. This was acceptable thinking because a Pow-Wow considered the snake to represent the evil in the Garden of Eden story in the Bible, so it was okay to kill that life form through sympathetic magick. Today, we realize that everything is connected to the All. Taking a life, simply because it is a snake and it bit you, is not the answer. To curse someone or something is dangerous business. First, most magickal people believe in the "Rule of Three"—what you send out, whether it be good or evil, comes back to you three times. The tricky part of this rule is that it can come back to you with three things, one big whopper of a thing, or it may hit someone you love. If you are only doing positive things, you will reap a threefold reward. If you are delving in no-no territory, your life and the lives of those you love will most likely deteriorate in short order.

In today's society, cursing is commonplace—people just color it with different words. It is amusing that Witches backpedal about the idea of cursing. Instead, they will do everything in their power to avoid harming anything or anyone, unlike other religious groups who tear the world apart with their holy wars. To the Pow-Wow, cursing was a useful form of protective magick. People one hundred years ago (and even today) were more likely to blame their ills on another person or mystical evil rather than take responsibility for their own actions (which probably brought on the problem in the first place). Today, many people have lost their personal power and create negativity through blindness. One hundred years ago there were more housewives trying to zap each other through simple charms and spells that they learned from "that Pow-Wow over yonder" than you would believe. Uncontrolled energy due to superstition ran high. The Christian religious base is partly responsible for this. In the Old Testament of the Bible, an eye for an eye was acceptable. Sadly, the rule of three did not come with the gift of a chant or a spell.

Chants written on paper were called "letters of protection" or "charms." In the previous chapters on herbs and healing, the conjuring bags have been explained. These were used for protective spells as well as banishing and cursing or hexing.

Banishing

To banish something is to literally make it go away. Banishing is not an act of cursing if it is done for warding measures. Pow-Wows were great at banishing all sorts of things, from physical items and people to astral boogies. Herbs for banishing were St. John's wort, basil, angelica, yarrow, rosemary, rue, vervain, and asafoetida. The element for banishing was most often fire. Although there were several charms for banishing, rituals were performed as well in which a knife was painted red and ritually used to cut negative astral ties from an individual or animal. A loaf of brown bread is also placed in the magick circle. As the spell begins, the Pow-Wow walks widdershins around the person who thinks he or she is being attacked by negative magick. The spell for such a ritual, written by Thor and Audrey Sheil, is this:

> *(Name) strolled through a red forest*
> *And in the red forest there was a red barn*
> *In the red barn there was a red table, surrounded by red straw*
> *On the red table lay a red knife*
> *Beside the red knife was a loaf of red bread*
> *Cut the red bread*
> *The evil attached to (name) is dead.*
> *Say dead.*
> *Now it be so.*

On the line, "the evil attached ..." forcefully bring the knife down and stab the bread.

A Chant to Banish Caterpillars or other Field and Garden Pests

The Lord and Lady went out upon the field.
They ploughed up three rows and plowed up three (name the pest).
The first was white, the second was black, and the third was red.
Say dead.
Dead.
Now all the (pests) are dead.
It is made so.

Like other charms, this is to be repeated three times. As with the healing charms, this one leads you from past (white) to the future (black) through a present action (red), allowing the subconscious to perform the magickal act through visualization of the charm. The last line, "it is made so," is a direct command, slightly different than some of the previous charms. Again, the colors are named: white is the past, red is the present, and black is the future. In this case, you also can visualize a new pest (white), the act of destroying the pest (red as in blood), and the death of the pest (black is often associated with death).

A different version of this charm is:

Mary, God's Mother, traversed the land
Holding three worms in her hand
One was white, the other was black, the third was red.
Now they are dead.
Dead, Dead, Dead!

The charm was said three times while stroking a person or an animal who has been afflicted with worms. At the end of each repetition the Pow-Wow would strike the patient on the back. This is an excellent example of a Triple Charm. To rid your dog or cat of fleas, substitute the word "fleas" in place of "worms."

Curing a Snake Bite

"We consider this secret worth the cost of this book alone," states *The Guide to Health or Household Instructor*. Although I don't approve of this curse, it shows the formulation of many of the curses.

Repeat the following three times, each time raising energy over the patient from wound to foot:

> *God created all things and they were good.*
> *Thou only serpent art damned.*
> *Cursed be thou sting.*
> *In the name of God, the Father, the Son, and Holy Ghost.*
> *Zing, Zing, Zing.*

This will surely kill the snake.

Turning Back Energy

Turning back negative energy to the sender is a common practice in the Craft. If someone purposely tries to harm you, casts about malicious statements, or in some way feels it is his or her personal goal to cause you difficulties, you are permitted to send back the unfortunate energy that was sent to you in the first place. You are not permitted to create your own negative energy to go along with it. This means that you must perform any ritual or spell without anger—no easy task if your blood pressure is high. You can deflect or return, but you may not create. To do so would be to break your vow of initiation. To do so in anger would be a curse.

To an individual who is not familiar with magickal people, this may not mean a lot. So what is a vow, anyway? But to Witches, the vow taken during the initiation process is more binding than any modern marriage promise. If a Witch breaks his or her vow, he or she will suffer the consequences. Pow-Wow artists designed numerous chants and spells to turn back evil or negative influences both to protect the community and to release them from any intended malicious harm. The process of "turning back" is far better than suffering the consequences of creating more horror in the world.

Interesting Ways to Turn Back Evil

PINCH IT OUT

If you believe that someone is intentionally sending evil your way, take your shirt, turn it inside out, pinch it in the hinges of your bedroom door, and leave it there all night.

SHINE IT UP

You can also shine your best brass or copper pot and say:

Magick kettle shine for me
Deflect that evil energy.
Send it back now three times three
May curses and slander not find me.
As I will, so mote it be.

Hang the pot in the most used room of the house, usually the kitchen or dining room.

Wash It Out

Creek stones and an earthen bowl of water are used in this ritual. Its purpose is to deflect negativity. Fill the bowl nearly full of creek stones, then fill the bowl with water. The chant used here is:

Bowl of reflection
Stones of protection
May the reason of my harm
Feel the power of this charm.
Sisters three come work for me
Bowl detect
Stones deflect
And water reflect
Peace and harmony now come to me.
As I will, so mote it be.

Change the water once a week and renew the chant. Throw the old water on your doorstep. The Sisters of the Wyrrd are incorporated here. The bowl stands for the first sister, she of the past; the stones stand for the present and second sister; the third action, that of reflection, is the sister of the future.

Soak It Up

Often an onion was halved and dropped into a canning jar. When it rooted, it was thrown away and replaced. The onion was said to soak up evil or negative vibrations from anyone who entered the house.

The Twisting Vine Spell

The protection jar is a variation of the creek stone bowl. Find a ceramic jar or make one yourself. Empower creek stones for protection, add one red agate and one crystal, sprinkle the stones with spring water, place them in the jar, then fill the remainder of the jar with ivy. As you are filling the jar, chant the word "protection" over and over again. Place the jar in your living room to protect your home when you are away and turn back evil influences when you are home.

Jar be sensitive
Jar be smart
Ivy twist evil
Around its own heart
Who dare to break into my home without invitation
Send them back out with great deprivation!

I originally made this jar for an actress friend of mine who has an apartment in New York City. Because she travels a great deal to go on location at different areas of the country, she asked for something to leave in her apartment to protect her things. I handed her this jar four years ago and she has never been the victim of a crime in the "Big Apple."

SEND IT BACK WITH LAMP BLACK

When Pow-Wow began, there was no such item as a photograph. If you wanted to stop a particular person from harming you and send back the negative energy, you would burn a candle coated with lamp black (the soot that collects on a kerosene lamp chimney). Next you needed something from the person who was giving you so much trouble, such as fingernail clippings, a lock of hair, etc. Human contagions were items that had been cast off by the body and no longer needed, such as hair, menstrual blood, fingernails, etc. This is contagious magick.

On a small mirror place the personal item and a slip of paper with the person's name on it, and cover them with salt. Wrap the mirror and its contents with a black cloth and bury it at a crossroads at sunrise on the day of the Full Moon. You will surely be freed. This type of amulet magick is to be done in total secrecy.

PUT IT IN A JAR

As disgusting as this spell may appear, it is a traditional method used by various cultures over the centuries. The use of urine is an animalistic one, as animals are known to mark their territory with it and ward off trespassers.

Place three rusty nails (it is best if they are from an old barn) in a jar with the person's name who is slandering you written on a piece of paper. If it was possible, one was to procure a contagious magickal example, such as fingernail clippings. Sprinkle tobacco or gag root (the original spell called for nightshade) over the paper and nails. Pour in an ounce of vinegar. Urinate in the jar at midnight. Cap the bottle tightly, seal it with black wax, and shake it three times. Repeat the following chant each time you shake the jar, then bury it off of your property. Some Pow-Wows waited to bury it until the Waning Moon; however, having the jar around in my house for a full month would make me nervous.

> *Witches' jar, charm, and nail*
> *Banish evil, turn thy tail*
> *Protect me from mine enemies*
> *Sisters three watch out for me*
> *One is nail, the other herb*
> *The third about me protection girds.*
> *Take this hexer away from me.*
> *Deadly nightshade let them see*
> *Universal Light cover me*
> *As I will, so mote it be!*

If you really wanted to get down and dirty you would draw a pentacle on the floor, put a candle dressed with lamp black at each point, place the jar in the center of the pentacle, and say:

> *Glowing pentacle burn bright with light*
> *As shall (person's name) meet his own evil this night*
> *May he/she suffer what they sent to me*
> *Until I will to set them free.*
> *Cursed be mine enemy*
> *Sisters three watch out for me*
> *The first protects me*
> *The second rejects thee*
> *The third brings harmony back to me*
> *As I will, so mote it be!*

At first glance this appears to be black magick because of the use of the pentacle. Research tells us that the pentacle is not an evil symbol. The upright star enclosed within a circle stands for the four elements, the spirit of humanity, and the circle of the universe. It has been known throughout the ages as a protective mechanism, not a harmful one. The spell ensures turning back any evil without a doubt as to the intent. However, the spell gives a rider that once you feel they've had a good taste of their own medicine, you can stop it, unlike other spells that simply turn back and the heck with it. This spell was especially effective when done on a Full Moon, the Dark of the Moon, or during a lunar eclipse.

Now, you are thinking, when would I use such a spell? I'll be happy to give you an example. A friend of mine was accused of child molestation (which he didn't do). His accuser was actually the perpetrator of the crime and threw the blame on my friend in order to save his own skin. Needless to say, my Witch friend threw the situation right back into the kettle where it belonged and the actual criminal was subsequently arrested, tried, and put in jail. Although I have rarely used this spell, I can honestly tell you that it has worked for me every time.

Star It Out

One of the easiest ways to get rid of someone who is in your face is to envision a blazing blue pentacle on his or her forehead. In your mind, simply say, "I banish thee in the name of the positive powers of the universe!" I cannot tell you how many times this has worked for me. It even works on intoxicated individuals and those people who are taking both major prescription drugs and illegal ones.

Freeze It Out

One of the oldest Pow-Wow customs in my home town is "freezing out" the person who is bothering you or sending evil your way. Take a picture of the person or something that belongs to him or her and put it in a plastic freezer bag. If you can't find a picture or something personal, write the person's full name on a piece of paper and put that in the bag. Add a touch of vervain. Seal the bag and throw it into your freezer. Slam the door and say, "Chill out!" This works just about every time and is so popular with the ladies of my Circle that we get a kick out of listing who may be in our freezer this week! Fun aside, this is a totally harmless way to work with negative energy that is coming your way. It doesn't hurt anyone and neutralizes the situation. Granted, it is not "big guns" magick, but it fulfills a purpose when needed.

Stopping a Crime or Bringing a Criminal to Justice

There are many chants and spells to bring justice when harm has been done by a criminal act. This one makes a thief stand still so he or she can be caught.

> *I borrow the power from the Lord and the Lady.*
> *What I shall bind with Pagan hands shall be bound.*
> *All manner of thieves shall be spellbound by the Power of the Lady.*
> *And not be able to walk forward or backward until I see them with my*
> *own eyes and leave them with mine own tongue, except it be that they*

count for me all the stones that may be between heaven and earth, all raindrops, all the leaves and all the grasses in the world until they are caught by the authorities and repent to their God.
So mote it be.

By employing an infinite act, the Pow-Wow is actually controlling all avenues of escape, both within his or her own unconscious mind and that of the criminal. While reciting this spell, you should be walking. This is also a good spell to use if you are looking for someone or wish to see someone. Again, you are on the line here regarding ethics. However, there are always exceptions to the rule. Perhaps your child has been injured, or your husband is traveling and you want him to stay put so you can find him. In that case you would want to reword the spell for a softer result. Or, perhaps you could use this one on a hit-and-run case or some other criminal activity. In actuality you are not harming the person, you are simply taking away his or her travel papers.

This spell could manifest in the breakdown of the person's car or some other type of situation that would keep the criminal from escaping. It is wise to be careful and reword the spell should you not want to personally see the criminal. The Christian version of this incantation instructs the user to repeat the Lord's Prayer as well. One must also take into consideration that there were no "authorities" when the chant was originally written and it called for the thief to stand still until you could catch him or her yourself, not until the authorities got there.

There is also a "release" for this spell. Should the thief remain alive, the sun was not supposed to shine on him or her before the thief was let go by yourself, either by invoking St. John or by saying:

My words which have bound thee shall give thee freedom.

A variation for this spell is as follows:

Thus shall rule it by the Lady and the Lord. Thirty-three angels speak to each other coming to administer in the company of Aradia. "I have bound with a band through my mother Diana's hand; therefore, the thieves are bound even by the hand of my Father, her consort. If they have stolen mine own they shall stand still like a buck in the forest, they shall stand like a stake in the field and shall count all the stones upon the earth and the stars in the heavens, thus ruled by my Mother and Father. I command every spirit between the worlds to be master over this thief and he be burdened by the stolen goods or the money he shall receive thereafter. He canst remove from the spot as long as my tongue

*does not give him leave. This I command by the Holy Virgin, the Holy
Mother, and the Holy Wise Woman."*

To Catch a Thief in Progress

If you are unlucky (or lucky, depending upon your point of view) enough to
witness a crime, here is a way to stop the criminal:

*Thou driver and footman, you are coming under my lair, you are scat-
tered! Thy barrel, thy gun, and thy knife are bound; thy hands are
enchanted and bound. In the name of the Father, the Son, and the
Holy Ghost!*

This must be spoken three times.
If for some reason you decide to let the thief go (which makes one
wonder if this spell was used for a variety of purposes other than thieves—
like to catch the eye of an interesting young man or woman), you would say
the following:

*You driver and footman, whom I here conjured at this time, you may
pass on in the name of my God, through Her will and His word; drive
ye now and pass.*

Originally the word "driver" was "horseman," but envisioning a horseman robbing a bank these days would make the spell out of place by time.
A variation to this charm is as follows:

*There are three lilies standing upon the grave of mine ancestors. The
first is for courage, the other is for the blood of sacrifice, and the third
is for the will of the Lady. Stand still, thief! No more than did the inno-
cents free themselves from the burning pyres of the Witch finders, I command the four elements to hold thee still!*

This charm is much like the Triple Charms and could be written thus:

*Three sisters stood upon the grave of mine ancestors
Three lilies they beheld in their hands
The first sister said, "I am for courage"
The second replied, "I am for the blood of sacrifice"
And the third demanded, "Stand still, thief, for I am the will of the
Lady!"
And it is so.*

To Win at Every Game You Play

Tie the heart of a flittermouse (bat) with a red silk string to the right arm and you will win every card game you engage in. Since none of us have any desire to murder a bat to win a game, instead one could conjure the spirit essence of a bat and load it into the red string. Be sure you ask for permission first or there may be more bats in your belfry than you anticipated!

How to Relieve a Person Who Has Been Bewitched

Three false tongues have bound thee, three holy tongues have spoken for thee.
The First is the Maiden, the Second is the Mother, and the Third is the Crone.
They will give you blood, flesh, peace, and comfort down to thy bones.

To be "bewitched" may not necessarily mean the actual use of black magick, it can also be interpreted as someone who is being unduly influenced under a variety of circumstances. The old adage "love is blind" is not merely a saying. Often both women and men are fooled by what they wish to have rather than what they have actually managed to capture. "Wolf in sheep's clothing" is another good saying to nail down the point. This spell is useful to see the evil intent lurking underneath. There are a great many references to being bewitched, especially in the Hohman material (*Long Lost Friend*), which was presented to the public in 1820. It could be, then, that as early as 1800 there were individuals who feared the immigration of the elite Germans and the Hexmeisters because they knew darn well they had left them behind in the Old Country and it wasn't beyond them to come to the Americas, too.

How to Escape an Attack

I breathe upon thee.
Three drops of blood I take from thee—the first out of thy heart
The second from thy liver
And the third out of thy vital spirit.
In this I deprive thee of thy strength and thy manliness!

This spell was used both for physical and mental attack. If the banker was a bad guy and out to sell your land from under you, this spell would do the trick. Likewise, if you were walking home from the church social and Sam's hired hand was out to make a gift of your virginity to himself, you'd certainly put it to good use. Half the time just knowing the chant and yelling it out was enough to scare off the superstitious types.

The Takinoff

Perhaps the most well known of all the charms and spells used to get rid of evil or to cure infection and wasting away of the flesh was called the "takinoff," which meant "the taking off of negative vibrations or influences." One of the first things a Pow-Wow artist would do for you was this procedure, whether you were sick, unhappy, or just felt a little "off."

Often a skein of red yarn is kept handy to perform this spell. The person is to lie down on the floor on his or her stomach. The yarn is measured from the crown of the head to the heel, then down to the big toe and cut from the skein. The patient then sits in a chair and offers the Pow-Wow his or her foot. The length of yarn is measured on the sole of the foot seven times. If after the seventh time there is extra yarn, there is no evil on the patient. If, however, the measurement was short, there definitely was a problem. The yarn is burned to "take off" the malady. If the yarn was too long, it was burned anyway, "just in case."

Another way of performing the takinoff was to take a piece of red thread and measure the body of the afflicted from head to toe. Wrap it around your ankle or wrist, then walk around the kitchen table widdershins (counterclockwise) either the number of years you are or seven times. The string would be taken off the wrist or ankle and either thrown in the hearth to burn or given to the patient to take home and place in the hinge of a well used door. When the string was broken by the repeated motion of the hinge, the spell (or whatever badness ailed you) would be taken off.

Although this may be thought of as a silly practice, its roots go very deep in our ancestry. When a Witch is initiated into the mysteries, he or she is measured by a length of cord. This cord usually stays with the coven until you either die or move. The cord was used to call you in times of danger and keep you from ratting on your fellow coven members. If you were solitary, the cord was given to you and you were to care for it until you died, leaving instructions that it was to be buried with you. The cords were also used in handfasting ceremonies, where the two were joined to create the marriage entity, or symbolically bound together to cause a major change for the covendom.

In almost every interview I conducted for the research of this book, I was told about the procedure of the takinoff. It was used to take weight off, put weight on, get rid of an illness, get rid of bad influences, send back evil to whomever was plaguing you, cleanse your aura of psychic debris, etc. It was an all-purpose practice that could manifest a variety of outcomes.

Many of the chants and spells in this book were plugged into the practice of the takinoff, though it was rarely used with charms for stopping blood or healing burns—those spells were considered powerful enough on their own. Besides, in such emergency cases, who has time to run for red thread and start running around the kitchen table? A good chant for the takinoff is:

> *Turner be turned*
> *Burner be burned*
> *Angels of light*
> *Assist my plight*

The takinoff is a marvelous icebreaker with groups or new people coming to see you. It is fun, you laugh a lot (especially if you have many people doing it), and they all feel great after it is done, including you. I have had a large number of students who have practiced this procedure with both success and smiles.

To Make Your Enemy Your Friend

Have you ever met a person who just seems to hate you at first sight and does his or her very best to ensure that your life henceforth is miserable? What is really amazing is that you think you would really like that person if he or she didn't hate you so much. Take a brown clay or enamel bowl or jar and fill it with brown sugar. Sprinkle the top with basil (known to cause sympathy between warring factions). Write the person's name on a piece of paper and bury it in the mixture. Draw a solar (equal-armed) cross in the mixture and put a brown candle in the middle.

> *Thine cussedness I will overcome*
> *In days of nine with the setting sun*
> *I'll have thy friendship in my hand*
> *Through thick and thin it will stand.*
> *I choose not to harm but to heal the wound*
> *Love comes now by the Witches' Tune!*
> *So be it!*

A Triple Charm to Bind and Bring Justice

This charm (from *Old Norse Charms, Spoken Spells and Rhymes* by Thor and Audrey Sheil) requires a piece of red yarn. As each sister is invoked, a knot is tied. The yarn will be knotted nine times by the end of the spell.

> *Three sisters came across the land*
> *Each held cords in her hands*

The first one found him/her
The second one bound him/her
The third one dragged him/her away.

This charm has a bizarre story attached to the first time I employed it. We live in an area of low crime, so when something outlandish does happen, everyone is all in a flutter. One summer the news hit the paper and air waves that a young woman had been raped by several men at a local shopping mall in broad daylight. We were all aghast, of course, and our ire was truly up. What to do?

When people ask me about working for situations where permission cannot be granted by the supposed recipient, I tell them the following things.

First, if it is a situation in which you would mundanely assist the individual, then using your magickal skills is not inappropriate. For example, if you see a crime in progress and are the type of person who would do something about it, whether by calling the police or rushing in yourself, then working magick in the same instance would be acceptable. It is a part of you, and therefore a skill you have learned. If you are the type of person who would simply look the other way, magick should not be employed.

Second, if you want to help someone but are unable to ask his or her permission, you can call upon the astral guardians of that person and ask their permission to work for the person. If your spell or formula does not work, then permission was denied. A case in point here would be a person in a coma who certainly can't be contacted in the mundane sense.

Our circle decided to work on catching the perpetrators of the rape. In a ceremony the night before, I asked the guardians of the young woman and of the men to allow the working to take place. I put some heavy energy into the entire ritual using the chant above. The next evening, our circle worked for justice.

A few months went by and nothing was heard. People were afraid to go to the shopping center. It was on the news about how lax security was there and the whole thing just balled into a general mess. Members of the circle would often ponder on what had happened to "our work." There was no answer, until one day, the horrendous news came. The young woman hadn't been raped at all! She admitted the entire escapade was a hoax! We were flabbergasted and angry. There are enough women in the world who find themselves entangled in the violence of a rape experience who have a terrible time proving their innocence (as if they were the criminals in the first place). Then, to have someone lie about such an awful thing was inconceivable to us.

However, justice (which is what we called for with this spell) was most definitely done. The real crime came to light—the young woman's treachery.

Dealing with Fear

Fear, when you are in danger, can definitely be a mind-killer. There is one particular phrase that pops up often in both Pow-Wow and Craft texts:

I stand in circles of light that nothing may cross.

It is simple, and it works beautifully whether you are out for normal protection magick or feel that you are in the line of immediate attack.

To Stop a Dangerous Storm

Mimic the cooing sound of a dove three times, then repeat this charm thrice. End it with a second succession of cooing sounds.

Morrighan, Morrighan hear my cry
Turn this storm—let it pass me by.
Morrighan, Morrighan in the sky
Turn thy tempest to blue sky.

My family and I have used and tested a great many of the charms in this book and you will find that most of the material has been run under some type of experiment. The very day I was working on transcribing the Morrighan spell for this chapter, a rather nasty storm blew up. Normally I like storms, thunder, lightning and all that jazzy stuff. On this particular early evening, both my daughters were at cheerleading and drill practice in an open field and I felt we could dispense with such a show for just one day.

A friend of mine called me and said, "You know, they were predicting winds of 50 miles per hour over here [she is 16 miles away from me], and it is really carrying on. There is lightning and thunder just horrible and, frankly, I'm afraid to be on the phone. I just figured you were probably working and not paying attention to the news service. So, if any of your kids are out, get them in!"

I looked outside and sure enough, it was black. My girls were outside at the school and I was worried I wouldn't make it in time. I called out this spell in the required manner and sped to the school. There was plenty of time for me to pick them up before it hit, but as groups go, whoever was in charge was indecisive, hoping it would blow over and refusing to dismiss the girls. Although I was rather irritated at the time, being there under the cover of a concrete overhang allowed me to watch the most spectacular cloud movements I have ever seen. I have never seen a storm billow clouds so blackly in such unique patterns. The entire time I was chanting the spell in my head, hoping that if it didn't turn the storm away, it would at least limit its effects. Sure enough, we got a good thirty-minute downpour, but there was no wind at all and only three half-hearted bolts of lightning. We were all finally dismissed. An hour later, we were graced with a brilliant blue sky and a beautiful sunset.

The weather appeared to be particularly bleak during our town Harvest Festival. On the first night of the festival, the children march down the street in what is known as the Baby Parade. Since my kids were in the parade I had no desire to see them march home with a cold. Again I used the Morrighan spell and although the air "felt" like a storm, the main street of the town remained dry as a bone. Jean Kitzig was coming into town from the highway. She walked in my door and said, "You were at it again, huh? I know 'cos it is raining and sleeting on the other side of the highway and on this side it's dry as the desert! You can literally stand on this side of the highway, Silver, and watch a wall of rain!" After the parade was over, I released the Morrighan and lost one of my favorite handmade Halloween decorations. It blew off my door and shattered into several pieces. Guess she was trying to tell me something—like don't mess with the weather if it's not an emergency and that I owed her one. I didn't use it again after that time. It's a good thing, too, because some idiot would have tried to blame me for the tornado that tore through the area about a month later.

When People Think You're into Bad Magick

Once you really get involved in magick, whether it be Pow-Wow, Witchcraft, Druidism, etc., the word gets around. There is only so much you can do to control gossip. Your prime directive is to become involved in as many community functions as you can so people get to know you first and learn about your religion later. When they do discover that you deal with magick, most of them really don't care. It is hoped they like you for who you are and the good things you have done for the community rather than listening to half-truths whispered over the backyard fence.

The problem here is you can't know everyone on a first-name basis, and sooner or later some schmuck is going to harass you because of your faith. Although there is such a thing as freedom of religion in the United States, this edict is not faithfully followed by all its citizens. Sometimes situations arise by accident and mushroom into something far more dangerous. For example, last summer I needed to do an interview for the newspaper I work for and I arranged for a babysitter to come and stay with my kids for an hour or so. An hour before I was getting ready to leave, my oldest daughter came into the living room and told me that two brothers that lived down the street heard a babysitter was coming to watch the children (news travels fast on the block beat), and because she was an attractive teen known to them, they were planning on coming up to my house after I left to harass her.

At the time, I didn't realize my daughter had a friend with her. (My face was buried in my computer screen.) "Not if I have anything to do about it!" I snapped, and never turned around. "Tell them if they step one foot on my property they'll wish they never breathed because I'll call their parents." The girl who was with my daughter never stuck around long enough to hear the "I'll call their parents" part of the conversation. When I got back from the interview all the kids were in a tizzy. "Guess what! Guess what!" exclaimed the visiting little girl. "Remember that kid and his brother who were going to come here and bother the babysitter?"

Yes, I remembered, and asked if they ever showed up. I was greeted with a chorus of "no's" with very big eyes. "So what happened?" I asked. Well, it appears that one brother came down with a case of appendicitis and the kids in the neighborhood were now blaming me for it. Oh, for heaven's sake. Unfortunately, the story did not stop here. There was a little girl on our block who played that story up for all it was worth, making my children miserable. She spread rumors all over the place about how we were all devil worshippers and did things to hurt children. I was vitally offended as I adore children and would never think of harming them. After all, I have four of my own, and they are breathing, well-fed, and happy. As summer moved into fall, I found that she was in one daughter's class at school, where her harassment continued. Luckily for us, we know many people in our town and the false tales from the little girl fell on deaf ears. However, it certainly reminds one of how the Salem mess really started—from the mouths of spiteful little girls.

Such incidents as this can hurt your feelings very badly, especially if you spend a great deal of your personal time helping and healing your friends and neighbors. It may be a free country, but magickal people are still subject to harassment from uneducated and fearful souls. The major lesson here is not to be mean and spiteful in return. Some of the women of my circle have had similar experiences, wherein they have been blamed for the mishaps of other people. One fellow was harassing a circle lady about her chosen religion and ended up in an auto wreck two days later. He blamed it on her, not the fact that he was intoxicated while driving.

A third incident began in a humorous vein but ended up rather sadly. One Halloween I took my kids trick-or-treating. My eldest girl decided to stay home and give out the candy as she felt she was too old to go door-to-door anymore. By 7:30 PM, we were just about done. My three other kids and a friend went to a house at the bottom of our street. I was standing on the corner waiting for them. Halloween is my favorite holiday (of course), and I was dressed as a witch with a skull face and carrying my youngest son's plastic pumpkin packed with candy.

I saw three boys go to our house, one carrying a musical instrument, then they meandered down toward me. They stopped at the curb across from me, picked up rocks, and threw them at me. They missed and hit my pumpkin. I was appalled. Talk about bad breeding! I had heard other instances earlier in the evening from passing parents about older kids throwing rocks at the little kids. In our small town I felt this was inconceivable. It also pissed me off.

So, as the third rock hit my pumpkin, I couldn't resist.

I hunched over and brayed, "I know who you are and I saw what you did!" (Remember that movie?)

Then I pointed my finger at them. "Keep thy nose to the ground! Goddess made thee and hound!"

Instead of running they stood there, opened-mouthed, staring at me. (It didn't hit me why until I realized what charm I had used and what it is for—to make dogs stand still. Well, I guess if people are acting like a pack of wild dogs, the charm works for them, too.) Finally, the bravest of the three said, "Who are you?"

"It doesn't matter who I am," I cackled. "But I know who you are!"

They still didn't move, but they didn't pick up any more rocks, either.

"Be gone!" I yelled, and they bolted.

When I got home, I asked my daughter who the kids were and she gave me their names. One of them was in her class at school. "Well, when you get to school on Monday," I said, "tell that kid I didn't appreciate him throwing rocks at me." I figured that if he knew who I really was, he wouldn't be frightened. He would also know that an adult had seen him who could identify the boys, and therefore would think twice about doing such cruel things again. My mistake.

On Monday, my daughter gave him the message, and he sputtered and stammered how sorry he was. I considered the matter closed.

Not so.

A week later he approached my daughter while she was at her locker. "My grandma died yesterday, and I know your mom did it!" he shrieked at her.

Geez, cut me a break, will ya?

My daughter was upset and wanted to know what to do about it. "Nothing," I said. "The child was dealing with two very stressful situations. First, he got caught doing something he shouldn't have and felt guilty and worried that I would call his parents. It is obvious he and his friends were the ones throwing rocks at the little children and he knew it was wrong. When his grandmother died, he tried to rationalize his guilt onto someone else—primarily me—which is ridiculous, but I can see how it happened. When someone close to you dies unexpectedly, you often try to blame someone for the loss of their love, whether it be the doctor, the hospital, the medical care in the ambulance, a member of the family, or in my case, the Witch who called him out."

However, I bet that kid won't be throwing rocks next Halloween.

South
Fertility
Creativity
Harvest
Abundance
Sun Energy
Designed by Silver RavenWolf

Pow~Wows and the Animal Connection

On the Issue of Familiars

The relationship between Pow-Wows and animals was as diverse as the magickal practice itself. Some saw them as friends and confidants (the storybook type of familiar), and others saw them as something to "use" to gain a specific end. There were those who thought only of animals when "control" was an issue, and of course animals were also thought of in the veterinary sense. Finally, there were Pow-Wows who didn't deal with animals at all.

First, I'd like to clear up the familiar issue. There are two types of familiars in magick—those of the breathing, earth plane, animal variety, and those of the conjuration variety. Something conjured may not necessarily be an animal—it could be anything from a griffin or a unicorn to a demon. It also can be a normal-type animal—the pet you had and loved for fifteen years, or the collective unconscious of a particular species. If anyone tries to tell you that indigenous peoples, Witches, or Pow-Wows didn't have familiars, this is not true.

Real Animals

Animals were considered an important part of Pow-Wow magick, and were both used and healed. For example, eggs laid on Friday were used by the

Pow-Wow for magickal and healing purposes. Some German folk of the times believed that if you named your pet dog "water" or "fire," it could not be charmed by one with evil intentions. Again we see the water/fire theory of the Heathen Germans. Most Pow-Wows did not bond with live animals. Yes, they had pets and livestock, but most did not consider the flesh and blood animal to be magickal while it was breathing. Notice I said "while it was breathing." There was a certain group of Pow-Wow artists who killed animals, just so they could use special parts of them.

For example, tying a bat's heart to your arm to be the winning gambler of the evening or smushing up a frog, drying it, and putting a little of this and a little of that into the mixture to create a substance that could open any lock or win the heart of the opposite sex. These people were great for slaughtering chickens and messing with the blood and feathers. At no time do the words "ritual killing" or "sacrifice" rear their little heads in historical documentation. This, to me, means that the animal was killed without honor—obviously these people were not a part of the ethical magickal crowd. There are other ways to achieve the same end without harming an animal—or a person, for that matter. However, before you think badly of the Pow-Wow, please consider there were no local occult stores to supply materials. Nor was there a local arts and crafts shop where items like black feathers, parchment paper, or red ink could be purchased. If you wanted something, you had to make it yourself. The Pow-Wow was more practical and operated from that mindset.

Those Pow-Wows who did have air-breathing, tail-wagging familiars were mostly individuals with the heritage of the indigenous peoples of America somewhere in their family line. They would often talk to animals, feed and care for the wildlife around their homes, and of course, bond with a special one or two.

Live Animal Bonding

Bonding with an animal, should the animal be cooperative, is not as difficult as you may think. You just need to take some time to do it. It is best done when the animal is between six months and two years old, but can occur after the age of two. First, you should be the primary care-giver to the animal. That means you are responsible for feeding it, giving it water, making sure it is trained properly in the mundane sense, etc. The animal must be healthy and well-adjusted. It needs to know that it is much loved. Don't be disappointed if the animal does not wish to cooperate with you on the bonding process. You may choose a familiar for yourself and instead it may favor your oldest daughter, your spouse, or another individual in an extended family environment. Familiars choose you, you don't choose them.

Pow-Wows and the Animal Connection

The basic procedure is a simple one with only one exception—it must be performed every night from Moon to Moon. If you begin at Full Moon then you must continue until the next one, and so on. With the animal either on your lap or at your side (whichever is comfortable for the species), ground and center yourself. Speak softly and tell the animal that you wish to bond with it and why. Shut your eyes and hold your hand over the body of the animal. Do not put your hand directly over its head; most animals dislike that intensely and will flinch no matter how much they adore you. With your eyes closed, feel the energy of the animal. Is it quick, cunning, smooth, wild? Very slowly, move your conscious mind into the body of the animal. Don't overtake its thought process—simply feel its existence. Sit quietly for a few moments and allow the animal to meld with your consciousness, then gently remove yourself (don't jerk away). Offer endearing words and perhaps a treat. This is one aspect of shapeshifting. Once the animal is comfortable sharing consciousness with you, you can call it to you by imagining it is in front of you and moving your mind into the creature's, calling its name. After a few trial runs, the animal will usually appear by your side.

The final "familiar" test is judging the reaction of the animal while you are working magick or healing. If the animal comes immediately by your side during the operation or sits directly outside the cast circle, you've got a winner. If it is totally disinterested and leaves the magickal area to snooze on the sofa in the living room, try a different animal.

I'd like to make a note here on direct eye contact. Wild animals and animals trained to attack will do so after prolonged direct eye contact. For some species this reaction is inbred, in others it is trained. So, before you look soulfully into that bear's eyes, consider if you'd like to keep all your body parts. There were Pow-Wows who did use direct eye contact to control wild animals and train pets; however, rest assured they were chanting their brains out under their breath or doing controlled mental techniques at the same time. If you intend to meld with animals in the wild, you can contact them from a distance. They do not need to be in your lap or by your side. By not attempting to touch them, you are honoring their wildness. In time, if they so choose, they will come to you. Please do not try melding with a wild animal during hunting season. Should the animal be killed, either by accident or on purpose, legend has it that you too may suffer the same fate, or at least some unfortunate side effects.

Alchemical Animals

Until the 1900s, most Pow-Wows believed in alchemical animals—today they are known as power animals or totems—whether they were born with the heritage of the indigenous peoples of the New World or with the German blood of the Old World, or often, both. An alchemical (power) animal holds special qualities in its collective unconscious that harmonize with the human of its choice. Power animals were (and are) friends, allies, protectors, healers, and messengers. It was not unusual for a person to have more than one species in resonance with his or her vibrations. Granted, some humans were better at connecting with power animals than others.

Alchemical pursuits were a great favorite of the Pow-Wow in the eighteenth and nineteenth centuries, and the topic was discussed in their theosophical and philosophical circles almost as much as astronomy and astrology. It was believed that to own the animal's skin was a primary function of shapeshifting and was used to call on the collective unconscious of the species—this is a type of alchemy, as the word means transmutational process. Often these people would use the spirit of one animal to overcome the spirit of another, reckoning themselves as the predator and their enemy the prey.

For example, if Jacob the Pow-Wow was cheated at market by Irwin Snyder, he may have gone home and performed a small ritual in which he would invoke the spirit of the wolf to represent himself and the spirit of a sheep to represent good old thieving Irwin. During the incantation, Jacob would throw a wolf skin over one of a lamb or sheep to symbolize his dominance over Irwin and cement a successful outcome to the situation—primarily that of Irwin paying up and making amends.

Although one may wish to entirely credit the indigenous peoples for the German usage of alchemical animals, such is not the case, as this practice was popular in Europe as far back as the time of Plato. However, I'm sure the beliefs of the Native Americans left no doubt in the Pennsylvania Germans' mind about the validity of the practice. After all, they were two absolutely separate societies that evolved without knowledge of each other, yet came together with many of the same mystical beliefs—including those regarding alchemical animals.

Animal Attributes

Although the Pow-Wow artist adapted well to the surrounding flora and often found reasonable substitutes in herbal work, he or she was not so quick to give up tried-and-true alchemical animals. After all, you could take them anywhere and it didn't cost you anything to keep them, nor did they require a specific habitat for survival. Often you will find spells for lions, vultures, and even elephants mixed in with those animals that were native to the New World such as asses, wolves, fox, sheep, and chickens.

The appearance and movements of animals were considered omens which could be favorable or unfavorable, depending upon the interpretation.

Pow-Wows and the Animal Connection

It can take years of study to excel at this, but you can become quite proficient by watching the animals in your locale for a few seasons. The following list covers a few of the animals used in Pow-Wow magick and the type of mystical associations they represented.

Bat: A bat was thought to bring good luck for participating in games of chance. Bat magick was also used to "see in the dark" and to see things in the astral. Bat and cat magick mixed together assured one the second sight as well as heightened intuition.

Chicken: Because cocks and hens were so plentiful, they were used often in Pow-Wow magick. Eggs, as mentioned before, were used to break hexes and dispel disease. The cock was often considered a bold bunch of feathers, and when the need arose for one to cast that cocky appearance, this bird was used. The black feathers of chickens were used to break hexes and ward off evil. Egg whites poured into a small mold and allowed to harden for one month were called Topacious Stones.

Distelfink: Although it once represented a real bird (the golden finch), its stylized variation appears on many Pennsylvania Dutch arts and crafts and was considered a bird of good luck and good fortune. The distelfink was also known as the thistlefinch because it ate thistle seed and used the thistle down in its nest. Two were often painted opposite each other to double one's luck. My grandmother Baker painted numerous distelfinks and tulips on her furniture. These items sat in her home for over fifty years.

Dove: The dove was used in two types of magick: that for love and for bringing about and predicting weather. Pictures of doves were stylistically drawn to bring happiness into a marriage or to bring two lovers together, representing harmony and peaceful surroundings. They were also used to resolve marital spats and disagreements. Dove feathers, as well as those of sparrows and swallows, were ground and used in conjuring bags for the same effect. To see doves in the morning meant a fine, clear day. If the day was stormy and you needed good weather, you would walk through your fields or to the top of a small hill, cooing in the face of the wind like a dove, using your breath to turn back the storm.

Eagle: You will find many portrayals of the eagle, a symbol of responsible power, in Pow-Wow magick and the Pennsylvania Dutch lifestyle. They were painted on furniture, used to decorate birth and baptismal certificates, found on quilts, and incorporated into hex signs. Eagles were proud, strong, and free. They represented the dreams of the New World, spiritual power, and heightened spirituality. Stylized double-headed eagles were often used in hex designs to promote double strength in courage, especially in a marriage. Alchemical eagle magick was used in making sound decisions and choosing the right path or type of magick to use.

Frog: The frog was said to be able to delineate one's true soul. In mundane magick, he was used (quite literally) to open locks and turn back hexes as well as control the weather. In alchemical magick he was a discerner of truth and connected with lunar energies.

Lion: The alchemical lion was extremely popular as he represented strength, bravery, and boldness. Placing the skin of this animal between the eyes or at the heart and looking into a mirror was done to bring these qualities into the spirit of the Pow-Wow. The only animal magick that could overtake lion magick was that of the cock.

Mule: The magick of the mule could make both men and women barren of offspring and property. Therefore, Pow-Wows did not keep mules on their property.

Nightingale: The nightingale was said to create eloquence and enable one to speak on just about any topic without appearing foolish. Feathers of this bird were used in conjuring bags for this purpose, or placed in a favorite book of poems or scriptures that traveled with the Pow-Wow. The feathers of a nightingale were said to move one to tears, to melt hearts of ice, and to be an aid in arguing issues where an injustice needed to be corrected.

Owl: The owl was considered extraordinarily wise, but it was also the pathway to any alchemical animal magick. The owl was often invoked or consulted before other animals were considered or used. To have an owl outside your window was a signal that it was time to work magick for wisdom.

Raven: The raven is really a very big crow, and was considered the messenger between the worlds. The owl, as mentioned earlier, represented the gate or guardian; the raven had the capability to bring messages from the astral to the Pow-Wow. Raven magick also assists in breaking down fears and dominating an unpleasant situation through the use of magick. Feathers of the raven were often placed in conjuring bags for shapeshifting, divination, and manipulating spiritual laws in the physical realm.

Unicorn: Unicorns were seen as the traditional symbol of purity (as only a virgin could capture one), and were often drawn on birth certificates to ward off evil and impure thoughts that may be set against the child.

Vulture: The vulture was used as a spy and invoked for wisdom. In Egypt, the vulture was respected and honored as one who carried great intuitive prowess as well as logical and fair thought. Vultures were also the guardians of herb magick.

Wolf: The wolf was seen as a protector as well as a predator. Pow-Wows were careful with wolf magick so as not to induce a werewolf scare. Many Pennsylvania Dutch believed werewolves to be left behind in the Old Country, and this was one legend/superstition that they wished to avoid if at all possible. Unlike many of the magickal animals listed here, the wolf did not appear in drawings or hex signs. Records show a great many spells for calling off wild dogs and it could be that these spells were originally designed to call off wolves in Germany and later in America. Wolf magick was primarily used in predatory spells—not meaning black magick, but used to balance an injustice.

Amulets

An amulet is an object that protects you from harm and can be made from anything found in nature or manufactured. Unlike the talisman, which is often designed to pull things toward you, the amulet's main function is to push energies away from you. If the amulet is natural, like a bear tooth or wolf claw, it is believed to have a power of its own, not power that you have instilled in it through ceremony. However, amulets work best if you meld your energies with what it represents to achieve the height of protection. Amulet magick is not considered "big guns" magick. Usually it is for short-term functions, like when you visit your mother-in-law and you don't feel like dealing with her rabid mouth because it gives you a headache. You might grab a red scarf as you go out the door and empower it to last for the length of your visit (which you hope will be as short as possible). Amulet magick can be timed so that the protective or healing function lasts for a few hours to a few days. The longest time for empowerment of an amulet is from one Moon cycle to another. Then the amulet will have to be refreshed or buried with honor.

Parts of animals—such as claws, teeth, and horns—were thought to contain magickal properties of their own. For instance, if a child was in the throes of teething, one tooth was to be taken from a three-year-old horse and hung about the child's neck on a red string. This was sure to cure the pain that was believed to be brought on by a malevolent spirit. To get rid of a mouse, take the hoof of a horse and place it in your kitchen. Wolves' teeth were coveted amulets to the Pow-Wow as they were thought to bring both protection and great power to the wearer. Fox tails were hung from the rafters of the attic to bring prosperity into the home and empower the owners with cunning in business deals.

It is presumed that one must believe in the amulet for it to work. Faith is the "start button." Without pushing the button of belief, the amulet simply wouldn't perform. Normally, amulets are thought to be protective in nature; however, the Pow-Wow often used them for healing purposes as well in an effort to push negative energy away from the client. Hexmeisters were known to use saltpeter as an amulet of protection, though in most cases it was primarily used for show, and of course the Braucher (herb doctor) used herbs for amulets as well. The Christianized version of Pow-Wow was fairly quiet about the use of animal magick, and as the system moved into the 1900s little was said about animals other than to cure them of diseases. Stories from local sources continue to support the use of animal magick by the descendants of indigenous people to the present day.

The Web of the Wyrrd: Divination

Earlier in this text we talked a bit about the Sisters of the Wyrrd (also known as the Norns). You are invoking these Sisters when you work with the runes. Hence, the chants called Triple Charms relate specifically to this interesting trilogy of archetypes. Although each individual has a personal life-tapestry fashioned by the Sisters, each tapestry is also woven into the universe and can be thought of as much like the Akashic records of the famed Arthur Ford. If you are of Germanic descent, it is believed that it is easier for you to tap into the Web of the Wyrrd and access information through what Thor Sheil of Trollwise Press calls the "folk soul," though many magicians believe that those of Celtic descent and practices have equal access.

The Sisters of the Wyrrd had unique names and personality traits. Urd represented the past and is the oldest of the three. She is viewed as the most experienced and knowledgeable of the Sisters because of her age. In the Craft, she would represent the Crone or Hecate. It was she who received the souls of the dead. Her color is white.

Verdandi, the second Sister, represents the present. Her color is red. She is a maternal figure and in the Craft would be akin to the Mother image, such as Diana or Rhiannon. The third and youngest of the Sisters is Skuld. Her color is black. She rules the future, symbolizing the Maiden and choices to be made. We could see her as Persephone or perhaps the Morrighan. She is the destroyer, because she removes the future from humans by cutting the thread of life.

I agree with Freya Aswynn in her book *Leaves of Yggdrasil* wherein she states that the Sisters are rather underestimated in modern Odinist and

Heathen literature. Clearly the Pow-Wows thought them important indeed, as many of their charms called on the assistance of the Norns. As mentioned earlier, the Sisters each have their own color: white, red, and black. Assignment of the colors to one Sister or another depends on the historical source. Some believe that Urd's color is black, followed by Verdandi with red and Skuld with white. Others assign white to Urd, red to Verdandi, and black to Skuld. Remember that the Pow-Wows used only three colors in their magickal practices—mostly white and red, and sometimes black. No other colors were employed in basic magickal practices. The only exception are the hex signs, but we'll cover them later.

Perhaps the original basis for Pow-Wow, beyond German Witchcraft, is descended from a magickal system that revolved around the Norns. We have concluded that Pow-Wow was German Witchcraft filled with country magickal practices and folk remedies. We have also pretty much determined that German Witchcraft is derived from Odinist, Teutonic, and/or Heathen principles. Would it be so odd to believe that these three Sisters were far more popular than our modern historians have led us to believe?

We know that many religions began with matriarchal intent and slowly flipped to patriarchal dominance. However, Odinist, Teutonic, and Heathen principles are structured with more balance between the male/female energies. Perhaps the Norns were the original matriarchal Triple Goddess of those cultures. When the idea of a balanced system came along, they were transformed into the Goddess Freya/Frigga, who also stands for Witchcraft. I told you this book would give you something to debate. You doubted me—ha! But sometimes what may seem the most ridiculous is the most logical.

If you enjoy working with archetypal forms, the Norns make an excellent connection to the Pow-Wow system. Candles of white, red, and black can be placed on your altar to draw the energies of the Sisters into your work. Meditation practices can be employed to meet each Sister and gather valuable information and insights regarding difficulties you may face in your life. I have found the Sisters very valuable in relation to people problems. I often light the three colored candles, sit before the altar, and talk to the Norns about difficulties or confusing behavioral patterns exhibited by strangers and friends alike. Sometimes I petition the Sisters by writing down exactly how I see a situation and place this synopsis on the altar overnight, or even for a few days, until I receive the answer or solution I need.

Perhaps the most unusual use of the Norns in my life comes from my experimentation in astral travel and bi-location techniques. Briefly, this is the ability of the spirit (astral) or the mind (bi-location) to travel anywhere in time or place while the body remains stationary, in either a meditative or sleep state. If you wish to contact someone who may not be too thrilled at your presence, you can work with the Sisters first to ensure that you are operating along ethical lines. For example, let's say your boss is really giving you a bad time. No matter how hard you try, you can't figure out his reasoning. Your job performance has been good, you haven't used much sick time, and you are not the office gossip. Nevertheless, you've been catching flack. After you have considered all your options, you may feel that an astral visit to set the record straight is necessary. This is when you would meditate at your altar and call upon the Norns to determine the ethical procedure for contact.

First, light the three candles (white, red, and black). Breathe deeply several times until you are calm, grounded, and centered, as in a healing exercise. Imagine yourself encased in a big blue bubble. If you like, do the Lesser Banishing Ritual as given in the Appendix. In your mind, call upon the Sisters and wait until they appear in your meditation state. Don't feel foolish. Talk to them; it is not silly. Tell them what is troubling you and that you would like to visit Mr. Grump in the astral to set the record straight. You must give your word that you will not coerce the grump. You simply wish the time and ability to discover the root of the problem and tell him how you feel. Let the Sisters now show you the tapestry of the universe. To me it appears as a giant web, with the astral lines of each human connected here and there, as they are connected in life. One of the Sisters may show you the line to the person whom you wish to contact. Gently take hold of that line and follow it until you reach the essence of Mr. Grump. The Sisters will travel with you.

Tell Mr. Grump exactly how you feel; if you like, ask him to reveal to you what the difficulty may be. Remember to ask politely. In this way you are not inhibiting Mr. Grump's free will. I don't think the Norns would be especially open to future requests for their help, should you go back on your word. When you are through, count up from your meditative state from one to ten, then open your eyes and tell yourself you are wide awake and feeling good. Thank the Norns and resume your normal routine.

Ancient Germans and Divination

After A.D. 743, divination was illegal in Germany. The practice didn't stop because of the new laws, but it simply went underground as most magickal practices are apt to do at one time or another. Those in power at the time felt that the people were relying too heavily on the fortunetelling process. This is not an illogical mode of thought. Today, there are many bogus fortunetellers who will fleece you by taking advantage of your fears and troubles. Of course, not all fortunetellers (or diviners) are like that, but if someone starts asking your for your bank account number or requesting a payment of $500 to remove that negative spell that your sister-in-law put on you—head for the door. One cannot use a divinatory system to determine every move to be made. This is silly. Divination should be saved for important matters that you have already pondered extensively, not whether you should go to the bathroom at 1:00 or 3:15.

Through the information given to us by the Roman writer Tacitus, we are told that the ancient Germanic peoples often used the practice of casting lots to determine the outcome of a situation. Sometimes the situation called for the settlement of an argument or a choice in battle plans. Lots were also used to determine the sacrifice for a particular ritual. The lots themselves were made each time from the bark of a tree and carved with various symbols, then cast upon a white cloth. The act of divination was considered a religious practice and the energies of the divine were drawn down (or up, as the case may be) through both brief and complex rituals performed by the older women of the tribe. The observance of the heavens, weather patterns, and the movements of animals were often consulted for divinatory purposes. To divine was not to "fortune tell." Divining was a truly religious experience in which the seer would petition Divinity on how to proceed in important life matters. Lot casting was a serious act, and done with much pomp and fanfare. The runes are an example of tools for lot casting.

Basic Overview of the Runes

I purchased my first set of runes in 1986 and have been using them in various magickal and divinatory applications since that time. My introduction to the runes wasn't even my idea. I was reading the Tarot at the time and a fellow occultist mentioned that she normally didn't read the cards for herself. She preferred the runes for personal divination and recommended that I buy a set and see what I could do with them. Since that time many wonderful books have hit the market concerning these magickal little sigils. Even so, you can't believe everything you read about the runes in the historical sense as they are modernized to fit the present day. Most of the information is extrapolation. Pow-Wows did indeed employ the vast powers of this magickal system in both healing and folk practices. Runes were drawn on plants, on the ground, and especially in the air over a client.

In personal study, I have found the runes to be most beneficial. Although I use them for divination, their capabilities for enabling you to control your environment through dreamscaping, vision questing, and magick are astounding. The word "rune" means "mystery." Unlike the Tarot and other divinatory tools, the runes are an integral part of a religious system and have their own pantheon of Gods and Goddesses. There are three main pantheons that can be attributed to the runes: Nordic (such as Odinists), English (the Celtic and Druidic peoples—Anglo-Saxon), and German. Each alphabet has specific names and characteristics that are given to the sigils and deities. To appreciate the runes fully, you should delve deeply into their corresponding pantheons. This doesn't mean that you must know all about these religious systems to begin your work with runes. When I began my personal study, I knew very little about the pantheons that encompassed them, yet I was still highly successful with their use.

According to Donald Tyson (author of *Rune Magic,* Llewellyn Publications), there are three main branches of the runes. The oldest rune alphabet is the German futhark of 24 runes. This is the root from which all later rune alphabets sprang. In England, this ancient German futhark was expanded, first to 28 runes, and later to 33 runes (the original 24 German runes, with 4 or 9 new ones.). Around the same time the German runes were being expanded in England, they were being contracted in Scandinavia into the 16-rune reduced Norse futhark, which had two main forms, the Danish and the Swedish-Norwegian. Both types of Scandinavian rune alphabets have 16 runes, but the shapes of some of these runes differ between the alphabets. "Each of these three main rune alphabets," says Donald Tyson, "has its own name variants for the runes it contains. At root, all rune alphabets are based on the 24-rune German futhark, but they have been modified to meet the linguistic needs of the people using them."

The runes are a specific system of magickal writing and their age is about as old as the hills (which I feel is more truth than cliché), meaning no one really knows how old they are. The cultures from which they sprung were wild, brazen, and strong, not refined like those of the Egyptians. Perhaps this is why they are so successful—they are uncorrupted by civilization. I deal with 24 runes, with each corresponding to a phonetic sound, its own divinatory meaning, its own deity, and its own magickal use. In my opinion, the runes are far more powerful as a magickal vehicle than the Tarot. They also mix exceedingly well with other tools.

The Germanic runes (those that are usually most familiar) are called the Elder Futhark. This name is based on the sequence of the rune row in its fixed order (F-U-Th-A-R-K), much like saying A B C D E, etc. The futhark is divided into three sections, or aettir. Each section, or aett, consists of eight runes in a fixed order. The first aett deals with deities and their dominion, the second corresponds with necessary forces to bring about change, and the third deals with conditions, usually human in nature.

Bind Runes

Bind runes are a very important aspect of the runic system, especially where magick is employed. A bind rune is created when two or more runes are drawn together to bring about a desired outcome, such as protection, banishment, or movement. They are excellent talismans and provide their own force fields. These sigils were put on household wares, weapons, walls, clothing, and jewelry. They were also used in cooking and gardening. Some bind runes are traditional, such as the Galdor Staves. Others take bind runes and give them a more stylized look, making them appear more like Voudon veves rather than runes. Many of the bind runes you see in today's writings are modernized versions used to work in today's world. This does not negate their power and encourages anyone learning the system to create their own.

The information on runes here is given as it is used by Pow-Wows. Rarely did they employ the runes for divinatory purposes; rather they were considered powerful magickal tools, to be used with respect and dedication. Pow-Wows were not like the modern fortunetellers of today, nor did they seek spiritual enlightenment through the divinatory aspect of the runic system. Runes were considered a practical way to reach a desired end in the physical plane. Should you wish to learn how to divine with the runes, by all

The Runes

Fehu	ᚠ
Uruz	ᚢ
Thurisaz	ᚦ
Ansuz	ᚨ
Raido	ᚱ
Kenaz	ᚲ
Gebo	ᚷ
Wunjo	ᚹ
Hagalaz	ᚺ
Nauthiz	ᚾ
Isa	ᛁ
Jera	ᛃ
Eihwaz	ᛇ
Perth	ᛈ
Algiz	ᛉ
Sowilo	ᛋ
Tiwaz	ᛏ
Berkano	ᛒ
Ehwaz	ᛖ
Mannaz	ᛗ
Laguz	ᛚ
Inguz	ᛝ
Dagaz	ᛞ
Othala	ᛟ

means do so. They work quite well as a spiritual accompaniment to the human psyche.

The Germanic Runes

Fehu (Fe): Cattle. Stands for the creative aspects of fire and is female in nature. It is invoked for love, war, and Witchcraft. A good fortune rune, it allows you to draw wealth to you and maintain it. Fehu is a rune of new beginnings and expansive energy. Used with a healing rune, it acts as a catalyst/energy source. Fehu carries her own warning. Her gifts of good fortune must be shared, or else the rune will either destroy us or leave us worse off than we were before. Excellent in bind runes to bring in energy.

Uruz (Auroch): The auroch is an extinct European bison that was considered extraordinarily ferocious. This is a masculine rune that corresponds to the fierce power of ice, as in the movement of the glaciers. Therefore, akin to a glacier, Auroch moves with determination and purifies all it touches. Patience, courage, persistence, and strength are all qualities of this rune. It can be invoked for defense, crop fertility, good weather, strength, and healing. Excellent in bind runes for healing purposes.

Thurisaz (Thurs): Devil. Thurisaz is seen as the forces of opposition and chaos in the world and is the negative balance in the scales of nature. It is the shadow self of each person or positive deity. Thurisaz represents fire in its uncontrolled form and is the driving force behind a curse. Of all the runes, it is by far the most dangerous and can easily backfire. It was known as a war rune—one invoked to cause unmitigated fear and panic in opponents. The rune Isa is used as a protective backdrop. Although extraordinarily destructive, it is also extremely protective. A ring of Thurisaz runes will keep out anything harmful or destructive.

Ansuz: Ansuz is invoked for wisdom and occult knowledge from a higher, positive source. Its element is air and it is associated with the sacred breath. In Pow-Wow, Ansuz would be used during the faith healing process and is one of the runes that should be invoked by signing with the hand. It is often thought of as Odin's rune and has the highest vibration of the runes. Ansuz represents intelligence and reason and therefore corresponds well to the written word and all sorts of messages. It is used in invisibility spells, for healing, and for cursing.

Raido: Raido literally makes things go. It represents the act of being in charge and of motion and allows you to control particular situations. Where Fehu makes things go, Raido represents the directed pathway on which it will travel. The primary element of this rune is fire. Raido is invoked as a conduit for taking control and beginning new projects. It is also good for legal matters and protecting any type of wheeled machinery.

Kenaz: Kenaz is to be seen as the divine torch, clarity of thought, and insight. Kenaz is invoked for protection, teaching, love, war, and Witchcraft. The element of fire in its beneficial form is shown here and is used in astral travel and to expose what is hidden. Kenaz can be used as a weapon to get rid of unwanted influences.

Gebo: The magickal connotation of Gebo is to balance. It is the rune of partnership, whether you are speaking of two opposing or agreeing forces. Gebo is invoked to enhance exchange of data, ideas, or feelings. A rune of the element of air, it moves swiftly in many situations. It works well to bind two runes together and is used both in blessings and cursings. Gebo is the rune of honor and self-sacrifice.

Wunjo: Wunjo is truly a happy rune, one of joy and pleasure. It stands for blessings, fertility, gifts, light, and perfection. It is a fruitful rune and ensures proper payment for efforts extended. Wunjo is a harmonious rune. Combined with Raido, it will control and direct the will to a joyful conclusion. With Gebo, it brings one into harmony with divine will. The most beneficial aspect of this rune is its ability to exert one's will to facilitate wishes coming true.

Hagalaz: Hagalaz stands for the seed of ice and liberation through drastic means. It is disruptive and causes change. Invoked, it can create confusion and disruption but it is also excellent in staving off astral attacks. It is used for protecting barns or homes from storms. Hagalaz indicates a need for change, a journey into the underworld of the subconscious to bring about positive transmutation. Hagalaz is an interesting rune, for it can turn someone's past against him or her to precipitate a positive change. This is the rune of Urd, the eldest Sister of the Wyrrd.

Nauthiz: Nauthiz is a good stress reliever as it allow you to reach deep inside yourself and bringing forth personal inspiration. Nauthiz is associated with Skuld, the third and youngest Sister of the Wyrrd. Runes that follow this one indicate what is needed in order to bring about the desired future. Nauthiz was considered a war rune as its energies were used to stop and deflect incoming fire or magickal attack. To see Nauthiz in the world around you is an indication that a mistake has been made, a warning that there may be some unacknowledged needs to which you should attend.

Isa: Isa is the rune of Verandi, the Wyrrd Sister who rules the present. She stops unrestrained growth and can freeze activity for a full three months, where the present situation is destined to remain the same for a short period of time. Isa is ice. Invoked, she is used to freeze another's actions and can negate disruptive influences, whether they are magickal or physical in nature. Isa can be destructive by not allowing needed movement.

Jera: Jera represents harvest and is a cyclical rune of reward. It represents a gentle flow of change rather than one of fast pace. It is a friendly, smooth-moving rune, used for timing in magickal operations. It can be used to speed things up or slow things down. Jera's change is lasting and is great for assisting those in need.

Eihwaz: Eihwaz stands for eternity and a world without time. It is a "go for it" rune, but should not be used lightly due to its relationship to the yew tree, the tree of death. Powerful in death spells, it is an excellent conduit for reaching ghostly realms and represents the Tree of Yggdrasil—the tree of life. Eihwaz was the rune of the hunter and can be invoked when searching for a person, place, or thing. It can be used to find a job or a home. It is a good bind rune, providing it is used properly.

Perth: Perth is a rune of secrets and hidden knowledge and is the material used by the Norns to weave the tapestry of one's fate. It often foretells an initiation experience, rebirth, or a discovery of great import. Invoked, it is useful for contacting the Norns, past life regression work, and divination. It is a good rune to contact the collective unconscious of the folk soul. Perth is a rune of psychism, childbirth, and marital fidelity and is often explained as the evolutionary process. Perth symbolism often appears when a great change is about to take place, one that has been hidden from the mind of its main participant.

Algiz: Algiz is the main rune of protection and acts as a powerful conductor. It is said to represent the horns of a stag or elk. Invoked, Algiz is an excellent shield for everything from guarding letters through the postal system to protecting your home. It is also used when you fear a magickal working may have some unpleasant repercussions that you wish to avoid.

Sowilo: Sowilo is the sigil of the sun. Like lightning, it has a nasty habit of striking suddenly, when you are least prepared to deal with a situation. Often its inspiration is from some type of divine source and the message that it brings is a needed one in order for you to reach your desired goals. Sowilo can be a slap in the face, indicating you were blinded by someone or something and now you need to wake up. Invoked, Sowilo is used in healing to draw divine energy to the needed area or person.

Tiwaz: Much like Maat in Egyptian symbology, Tiwaz is pure justice. Invoked for courage, honor, justice, dedication, and bravery in a difficult situation, Tiwaz lends justice to the deserving. Good when drawing up contracts, rules of play, and excellent as a bind rune in legal issues.

Berkano: Berkano is the patron of mothers, children, and women's mysteries. It provides both emotional and physical security and is the rune of the mysteries of the Wyrrd. Berkano is a soft and maternal rune. Invoke Berkano for childbirth, problems involving children and marital affairs, women's illness, and where things need to grow.

Ehwaz: Ehwaz is the symbol of the horseman or war horse. It is a rune that flows and adjusts to new issues or problems. Although often thought of as male in nature, it tends more toward the female energies. Invoked, Ehwaz can bring people together or split them apart. It allows one to take control of a situation or issue and can create links for good or ill.

Mannaz: Mannaz is a people rune. It deals with the cooperation between people for a beneficial end and with the thought process of humanity when it eventually takes a verbal, written, or legal form. Invoked, Mannaz can provide an intellectual edge over an opponent. As a bind rune with Perth and Eihwaz, it is useful in contacting the dead.

Laguz: Laguz is the rune of flow and sorcery and is used to gain access to someone's mind, to send thoughts, and to facilitate mutual feelings. Its element is water and its gender is feminine. Invoked, it enables one to form things by visualization with ease for attracting a love interest, healing, or visiting someone in dreamtime to talk seriously and honestly with them about a particular issue of mutual concern.

Inguz: Inguz is a type of fertile magick circle. It contains strong foundations and room to grow. As a bind rune, it is used as a vessel of gestation—the other runes are placed inside the vehicle of Inguz. Invoked, Inguz is a doorway to the astral, yet provides the necessary grounding for the journey. Inguz is a cyclical rune where sowing, nurturing, and growth are evident.

Dagaz: Dagaz is a rune that indicates a breakthrough of exciting proportions. It marks the end of a cycle or era and the promise of something new and better. Dagaz is a catalyst rune in an uplifting and happy sense. Invoked, this rune brings light and transformation into a situation. It can also be used as a rune of protection and to hide things in the astral and the physical. With Dagaz placed at the four quarters of a magick circle, your work will go unnoticed by outsiders. Dagaz is mysterious and is said to render the wearer invisible.

Othala: Othala deals with ancestral property, both physical and nonphysical, as well as one's heritage. Invoked, Othala brings ancestral power and supports values and traditions of the family. Othala gives access to the universal folk soul and provides a sense of togetherness. It is also used in centering either an issue or one's self.

Loading

Whether you have constructed a bind rune or drawn a simple rune to stand alone, it must be activated or loaded much like one enchants an herb before it is used. Holding the rune in your hand, you must clearly state your intent. Indeed, you are giving the rune a task or mission to perform. Visualize the results much as you would while using a Triple Charm. The issue was a certain way, now you want to do something to correct or enhance it, and it will bring a specific desired result.

As with the herbs, you should next envision colored energy surrounding the rune, much like a protective bubble or shield. This will hold the magickal power of the rune and fix it to your visualization process (or spell), holding it to the object upon which you have inscribed the rune. You also should consider that you are contacting an ancient and powerful pantheon to bring your desires. They should be called with honor and reverence.

Chants and Charms

Using runes with Pow-Wow chants and charms brings the original ancestry of the magick to bear in the process, whether it be a chant of healing, protection, or binding. Throughout this text I have mixed many of the facets of the Pow-Wow system—including herbs, conjuring bags, and of course, the spoken charms—with the runes. The Pow-Wow system encourages self-exploration; mixing and matching charms, herbs, and runes to see which works the best for the practitioner is expected. In essence, it is the only way you and your knowledge will grow toward adeptship.

A word of caution: The runes are not a New-Age toy, and a rune expert is not someone who picks up two or three books and is then prepared to teach them. I am not a rune expert or teacher, though I love them, use them, and encourage others to learn them. If you are not diligent and ethical with the runes, you can make huge magickal messes. You must be careful and diligent in your learning and experimentation.

A Simpler Form of Casting Lots

There are, of course, much simpler ways to cast lots, especially if you have a yes or no question in mind. Creek stones are wonderful for this and you can have a family outing to gather them. After some contemplation and perhaps a meditation invoking the Sisters of the Wyrrd, choose 13 stones from a living body of water (creek, stream, lake, etc.) to represent a yes answer. They should be all the same color and of equal size and shape if at all possible. Place them on a white cloth, dry each one carefully, and concentrate on the fact that you are creating a divination tool. Bless the stones and set them aside. Return to the water and choose 13 more stones of another color, or take a hike in the woods and gather them as you walk along. Make sure you can clearly tell the difference between these stones and the stones you have collected before. These new stones will be for a no answer. Follow the same ritual of drying and blessing.

When you return home, find a bowl in which all the stones will easily fit. Pour the stones into the container and hold it up and invoke the Norns, asking them for their blessings and wisdom. Think of a yes or no question, shut your eyes, and stir the stones with your right hand three times. Now grab a handful and lay them out on a white cloth. If there are more of the yes stones, then your answer is yes. Conversely, if there are more no stones on your cloth, the answer is definitely no. If there are an equal number of both colors, then the outcome is undecided. Some diviners place an extra odd colored stone in the bunch. If this one is drawn it means the outcome is set, but the answer is not in your best interest now.

Knife Divination

Knives are used as direction finders. For example, if you lost something in your home, you would go to the center of the house, place the knife on a flat surface, and spin it. The direction in which the knife points is where the item can be found. You can also name compass points for divination purposes. For example, if you want to know who loves you—Tom, Harry, Bill, or the unknown knight in shining armor—assign each point with a person's name—East for Bill, South for Harry, etc. Spin the knife. The name closest to the point is the fella who likes you the most. Of course, it could fall directly between two, in which case you've got a fun choice ahead of you.

Needles and Pins

Pins and needles were very popular as divinatory tools, especially in the later years of Pow-Wow. To determine whether the future looks good or ill, float 13 pins coated with vegetable or virgin olive oil in a small bowl filled with spring water. If any of the pins cross, the future of the issue is not good. Of course the most famous divinatory use of the needle is in determining the sex of an unborn baby. Thread the needle with red thread and suspend it over the mother's stomach. If the needle moves in a clockwise motion, it will be a boy. A counterclockwise motion predicts a girl.

Wind Divination

To work with the wind as an oracular tool, you will have to put in some extra effort and study time. Much of the outcome depends on your location. Again, you must connect with the elements and forces around you to perform this art. First, you will have to begin a seasonal diary. Each day, list the direction the wind is blowing when you rise in the morning. I suggest that you use a compass to make your notes more accurate. In the evening, at the end of the entry, you should indicate what type of day you had. Was it pleasant? Stressful? Extra special? You should also list world events, if they were important ones. Also make note of seasonal changes, Full Moons, eclipses, etc. During the year you will notice that the wind and the future do have specific correlations. For example, if the wind flows softly from the east, a bright day is ahead; if it blows strongly from the southwest, it will be a harsh day, etc. This can be a fun family project in which each member in the household participates in "tracking" the wind.

Birds and Omens

The ancient Germanic people used the eagle, crow, dove, and raven to foretell the future of specific issues and also to predict the weather. Should, for instance, you hear crows cawing in the morning, there is rain or snow on the way. If you hear the cooing of doves, then the day will turn out beautifully. I have used birds as weather indicators for the past two years. I have run several experiments and kept notes to determine their accuracy. They are not often wrong. You also can control the weather by either cawing like a crow into the wind to bring rain, or coo like a dove to bring better weather.

When working with birds, it is best to form a relationship with those that are indigenous to your area. It is necessary for you to do some vision questing or meditation for several mornings and evenings, a few minutes at a time, to connect with the birds around you. Setting up a bird feeder and bath is a delightful way to meet your birds and assist in protecting and caring for them. Since they are giving you answers to your questions, you should give them something in return.

Generally, the following birds predict fortunate outcomes: blackbirds, doves, ducks, hummingbirds, orioles, quail, pheasant, ravens, robins, sparrows, and wrens. Owls depict wisdom; the cry of the loon represents sadness. Numbers play an important role in dealing with birds. One can count their actual number or the number of their calls. Even numbers are considered favorable, and odd are thought to be unfavorable. When listening, one or two calls are a positive omen; four or more are negative. If there are a multitude of cries, the answer is not yet determined.

Summary

As you can see, Pow-Wows did not use elaborate modes of divination. Usually, oracular pursuits dealt more with omens and items of nature, or contact with the Sisters. Any type of divinatory tool or method requires patience, faith in oneself, and perseverance. It is understood that answers from divinatory questions are not cast in stone, and that the future can be changed— hence the reason for divining in the first place. It was (and is) a tool used to determine what was to come, and then as a magickal vehicle to change that outcome should it be undesirable.

Arts and Crafts of the Pennsylvania Germans

Everyday Art

Most Pow-Wows, like the surrounding communities they serviced, were not fond of large, showy paintings and drawings. What we consider art today had no place in the German home of the past. Art work was relegated to quilt making, needlework, pottery, carpentry, metal work, Himmelsbriefs, almanacs, and of course, the hex sign. The only items framed and hung on the walls were Himmelsbriefs and samplers, the latter usually made by the women of the home. By the time the American public and art scholars realized what they had in the realm of fantastic folk art, most of it was gone. When checking through libraries looking for information on art rendered by the Pennsylvania Germans between 1600 and 1800, you will not find references to magick. To historians, these art forms are nothing more than simple yet decorative designs of a simple people.

Absolute Denial

American historians are the worst perpetrators of the denial of magick in the Pennsylvania Dutch culture. You would think, at least, that the art critics held a broader viewpoint, but I have found their texts and information to be smug with narrow viewpoints. They leave no room for discussion—and many of these texts carry original copyright dates in the 1980s! Here is one example I found in *Arts of the Pennsylvania Germans*. It is a stuffy text published by the Henry Francis du Pont Winterthur Museum containing a collection of various viewpoints on traditional wood craftsmanship, architecture, earthenware, glass, metalwork, household textiles, and printing. One example showed a certificate (popular at the time) that bore a heart at the top, and in Hebrew were the letters JHWH (the highest name of God) and with the word "Adonai" at the point. The accompanying text reads, "This is one of Spangenberg's more modest certificates. His pedantic use of Hebrew (the letters of the divine name of God) may have impressed naive Pennsylvania Germans with their schoolmaster's erudition, but it well may be all the Hebrew he could write."

Throughout most historical documentation on the art forms of the Pennsylvania Dutch, little attention is paid to why the designs appear as they do. They are called "quaint" or "folksy," even "insistently symmetrical." Translations are conveniently made of material that is "Christian." No translations are given if the art form carried words that may be considered Heathen or Pagan in nature. In most erudite books, hex signs are not shown, nor is the Himmelsbrief mentioned by that particular name.

Occasionally, a historian will step over the line and mention "occult practices," using Hohman's book *(Long Lost Friend)* as an example. However, they believed the magick of the Germans to be nothing more than journalistic sensationalism and a small part of the culture in general. Those historians who followed up on occult information were rare. Obviously, most of them don't bother to visit senior citizen centers, but wander about in libraries to gather their material.

Homes of the Pennsylvania Germans in the early years of Pow-Wow were elegantly designed. Artistic grace was shown by the fluid lines of woodwork and doors, rather than by non-useful furnishings. Chests, clocks, and tables were carved, then painted with bright designs affording all the art work needed to "dress up" a home. A few pieces of pottery may be seen here and there, but you will not see the clutter we all enjoy today until after the Second World War. Interestingly enough, neither the Pow-Wows nor the German community at large cared much for jewelry.

The Hex Sign

Let's end the argument before it begins. The Amish and Mennonites and other plain sects did not use hex signs in the past, nor do they use them now. Indeed, the Amish have strict rules on graven images and designs. Whenever I pick up an article on hex signs and the author tells me that the Amish use them, I know that the article was either not well researched or the writer interviewed a maverick of the lot. The big and splashy hex signs were a product of the "fancy" Dutch—Lutherans, Reformed, and other church people, including River Baptist.

The hex sign traveled right along with the Germanic peoples as they came to the New World. At first, the symbols were used specifically for magick and were considered an important part of the culture. And, just like a German, they performed more than one specific function. Only in the mid to late 1900s are they considered "chust for nice." Particular hex signs were also placed on houses and barns to let travelers of their own beliefs know that like minds and hospitality could be found on the farmstead; this is where, perhaps, the confusion of well-meaning historians steps in.

The Mennonites and Amish did, at one time, display symbols to let travelers know the particular religious faith the farmstead followed. These signs were not of the traditional, colorful hex sign variety. At a later date these same faiths took to erecting signs with short religious passages for the same purposes. However, I'm not sure if the writing seen on a barn in Talmage, Lancaster County, Pennsylvania in 1968 was a sign posted to welcome strangers. It reads (in block letters that cover one-third of the area of the barn) "Thou Shalt Not Covet Thy Neighbor's Wife." (Hmmm … I wonder if that farmer was a Leo? Just kidding.) And, while we are at the point of correcting some minor historical errors, a Hexenmeister is *not* a person who paints hex signs. Remember, in America, the Hexenmeister was the bad guy! A hexologist paints and studies hex signs.

Hex signs, as understood today, are colorful designs encompassed by a circle. Many of the inner designs are made up of geometric patterns, although one will find stylized animals here and there among them, the most popular being the eagle, the unicorn, and the well-loved distelfink. The heads of horses and cattle figure prominently on livestock barns. The familiar hex sign is normally seen on a barn, house, or some type of out-building and occasionally on a wagon. They were not hung in the home until the folklore craze emerged in the mid-1900s. And, surprisingly enough, they were by that time considered a quaint pictorial, based on superstition that may come true, if you were lucky. Local peoples were, and still are, divided on the effectiveness of the hex sign. Some believed in and used them, others thought them silly, and many considered them blasphemous. To be absolutely honest, there is no central source of knowledge about hex signs. Like the system of Pow-Wow itself, much of the legends and lore, meanings, and fine magickal tuning of hex signs was oral in nature, lost as society moved forward into this technological era.

Where Did Hex Signs Come From?

This is a difficult question. A hex sign is a magickal sigil, a geometric or stylized design encompassed by a circle. Magickal designs are as old as time itself. Circular designs are found all over historical Europe and ancient Asia, even back to the Mesopotamians. Occultists know that the circle in the symbol stands as a magick circle to either hold power in, concentrate power, or keep bad energies out. The hex sign circle stands for the continuity of the cycle of the wheel—never ending, never beginning. Circle imagery also idealizes the magnificent cauldron of life, the place of creation, as circles are energetically female and angles considered male.

From an artistic point of view, the circle also adds symmetry to the design, making it stand alone to the eye and giving the impression of perfect balance. Hex signs encompassed by circles were found on buildings, but the same inner designs, often minus the circle, were used on furniture, pottery, and of course, those lovely quilts we'd all like to have but few of us can afford.

Earlier in this book we talked about the history of Pow-Wow beginning with the 1600s, but touching on a few of the centuries before. To understand hex signs, however, we need to travel further back in time, to when the Germanic tribes and clans were overthrown by Caesar and his Roman legions. Although this is not the starting point of the designs, it was the beginning of written documentation and the end of oral traditions. When we think of Europe today, we have a bad habit of assuming the countries are locked into place. We often assume that as it is now, it always was. We think of countries, boundaries, and travel brochures. We do not think of tribes and clans as the society. There is a resurgence today, especially for those interested in Wicca and other alternative religions, to study the nature of the ancient Celts and Gauls. This is difficult because little information remains to lead to exact conclusions about anything. Depending on what you read, Julius Caesar can be considered a progressive founder of civilization or a murderous destroyer of life and earth-centered magick. Yet it is Caesar's chronicles that give us written confirmation of how the world appeared—through his eyes, of course—at the advent of a written word that connected the Brits, Gauls, and Germanic clans. Before his time, most European history was oral in nature. Caesar and his legions mixed cultures that had either never heard of each other or warred constantly against one another.

Caesar amassed a melting pot of cultures and traditions that would change the world forever. Because Caesar dumped all barbarian beliefs together, mixed the many tribes as slaves, and installed Roman rule and elaborate trading systems for those left behind, which information came from which tribe is difficult to ascertain. We do know that tribal cultures followed, as we have mentioned earlier, and connected with elemental energy patterns and local power matrices. These patterns were turned into symmetrical designs found in jewelry, on shields, and on war implements. The patterns themselves were universal in nature, though they may have represented one deity to a local tribe, and another to a tribe miles away. To them, the energy stayed the same. The Source from which the deity sprang was considered universal.

Unlike the Greek and Roman cultures—who had specific deities known in their cultures, with the same attributes, lineage, and personality characteristics as well as standard body structures—the ancient Celtic and Germanic tribes put more emphasis on the energy patterns of the Source rather than the creation of a human archetype. Rarely did they immortalize their deities in stone or on shields. It was the Source that mattered, and the Source was depicted in universal designs to assist in focusing power either toward or away from the design. It is from these glorious and powerful designs that the hex sign was born.

When you glance at a hex sign your eye either focuses into the design, or picks up the core and moves out. As a result, with your gaze, you create a sacred spiral, a symbol used since the dawn of humankind to represent the connection of universal energies. In the spiral, you can feel the descent of the Goddess or the ascension of your spirit to the Divine. Therefore, every time a human looks at a hex sign, he or she has become part of the pattern and assists in moving the energy either in or out. The person becomes a part of the magickal dance, synchronizing and manifesting the magick the design represents.

One of the failings of people today is that we get too technical. We must remember that we are dealing with tribal and clan thought forms, feelings, and intuitions. The real secret of the original hex signs is that each line is connected. Every line from the center of the drawing out must touch another, thereby never breaking the energy-building process. Yes, I know there are certain hex signs that have extra little symbols floating around in them, but the basic design itself is a continuous line drawing. Where the inner design is not continuous, notice that it moves the eye in the shape of a clockwise spiral and allows your eye to flow easily out to the next line, thereby not allowing you to break the pattern unless you consciously do so.

Part of the problem today is discerning which hex signs are old, dating back to their first appearance in Europe and beyond, and which are of the newer variety, designed to interest tourists. I am not saying that one type is more magickal than the other, but in investigating the source we can better determine the original function of the hex sign.

In their book *Hexology, first* published in 1962, Jacob and Jane Zook tell us the following: "Searching and researching through many books, I find the Double Rosette is the beginning of all hex signs … This sign was cut in stone, and set in the side of an entrance of an Old Greek church in Athens in the year 1453."

A different historian, Dr. Preston A. Barba, in his work *Pennsylvania German Tomb Stones: A Study in Folk Art* (no publishing house listed), tells us that the rosette design was found all over the world, from Ephesus to the Keystone State. "This design can be found on the temple steps of ancient Ephesus, on the walls of the Byzantine Metropole Church of Athens, on the bronze doors opening to the shrine of Eyoub Ensari at Istanbul, and on the walls of a synagogue in Allentown, Pennsylvania."

If one considers the natural progression of hex signs, they were created first in geometric form, progressed to the idea of adding totem animals (such as the double-headed eagle, the unicorn, and the distelfink), and went on to creating family insignias (much like the old coat of arms). Items like hearts, shamrocks, and tulips were added at a much later date. Some modern hex signs include words such as "welcome," "love," and family names.

Flower Stars: **Blummesterne**

The single and double rosettes were called *blummesterne* (flower-stars), *blumma* (flowers), or *dullebawne* (tulips—not to be mistaken for the definite tulip heads on more modern hex signs) by the Pennsylvania Germans. The numerical basis for the rosette is six—it takes six circles with the same radius to create the design. Three would represent the feminine aspect of Maiden, Mother, and Crone; the other three represent the male aspect of Hunter or Son, Consort, and Father. Together the six circles make the whole, with no energy overpowering, symbolizing a state of perfect balance.

The rosette also looks very much like a fully opened tulip, and tulips were often considered symbols of the Witches' cauldron. In fact, many Pennsylvania Germans called the rosette the *hexefus*, meaning Witches' foot or

Witches' cauldron. A single rosette design (see illustration) was commonly used to ward off bad luck and other nasties.

In this illustration your eye is led from the center of the design out, therefore taking the divine energy from within yourself out through the represented archetypes to connect with the Source. In the 1900s, the little stylized tulip heads often replaced the rosettes in hex signs where many issues were handled by one sign, and the focus (major design) was a star or fertility chevron.

It is well known that early Christian rulers (after A.D. 389) used Pagan workers to build their churches, which were often constructed on sacred Pagan ground to bring the people to the building. Could the rosette design found on the Athenian church have been a message from a Pagan artisan telling his people that this church was indeed resting upon an ancient sacred site, a place where both the God and the Goddess energies were mutually accepted by the people? We may never know.

Rosettes seemed to be incorporated to reach the Divine or to indicate where the Source or Divine being can be reached. Silver amulets, once worn by pregnant women in Sudan, were inscribed in Arabic and carried the single rosette design. In this case, the woman represented the cauldron of birth and wore the insignia both as protection and to bring the Divine into the child she was carrying. It was also to let others know that she carried the seed of life with her and was therefore sacrosanct to the world of men.

Although there are a variety of hex signs today, several senior citizens of the area say that before 1900, the only designs used on barns and outside of homes were rosettes or stars. Therefore, it would appear that all designs thereafter were either variations of these patterns or were invented by hexologists or barn painters in the 1900s.

Barn Painters

Barn painters were a different breed and not especially magickal. Those interviewed in 1968 indicated that the owners of the establishments they worked for (the farmers who owned the barns) rarely asked for specific signs to be painted. Most often they left it up to the painters themselves. Now we see there were two types of individuals interested in the signs: the hexologists (those who wanted the magick) and the barn painters (those who cared little for magick but were very concerned about design and making money). When you look at pictures of barns painted in the sixties, seventies, and up to the present, a singular design is used on the barn to give the building a continuity. Though these hex signs are spaced at intervals of three or four on each side of the barn and one on each end, the design used never varies in color, size, or symbolism.

Stars: Schtanna

The star, regardless of the number of points, is the oldest known protection design known to humankind. Some say it could be a reminder of our stellar ancestors, but no one knows for sure. Stars ranging from the traditional five points to patterns containing sixteen points (called triple stars) were extremely popular hex signs for barns and other outbuildings. The star (beginning with the five points) is not to be confused with the four chevrons (star-like points) that symbolized the four directions, the four quarters, the four watchtowers, and the four elements, as in a ritual circle—therefore a star pattern always begins with five points. (However, the triple star has sixteen points, the extra point being for the unknown.)

The five-pointed star enclosed in a magick circle is an ancient symbol of protection. It is rumored that King Solomon wore the pentacle on his left hand. The points of the upright pentacle stand for the elements of air, fire, water, earth, and the top pinnacle represents the spirit of humankind. The outer circle is considered the magick circle, representing the universe and connecting the elements to humanity. An inverted pentagram is never seen on a hex sign, nor is it used in Wicca or Witchcraft. It is used in horror movies to represent evil and has been linked to Satanism. Therefore, I repeat, the pentacle/pentagram/five-pointed star is not a symbol of evil, as long as it is upright. According to various historians, the pentagram/pentacle has been found on early Sumerian pottery.

The five-pointed star on a hex sign is a basic protection and good luck charm for the owner. In later years, a few farmers would request that a picture of the type of animal housed in the barn be painted within the star. The six-pointed star (often called the Star of David today), although occasionally used, was not a particular favorite for general hexology use. It was popular, however, with those who used *The Sixth and Seventh Books of Moses*. Donald Tyson relates the following: "The star of David is more properly called the 'shield of David'—magen David. See Gershom Scholem, Kabbalah, pp. 362-8. Scholem notes that the hexagram was often found inscribed alongside the pentagram and swastika—three very unlikely symbolic bedfellows, at least to our modern perception."

Far more popular were the double and triple stars. The double star, often called the morning star, is symbolic of many ancient cultures and religions in which the first rays of sun were honored to bring good fortune, love, and fertility to the individual who took the time to face the sun and honor the source from whence it came. (See illustration.)

The morning star is definitely a symbol of life, hope, light, energy, and harmony. The image of two stars locked together to make one design shows the joining of male and female energies to make a third energy, that of the whole. Stars, especially double ones, were often worked into quilt designs and samplers to decorate the inside of the home. As the Germanic tribes of old sang the song of the morning, so did the Germanic peoples of Pennsylvania honor the Sun's rising across the seas and into the New World with the double star hex sign. The eight-pointed star often seen is not a star at all, but a double element chevron, meaning fertility.

Elemental Signs

Weather magick is something at which we would all like to be proficient. However, if we mess with the weather, we may be causing distress to the land patterns around us. To create a storm just for the heck of it is unethical; however, since weather magick is relatively easy to do, you will find many fledgling magicians screwing with it. Not all stormy or sunny days are left entirely up to the choice of Mother Nature. Hex signs dealing with the weather were initially designed to work with the pattern of the land around them. They were created to bring harmony to the area (usually the farmstead) and hung on the barns (because the barn was usually the closest structure to the field).

The Rain, Sun, and Fertility Hex Sign

The rain, sun, and fertility sign was popular. (See illustration.) Star-like points (in groupings of four) represented the four directions as well as the sun. The double cluster shown in the example is also equated with fertility. The teardrop shapes stood for rain; an eight-sided rosette in the center represented fertility, the act of growing. The symbol itself grows out from the center, much like a seed would do. The scallop border, with waves pointing outward, continues the design into the world of the invisible to manifest back into the world of form in a complete cycle.

Scallops or waves represent flow and movement, like water and emotions. This is much like the suit of Cups in the Tarot deck. The inverted scallops (next to the raindrops) express the need for rain to nourish the rosette (seed) to create abundance in the fields. You would not think that this hex sign would be found on a quilt or on a blanket chest due to its association with weather and land pattern magick, except that Professor Johnny Ott claimed an additional use for the sign, recorded in the Zook's book *(Hexology)*.

Professor Johnny Ott, a popular character in Lancaster County, did a whopping business as a hexologist until his death in 1964. He was a full-time hex artist and not a barn painter. His nocturnal habits often raised as eyebrow or two, as he would arise at 6:30 in the evening, work all night, and retire around 7:00 in the morning. "These signs really pay off sometimes," he is quoted as saying. "A man came to me from Long Island, New York, and said, 'Six months ago I bought a two-foot rain, sun, and fertility [hex sign]. Now we are going to have a baby. Now my next door neighbor wants a baby [and] I have to have another sign!'"

If you were experiencing a drought, you would not choose the sun and fertility sign. Instead you would hang your rain sign outside. (See example.) This hex has one function and one function only: to bring rain. The teardrops move in a spiraling motion outward and the scallops face out, shooting the desire into the realm of spirit to manifest in the world of the physical.

Unlike the rain, sun, and fertility sign we first examined, this one would definitely be portable. Professor Johnny Ott had this to say about the rain sign: "I took Joe a rain sign up [and] told him to put it out when he wants rain [for good fishing]. When [it rained] enough, [he should] take it in. He went away and left it out. The rain came and washed away the shed where the hex sign was on, and did five million dollars in damage along the Delaware river [in] 1955." So, if you choose to use this sign, for pity's sake don't go away on vacation and leave it out—you might not have anything to come home to!

To show that a family followed the wheel of the year and the succession of seasons, the next illustration would most likely tell a traveler that a particular farmstead followed the teachings of the wise.

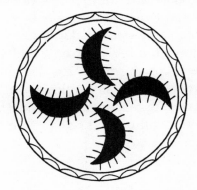

Crescent moons are very old symbols indeed. Popular from Arabia through Europe, the crescent moon is often considered a symbol of the Goddess and the movement of the Moon through the heavens. Unlike we progressive Americans who follow the cycle of the Moon from Full to New (light to dark), the Germanic tribes followed it from dark to light, or New to Full. The moons in this design move in a spiral motion to create the dance of the seasons.

Love and Romance

Hex signs for love and romance are considered relatively new to the magickal family of signage. They were not of the original barn sign variety, nor were they usually hung outside the home, but found a place on a kitchen or dining room wall (circa the mid to late 1900s). Often depicted with hearts, stylized tulips (for the cauldron of life), scallops (for the movement of emotions), and braiding around the outer ring of the circle (to bind two people together), these very cheery signs were given as gifts to young newlyweds and those more experienced couples who had difficulty getting along. (See illustration below.)

The double-headed eagle was another favorite sign to secure a marriage that was getting a little moldy around the edges. Depicted in the following design, the double-headed eagle was for clarity of vision (so you can see who is fooling who or if you are fooling yourself), and strength and courage to learn to give a little. The tulips (representing the cauldron of life) also stood for faith, hope, and charity, as well as invoking the powers of the three Sisters of the Wyrrd to weave the marriage back together. They also represent the Trinity of the Maiden, Mother, and Crone to instill the divine feminine into the marriage bond.

Professor Johnny Ott said this about one of his romance and love designs: "A lady from Edystone, Pennsylvania, complained [that] her husband slapped her around. I made her a love and romance [hex sign]. The next week she was back for two more for her relations." If you are a victim of domestic violence, I personally suggest you pull up stakes and seek professional help. However, feel free to hang up this hex sign on your way out the door.

Hex Signs and Magickal Applications

Hex signs, like other magickal systems, are created for a variety of purposes. As you would mix a potion or burn a candle for love, money, success, friendship, health, or protection in most magickal systems, so do hex signs have their own distinct patterns for these human needs. Hex signs usually were created to reach positive ends, not negative ones. The primary reason for this is that no one would be stupid enough to hang a hex sign on his or her property where the whole world could see and understand its evil intention of promoting a curse. To display a hex sign on your barn that held a curse for your neighbor would certainly be an invitation to a barn burning—namely yours. The closest thing to this is our fellow with the adultery passage, which, when you think about it, is pretty close to a curse after all. This is not to say that hex signs were not used in cursing. I'm sure they were, but like most tools used in cursing, they were buried or burned as part of the magickal act.

Hexology and Pow-Wow

Hexology is a magickal practice within itself. Because this practice was popular during the reign of the Pow-Wow the two systems are linked together by timing, but were they joined together in practice? In the beginning, I believe the answer was yes. Unfortunately, by the 1900s Pow-Wows were primarily faith healers. They were not artisans, nor were they skilled in the art of magick. Most Pow-Wows did not want to link their practice openly with the creation of hex signs as it lead to questions of magick and left their faith, and their healing expertise, open to debate.

In came the hexologist.

When Pow-Wow and hexology were separate practices, the Pow-Wow would recommend that clients seek the assistance of a hexologist on particular matters, such as protecting barns, homes, etc. After a while clients would simply seek the help of a hexologist and not go to the Pow-Wow. This is how a hexologist's practice grew, much like the practice of the Pow-Wow. However, Pow-Wows lasted longer than the hexologists. Back went the client to the Pow-Wow, who turned him or her over to the barn painter; but it was the Pow-Wow who described in detail the specific design that should be painted on the barn and applied the magick needed to make it work. Due to the secret nature of the charms so closely guarded by the Pow-Wow, outsiders did not know there was a specific magickal application to be performed with the display of the sign.

Since the designs were so familiar and the Pow-Wows never bothered to open their mouths about the process, many farmers simply circumvented the Pow-Wow and went to a barn painter themselves. It was still the same design, right? The question we now face is just how magickal was the design on a stand-alone basis—was the symbolism enough to produce the desired effect, or did the hexologist/Pow-Wow do something special to activate it?

Eventually, the farmers disregarded any thought of otherworldly applications as unnecessary and superstitious, much like they stopped working with the Pow-Wow practitioners. The difference was that they kept the hex designs to promote local tourism and washed the Pow-Wow down the proverbial tubes of time.

Where is the Magick in the Hex Sign?

Hex signs possess three levels of magick. Those incorporating geometric designs have a magick all in themselves, due to the repeated use of the symbolism over the centuries and the belief they spawned. Thoughts, after all, are things. Therefore, these designs, like the rosette and the star, do not need color or conscious activation to work. They have already been set into motion by the repeated thoughts of humankind over the march of generations.

The second level of magick is the application of color. Indeed, the major popularity of the signs in today's market comes more from the vibrant color application and the idea that they are delightful representations of deceased folk art. The supposed magickal intent gives it an extra unusual twist and is a nice marketing draw.

The colors used on the signs changed over the years. They advanced with the availability of technologically better paints and materials. The barns themselves were often red, with the doors and windows trimmed in white—definitely standard magickal colors. The white trim was said to keep the devil out of the barn because he could not get across the white line. When the line was painted around windows, the idea was to keep witches out, thereby coining the name "Witch windows." On quilts, however, the background was normally white. Why bother to go to the extra work of dyeing the material for the background when you could make delightful patterns with the colorful quilting blocks on top and retain the purity, through the color white, of the magickal intent?

The older hex signs (those recorded in the 1800s) had few colors— mainly red, white, black, and yellow when they were incorporated on barns. Inside the home, blue and green were added for quilts, samplers, and other art work. It wasn't really until the mid-1900s that unusual colors, like turquoise and tangerine, were painted directly on the barns by non-magickal barn painters. Professor Johnny Ott and individuals like him promoted the portable hex signs. These contemporary hex signs come in a variety of sizes and are made of pressed wooden (or heavy cardboard or even plastic) discs sealed with lacquers or painted with waterproof acrylic paints.

Often chevrons and star points were painted two-dimensionally, with half the point white and the other half black, signifying balance. In later years the same color would be used on each point, split by a lighter or darker variation, depending on how you look at it. Colors were always flat, meaning each block, chevron, rosette point, or star point was not shaded to look three-dimensional. Often the designs were outlined in black to keep the magick of the continuous line application and to make the design stand out. Original barn designs used either red or white backgrounds on each disc. Below is a list of colors that are currently used for hex signs.

Traditional Colors

White: White was considered an all-purpose color and normally used for backgrounds signifying the universe or purity of mind, much like the clean slate of a blackboard. This is the same aspect that one seeks before beginning a meditation. White also symbolizes the power of the Moon and the feminine aspect of life, as well as the element of water. White allows energies to flow.

Red: Back to the old symbolism here of power and the sacred blood of kings, sacrifice, passion, and strength. A good representation of the element of fire, whether you are thinking of power, charisma, lust, or creativity.

Yellow: Traditional meanings here—the Sun, fertility, connection to the God form, health in mind and body.

Black: Another traditional interpretation here is the one of protection. Black is really not a color at all, but the absence of color, the absence of light and pigment—a perfect choice to use as a thread to bind things together.

Newer Colors

Blue: Heavenly blue refers to the connection to God/Divinity, spirituality, and peace. Sometimes represents the element of air.

Violet: Represents those things that are sacred and at the highest spiritual level.

Green: Fertility; things and ideas that grow and prosper. Success. A good representation of the earth element.

Orange: Career and matters involving needed success and abundance of projects that have already begun. A link to solar aspects as well.

Brown: Friendship and strength. Found mostly on signs dealing with agriculture and earth elements.

When in the hands of magicians, the paints were often mixed with juices of particular herbs to enhance the power of the signs. Even minute amounts of menstrual blood, urine, spit, and semen were added for a desired result.

Blessing the Hex Sign

The third magickal application used in the creation of hex signs was the loading or ritual process done after the design was completed. It would be cleansed, consecrated, and blessed, just like any other magickal tool. Cleansing involves expelling negative energy that may have collected on it or attached to it. Now, how can this happen, if the sign is positive in nature? During the creation of any piece of artwork or magickal tool, your mind is not always at peace with the world. Although you are concentrating on the creative aspect of manifestation, your mind can be pretty busy sorting out events of the day, an argument with a friend, or even a feeling of uneasiness. Often magickal artwork is done to combat a problem, so your mind would often touch upon the unpleasant situation. This is good, as you will be putting the right amount of focus on the sign, but is bad because you could be instilling it with negative thoughts. Therefore, the cleansing part of the ritual is a must.

The next step would be to consecrate the sign. Consecration, remember, is the act of blessing something. It is the practice of giving it over to deity to work a divine purpose and be in harmony with the universe. This includes the energy patterns of the land around you.

The final step is to load or charge the sign with specific magickal intent. I don't recommend writing what your intent is anywhere on the sign. All magickal acts should be secret, between you and Divinity. If you must write anything, first work out the specific spell you wish to cast on paper. After it has been cast, burn the paper, giving the wish to the elements of fire and air to be carried into the unknown and manifested back to the physical world.

All cleansing, consecrating, and charging should be done within the confines of a magick circle at the correct astrological time to reap the best possible benefits. Much like creating holy water, you will bring your fingers together to form a triangle over the center of the hex sign and instill your desire within it. Some people prefer to hold their palms outstretched over the sign. Let the energy build and imagine your desire manifesting as a result of the sign. The time when the sign is hung on the property is also important. Don't let it hang around the house doing nothing, but put it in its intended place immediately after the ritual act.

Can you magickally activate a purchased hex sign? Yes indeed, although the outcome may take a little longer since it was not wrought by your hands, and you must remember to cleanse and consecrate it thoroughly. If the desired results are not brought about in 30 days, consider that the sign may carry negative energy from the manufacturer. A second cleansing and consecration is in order. If another 30 days pass with no result, ditch the sign and either make one yourself, or purchase a new one from another company.

Most magickal applications work either from Moon to Moon or over a period of 30 days, whichever applies. This means that if I design a sign over a Full Moon, most likely I will begin to see the benefits around the next Full Moon. We are not Samantha from the *Bewitched* television series. If you need your sign to work a little faster, be sure to include timing in your spell when it is cast over the sign.

You don't need many materials to design your own hex signs. A compass, ruler, pencil, paper, paints, and of course, a flat disc are necessary. For complete directions on designing and drawing your hex signs you can purchase a copy of Edred Thorsson's book *Northern Magic*, published by Llewellyn. To order them ready-made or procure patterns to try your hand at this type of magick, write to Jacob Zook's Hex Shops, Inc., P.O. Box 104, Paradise, Pennsylvania, 17562. (Thanks to Jacob Zook's Hex Shops, Inc. for providing the hex symbol illustrations for this chapter.)

The Dark Side of Pow-Wow

Speak not in the ears of a fool:
for he will despise the wisdom of your words.

—Proverbs 23:9

Yes or No?

During my many hours of research, I was often plagued with this question: did or did not the Pow-Wows of central Pennsylvania use the magicks of King Solomon and the lost teaching of Moses, often referred to *The Six and Seventh Books of Moses,* and *The Eighth, Ninth, and Tenth Books of Moses?* Are these teachings legitimate? Do they even work? Several historical texts and articles on Pow-Wow artists tantalizingly mention the use of the books, but never manage to come right out and say, "Yes, Pow-Wow artists used ceremonial magick," which is exactly what the these books represent. As many Pow-Wows became Christian, the use of these books became more prevalent.

Yvonne Milspaw, Ph.D., folklorist, local historian, authority on Pow-Wow, and professor at Harrisburg Area Community College, gave a talk in my town on the subject. It was a good lecture and connected with much I had already learned. In one particular segment of her presentation she showed overhead copies of a few pages from the aforementioned books. Her conclusion was, that while magickal in nature and known to be used in the era of the Pow-Wow, she felt that these books and the teachings therein were not used by the average local Pow-Wow artist. My conclusion is (drum roll, please) that she may be correct *and* incorrect.

Melting Pot of Magick

The magickal community in south-central Pennsylvania during the early 1900s and into the 1960s was filled with all types of religions and systems. There was indigenous people magick (shamanism), folk magick (cures and spells for healing and protection), traditional Witchcraft, the Free Masons, the Golden Dawn, the Rosicrucians—you name it. There were astrologers, spiritualists, and of course (let us not forget) the sorcerers. To the outsider, all this stuff simply fell under the heading of "Pow-Wow." To this day, residents of the area do not understand that the Pow-Wow community by the 1900s was a conglomeration of magickal people with a variety of beliefs and practices. A Pow-Wow artist could be of any faith, though most often worked under the cover of Christianity.

"Reading Yourself Fast"

According to Betty Snellenburg, a freelance writer for *Pennsylvania Folk Life* ("Four Interviews With Pow-Wowers," 1961), most Pow-Wows of that particular time did not use *Egyptian Secrets, Long Lost Friend,* or *The Sixth and Seventh Books of Moses.* One interviewee indicated that "there's some good and some bad in those books." This is quite true. All four interviewed agreed that they believed in the black arts, and one rather shady character boasted that he knew quite a bit about it, and could tell who had put a spell on whom. Only one of those interviewed, the gentleman mentioned previously, dealt with removing hexes for clients. It was believed that to read *The Sixth and Seventh Books of Moses* you were putting yourself in danger of "reading yourself fast." Sometimes a teacher would allow the student to read only certain pages of the volume and forbade reading others. It was felt that just by looking at those pages you could get "locked in" to evil.

The Dark Book

The Sixth and Seventh Books of Moses has carried with it a reputation of diabolical intent. It is no wonder, considering a great deal of it explains how to conjure both angels of good and ill repute. It also includes pictorial seals for uses such as conjuring grasshoppers and locusts, killing cattle with black smallpox and hail, or inundating the public or least favored friend with lice and similar vermin. Historians have disputed the validity of this work for years, screaming in no uncertain terms that it is all bogus. However, if it was so bogus, why was everyone afraid of even touching the book, let alone reading it? Nobody picks up a book of Grimm's Fairy Tales and thinks they are going to read themselves fast. If there is "really nothing to it," then why, in certain areas of Lancaster, Pennsylvania, can you buy many of the parchments shown in the book? To buy something is to use it, is it not? One summation can definitely be made—the tradition or system that is represented by *The Books of Moses* was primarily an oral one, with the texts used much like notes for a student, and it relied heavily on ceremonial magick.

Witches and Sorcerers: Is There a Difference after All?

To quote an authority, Gerald Gardner (in his book *The Meaning of Witchcraft,* 1959, Magickal Childe Publishing) says this, "Ceremonial magic, black or white, the magick of the grimoires, is something quite different from witchcraft, and has behind it a quite different set of ideas ... practiced in the Middle Ages, they were definitely Christian in outlook and phraseology."

Although the rituals and outlines in *The Sixth and Seventh Books of Moses* look like ceremonial magick, they have no sound history. Meaning, they are not of the Kabbalah (though certain aspects of it are listed), which is normally associated with ceremonial magick, nor does the verbiage belong to the O.T.O. (Crowley's gang) or the Rosicrucians. It does employ, however, Christian overtones, including the use of Psalms and the name of God, and of course, the many angels that can be contacted. It also appears that the book changes per publishing company, meaning that over the years different sections have been added to the original text. For example, my copy contains "The Sixth Book of Moses, Moses Magickal Spirit-Art" (translated from ancient Hebrew), which not only gives you the sigils but also discusses the magick of the Israelites, then moves on to Volume II, that tells of "Formulas of the magickal Kabala or the Magical Art of the Sixth and Seventh Books of Moses Together with an Extract from the genuine and true Clavicula of Solomon the King of Israel."

Part III indicates it was first printed and published by Andrew Luppius of Wesal, Duipburg, and Frankfurt (Germany) and sold in 1686. This area gives prayers, astrological information, and elemental guidelines, with the second division covering the use of Psalms. It is these Psalms that were considered appropriate for Pow-Wow students to read.

Conjuring

Certain types of ceremonial magick (read *The Mystical Qabalah* by Dione Fortune) use the understanding that spirits, whether they be good or bad, can be commanded by those "in the mystical know." By using the name of God, these spirits are in the power of the magician or sorcerer. Ray Buckland (in *The Meaning of Witchcraft*) tells us that "to conjure" initially meant "to swear an oath by," and the casting of the magick circle, in this case, literally was meant to protect the magician. A triangle is drawn outside the circle to house whatever you are calling. Notice I say "whatever," not "whomever."

The Similarities

All types of magical traditions and systems have similarities—and so it is with *The Books of Moses*. First, the area to be used must be cleansed and consecrated, just as in any other system. One must be initiated before attempting to work with the material, and once received, various passages in the book must be memorized—no reading the grimoire by candlelight here. There are certain times that are propitious and not so hot to command magickal intent.

There are also specific tools involved, namely a ram's horn (seen as a symbol of the God), the pentacle, a breastplate, candles, and a chalice containing holy water (the original symbol of the Goddess). The ram's horn is used to call the deities you wish to invoke. The ram's horn signifies the astrological sign of Capricorn, not the devil. (I'd like to make a small aside here. Witches are often linked with the ram and ram's horns. This is not true. Witches see their God-form as having the antlers of a stag, not the horns of the ram, nor do they normally employ rams or goats as totem animals.) Now for the last two items: the pentacle (originally a Christian symbol worn by King Solomon) is for protection and the breastplate denotes protection as well, along with your particular station.

This system also requires a book blessing (we haven't lost that), and of course the magick circle, which in this case requires one to either draw it on white paper or on sky-blue silk, with a circumference of 13 feet. Around this circle are written selected holy names, including Moses, Adonai, Jesus, Christus, and Aaron. In rituals, you must always wear the breastplate and face the rising of the sun. Astrological correspondences are vitally important as well.

Much of the material claims its cultural birth with the Samaritans (you remember the biblical story about the good Samaritan?) from the Culdees. According to this information, these people were much hated in their time and were considered sorcerers. It is claimed that Caspar, Melchior, and Balthazar were chosen arch-priests, shining lights among the eastern magicians—kings and teachers who eventually became the true gypsies. It should be noted that several areas of the book call upon these three kings for assistance in several matters (therefore calling in the energies of ancestral worship). It was believed that by using the words of power in this book one could call discarnate entities, including angels, Gods, Goddesses, and other rather unusual nasties, and compel them to do the sorcerer's bidding.

Magickal voice, as in most occult traditions, was extremely important. This is a technique where the weight, length, and breadth of uttered sounds (and words) are linked together in a pattern of energy that is then focused upon a particular need—a standard practice in almost all magickal endeavors. Incenses and oils were used during rites and spellcasting to assist the magician, and the practice of fasting was quite common.

The Differences

Many of the names listed in the book are attributed to the 72 rulers or evil spirits that were called upon by King Solomon and banished to the watery depths of the ocean. Most modern alternative religions do not invoke or summon entities that belong to the dark or negative side of magick. This "side" of magick is called the "left-hand path." When it is used, it is primarily to focus on dark things within ourselves that we choose to change, remove, or improve. The system/tradition is definitely male-oriented and dominated. Women were expressly forbidden to perform the rituals, though they were permitted to use the Psalm magick. Magickal traditions and religions normally favor balance between the male and female energies. To use the Psalm portion of *The Books of Moses* you will need a copy of the Bible, as the Psalms are not written with the explanation of their uses. Interestingly enough, the users of this odd system were definitely afraid of Witches. Today we know this is rather silly, as Witches are not evil practitioners but individuals who practice an earth-centered religion, believe in supreme good over evil, and take every effort to improve their lives as well as the lives of those around them. However, it could be that these practicing gents of the "dark books" were afraid of Witches for quite another reason. Those men who used this system didn't always walk the positive path, did not mind the rule of three, and definitely called, conjured, and cursed with some unsavory ends in mind. Only the Witch would know what they were doing, have an idea how they were doing it, and more importantly, both stop what they were doing and turn it back. No wonder they feared the Witch!

The religion used is Christian—this in itself is odd because most Christian sects expressly forbid the use of magick, sorcery, etc., and this is firmly stated in the Bible. I think what bothers me the most about *The Books of Moses* is a comment made by a friend of mine, MaraKay Rogers, who has spent years studying the Kabbalah, is Jewish, a ceremonial magician, and speaks fluent Hebrew. "It doesn't correspond to anything I've ever studied, and I've studied a great deal. Although there is plenty of Hebrew and reference to the Kabbalah, it simply doesn't correspond with the complete system in use today. There is a great deal that is noticeably missing. This leads me to believe that we are basically looking at a student's notes, and not the full realm of the study."

Donald Tyson relates the following. "It may not be very good Kabbalah, but it is definitely the magic of sacred words in Hebrew characters that defines the practical Kabbalah. In the Kabbalah, it is the words, particularly the names of God and the angels, that have power. Needless to say, this book is hopelessly corrupt, but I would not be surprised to discover that it was based on older Hebrew occult books (which were probably not very good themselves). It also contains many Gnostic elements. I do agree with MaraKay Rogers that this book is different from any other work on the Kabbalah currently available."

All this Fuss about Moses

For centuries, historians and theologians have argued vehemently on the issue of the correctness of the information that the Bible now contains. Where did it come from? Was it indeed written completely by Divine interference or were many very essential parts left out by power-hungry, women-hating men? (Or whatever other reason there might be.) Those today who follow the Bible to the last comma and quote tend to skim over the very real possibility of missing information, as well as the slurs made on women and magickal religions. I'm not bringing this point up to trash the Bible, no indeed. In fact, as a practitioner of Pow-Wow I use Bible verses, too. They work. However, should we not consider the possibility that a great deal of magickal information has been removed, making the Bible a teaching and historical text for ethics and morals, but not a handbook in magick, which it could very well have been at its inception? In fact, the earliest Semitic peoples were polytheistic (worshipping several Gods and Goddesses), and before the early Israelites developed their own religion they were Pagan in nature. For example, they made talismans, amulets, worked with the elements, and of course, practiced divination. It is well known that the "fathers" of the Israelites, before Abraham, practiced Paganism.

Moses, among other things and titles, was a practicing magician. His "miracles" were created with occult information and fueled by his own beliefs and his chosen Divinity—just like any other magickal practitioner. Many historians argue that the miracles of Moses were just as powerful and awe-inspiring as those of Jesus centuries later. The information in these books (meaning *The Sixth and Seventh Books of Moses* and *The Eighth, Ninth, and Tenth Books of Moses*) was said to be derived from the magickal writings of Moses—a compendium of lore he himself gathered over his lifetime. Moses was a very magickal guy.

So Where Does the Pow-Wow Come In?

When I was being taught by Preston Zerbe, I found that just about everything in his knowledge base was of the oral tradition as given to him by Gertie Guise. I noticed that he used Bible verses mixed with Heathen charms. And, I found that although he said he did not use these controversial texts, he did indeed practice Psalm magick, though he did not use the sigils, seals, signs, or papers shown in the books. It appears that his teacher related orally to him the methods from this text and failed to relate the source of this information. This is understandable because she was dealing with healing magick and its positive uses. She was not interested in unearthing lost treasures, bringing thieves to justice, or cursing her next-door neighbor with a black pox on his animals. Preston didn't need to know where the information came from, and he didn't ask—it would have been impolite.

Those individuals who used the darker side of the magicks contained in these texts would then be the Hexenmeisters, sorcerers, etc.; those who used the positive aspects would have been the Pow-Wows.

Hours of Devotion

As in many magickal and religious traditions, *The Books of Moses* contains instructions for hours of devotion. There are four times noted: sunrise (and the three hours following), noon, sunset, and midnight. The morning hours were said to be the strongest for prayers and spells to be answered. Logically, the mind would be fresh after a good night's sleep and therefore concentration at its peak until the hour before noon. Midnight, of course, was used for conjuring more unusual things and banishing, though morning was a great time for banishings, too.

The Magickal Psalms

Can anyone use the magickal Psalms? Anyone who believes in positive Divinity can use them with success. Naturally, if you are a Christian, there is no problem—this is your chosen religion. If you are of an alternative magickal one, you may perceive a difficulty that really isn't there unless you want to make it so.

In the end, all religions are the same. They all believe in a Supreme being, entity, or energy—it is only the name(s) that they are called by and the attributes that we give them that ultimately make them different. If Wicca is your chosen religion, you can change the wording of the Psalm so that it flows more with your belief system. The call to Father, Son, and Holy Ghost, remember, should not disturb you as in many religions the Holy Ghost is the Feminine Divine—therefore you are working with the triplicity of Deity. The magickal psalms can usually be viewed in four parts:

1. The recitation of the Psalm itself.
2. The calling out of a sacred name.
3. A specified act (such as writing on a piece of paper) or anointing.
4. A spell closure written as a prayer that addresses a specific need for a specific person and is designed to pull in the power of Divinity.

As with all Pow-Wow charms and spells, in most cases either the Psalm or the ending prayer (or both) was recited three times unless other instructions are given.

Much of the remainder of this chapter covers various Psalms and poems and their related prayers. For every Psalm in the Bible there is a magickal act and a prayer; however, they are not all listed in this chapter. Should you wish to completely study the magickal Psalms, I suggest you purchase *The Sixth and Seventh Books of Moses*.

If you are of an alternative religion, do not turn up your nose at the use of the Psalms, but simply redesign them to meet your needs. God is in every religion and in every corner of the universe, whether you call that force the Lord, the Lady, or Jesus Christ.

Our family has experimented with many of the Psalms with either the Christian religion and the Wiccan religion as a base with the same results. We have found that the magickal Psalms can be plugged into a full ritual, after the summons. For example, cleanse the room, cast the circle, call the quarters, invoke the chosen deity, and then use the Psalm as the petition for a work night. Then, energy would be raised. Or someone can recite the Psalm and the others in the circle can raise the energy. There would be a brief moment of meditation, grounding, and of course the thanking of the deities and dismissing of the circle. The Psalms listed below are ones we have used without difficulty. And, to the people who say changing the Godhead to feminine is blasphemy—well, it still works. God is sexless after all.

Following are just a few of the Psalms that have been used for centuries to obtain health, wealth, love, and provide protection. They can be used by themselves, in tandem with ritual, tailored around a chosen spell, with a conjuring bag, with candle magick, etc. Use your imagination and I am sure you will not be disappointed!

Psalm 3

The third Psalm is used expressly for backaches and headaches that just won't go away. For this particular healing you will need two black stones. During the recitation of the Psalm, run the stones over the client's body or head in conjunction with your chant.

Begin the healing by saying the individual's full name. Recite "And these signs shall follow those that believeth in my name ..." etc. Now recite the Psalm.

> *Goddess how they are increased that trouble me, many are they that rise up against me. Many there be which say of my soul, there is no help for him in Goddess.*
> *Selah!*
> *But thou, O Goddess, art a shield for me, my glory and the lifter up of mine head. I cried unto the Goddess and she heard me out of her holy hill.*
> *Selah!*
> *I laid me down and slept; I awaked; for the Goddess sustained me.*
> *I will not be afraid of ten thousands of people that have set themselves against me round about.*
> *Arise, sweet Goddess, and save me, for thou hast smitten all mine enemies upon the cheek and hast broken the teeth of the evil ones.*
> *Health belongeth unto the Goddess; thy blessing is upon her people.*
> *Selah!*

Blow three times on the painful area.
Recite the charm:

> *Hair and hide, flesh and blood, nerve and bone, no more pain than this stone.*

Blow three times on the painful area.
When you have finished, recite the following:

> *Adon (God) of the Universe, I call upon you as physician and healer. Heal me and relieve (person's name) pain in his/her (indicate where the pain is). They seek assistance from thy Divinity. May your action be swift. As I will, so mote it be. I thank you for your help this hour.*

Begin the procedure again and repeat twice more, making a total of three complete recitations.

Psalm 4

This one is for turning very bad luck around and requires a handful of five finger grass. Timing is important here. You will have to check the weather channel or your almanac to determine when the sun is to rise, as the spell is to be performed immediately before sunrise, and you must remain outside (or standing at the window) until you have watched the sun's rays billow over the horizon. Recite the Psalm and spell three times, then, as the sun rises, scatter the five finger grass before you.

Hear me, my God, who art as brilliant as the rays of the morning sun. Thou hast enlarged me when I was in distress; stir now with the rising of the sun and hear my call.
Oh ye sons and daughters of men, how long will ye turn my glory into shame? How long will ye love vanity and seek after only this?
Selah!
But know that the God of the Sun hath set apart the enlightened soul for the work of the Universe and he hears me now as I summon and call Him.
I offer the sacrifice of the five finger grass upon the land and I put my trust in my God.
Lord lift up the light with the rising of the sun upon me.
Thou hast put gladness in my heart, more than in the time that their corn and wine was increased.
I will walk always in the Light of the Sun, with peace and joy, for the energy raised within and around me makest me dwell in happiness and safety.

The prayer is as follows:

Jiheje (He is and He will be), I ask that I may prosper in thy ways, steps, and doings. Grant that my desire may be amply fulfilled, and let my wishes be satisfied even this day. So mote it be! Selah!

Don't forget to wait for the sunrise, then scatter the herb.

Psalm 10

Although this one is rather long, it is ideal for rapists, murderers, major thieves, etc. It is designed to turn back the evil that one has received and to stop it from happening to anyone else. The most important tool used is the altar, where you will literally heap your requests for seven days. It is a good idea to purchase an inexpensive plant hanger, the kind that you screw into the wall. We then take a basket, sometimes a hand-woven one or the metal three-tiered vegetable kind, and hang it from the extension. In the basket we place written requests for the week. For this particular magickal endeavor, only requests dealing with the subject will be placed in the basket. Each morning the petition listed below should be recited, along with its companion prayer, then your specific request should be placed in the basket. Repeat this procedure before you go to bed. By the end of the seven-day period, your basket should be heaping with your request.

On the evening of the seventh day, take out your cauldron or pot, recite the magickal piece, then burn all the papers. Scatter the ashes to the wind, asking the faeries of your area to help speed your petition on its way.

Why standest thou afar off, O Aradia? Why hidest thou thyself in times of our trouble? The wicked in his pride doth persecute the poor; the unprotected; let the wicked be taken in of their own devices that they have imagined.

For the wicked boasteth of his heart's desire, and has thrown deceit and hatred at our feet. His ways are always grievous; thy judgements are far above out of his sight: as for all his enemies, he puffeth at them. His heart is stiff and his mouth is full of curses, deceit, and fraud; under his tongue is mischief and vanity.

You can find him lurking in the villages: in the secret places doth he murder the innocent: his eyes are privily set against the poor. He lieth in wait secretly as a lion in his den: he lieth in wait to catch the poor: to rape the women and children: and draweth them into his net of evil. He hideth his face from the light of the universe and casts his gaze only in the dark.

Arise, O Aradia, and lift up thine hand: forget not your children. Thou art the healer, protector, and helper of thine children. We petition to aid them now and turn back the evil that has been sent to them. Break thou the arm of the wicked and the evil man: seek out his wickedness till thou find none.

Cast thine ear to me, O Aradia, so that we may no more be oppressed.

Spell:

Eel Mez (Strong God), may it be thy most holy will to heal the body and soul of (person's name) and free him/her from his/her plagues of oppression. Wilt thou strengthen him/her in soul and body and deliver him/her from the evil of (murder/rape/etc.). So mote it be! Selah!

Psalm 16

This Psalm has several apparent uses. To figure out who robbed you, take mud and sand from a stream bed, mix them together, then write the names of the individuals who you think may have stolen the goods from you on small pieces of paper. Put the mud mixture on the backs of the papers. Take a large bowl and fill it with spring water, then lay the papers inside. Repeat the magickal Psalm ten times along with the designated spell. The paper that floats to the surface first is supposed to contain the name of the thief.

The Psalm is also used to turn enemies into friends and sorrow into joy.

Preserve me, O Goddess, for in thee do I put my trust. Send me the energies of Earth Mother, in whom I delight. The lines of earth energy and magickal genealogy are my inheritance and bring me to pleasant places; yea, I have a goodly heritage.

I will bless the Goddess, who hath given me counsel; my reins also instruct me in the night seasons and the magick thereof. I have set the Goddess always before me: she is at my right hand and the God is at the left. They shall not be moved, nor shall I.

Therefore my heart is glad, and my glory rejoiceth: my flesh also shall rest in hope. For thou wilt not leave my soul in confusion: neither wilt thou suffer to lead me to be touched by evil.

Thou wilt show me the path of life and I shall walk it in fullness and joy forever more.

Spell:

Let it be thy will, Eel Caar, the Living God, to make known the name of the thief, who stole from me (name that which was stolen). Goddess grant that the name of the thief, if it is among the names, may arise before my eyes, and thus be made known to me and all those who are present, that thy name may be glorified. Grant this request for the sake of thy children. So mote it be! Selah!

Psalm 23

Use this Psalm for dreamscaping and vision questing to obtain information/wisdom. Before going to sleep at night, take a ritual bath sprinkled with chamomile and a little perfumed oil. It is best not to eat anything heavy and many instructions require some sort of fasting. If fasting is not a healthy thing for you to do, then at least refrain from meat, eggs, and fish. The idea is not to eat anything that was not given freely. Therefore, when choosing vegetables, do not eat the ones where the plant itself was destroyed.

The Lord is my shepherd: I shall not want.
He maketh me to lie down in green pastures: he leadeth me beside the still waters.
He restoreth my soul: he leadeth me in the paths of righteousness for Her name's sake. Yea, though I walk through the shadow of death, I will fear no evil, for thou art with me; thy rod and thy staff, they comfort me.
Thou preparest a table before me in the presence of mine enemies: thou anointest my head with oil; my cup runneth over.
Surely goodness and mercy shall follow me all the days of my life: and I will dwell in the house of the God and Goddess forever.

Spell:

Goddess of the Earth and Heavens, notwithstanding thy unutterable mighty power, exaltation, and glory, thou wilt still lend a listening ear to the request of thy child and will fulfill my desires. Hear my petition also, my God, and let it be pleasing to thy most holy will to reveal unto me in a dream whether (list information you wish to know here), as thou hast often revealed through dreams the fate of my foremothers. Grant me my petition for the sake of the universal energy. (Repeat the name "Jah" seven times.) So mote it be! Selah!

Psalms 41 and 43

These magickal Psalms are designed to bring aid if you have been either slandered or monetarily attacked. For example, if someone has slandered your name, spoiled your credit, and caused you to be seen in a false light by your friends, family, and community, and you have lost your job or have had your earnings reduced because of it, this is the Psalm for you. This is especially good for that dirty bird that got you kicked out of your job so that he or she could have it.

Recite both Psalms at prayer hours—meaning morning, noon, sunset, and midnight.

Blessed is she that considereth the poor: the Goddess will deliver me in the time of my troubles. The Goddess will preserve me, and keep me alive and I shall be blessed upon the earth and I will not be delivered into the hands of my enemies.
The Goddess will strengthen me and lead my attacker to his own evil. May the lips of the enemy die back, his words die in his throat, the evil spouted against me forgotten.

There are ones who, because of their own vanity, hate me and whisper with others against me and they wish to cause me great harm. I ask the Goddess and God to seek out these individuals and turn back the evil they sling like arrows at my heart. May their own evil disease cling fast to them.

I ask the Goddess to raise me up over these unfortunate beings, to give me strength. May positive energy flow from my body and whenever my name is heard or read, may it instill great love, compassion, and honesty, despite the lies against me.

I ask that I may triumph over my enemy yet retain my own integrity. Plead my case against the ungodly and deliver me from the deceitful and unjust. Send out thy light and thy truth and bring my petition underhill to the realm of the shining ones.

Psalm 133

Used to keep your old friends and make new ones, too.

Behold how good and how pleasant it is for brothers and sisters to dwell together in unity. It is like the precious ointment upon the head and the fivefold kiss of the God that brings the energies of Divinity into the seeker.

Psalm 134

To help you study or to be said upon entering college.

Behold, bless ye O Lady, all ye children of the God, numbered as stars in the heavens that twinkle at night. Lift up your hands as you draw in the energy of the Moon and the blessings of Divinity. The Goddess that made the heavens and the earth bless me as I endeavor to increase my wisdom and knowledge.

Psalm 150

A thank-you to the deity system you have used when a request you have asked for has been given or fulfilled. Sometimes we are so enthralled with the magick we have studied so tirelessly and worked so hard to achieve that we forget to honor the Universal Life Force. Before reciting this Psalm, light a candle of thanksgiving to the deity who assisted you, then speak the following words:

It is with deep thanks that I stand before the universal energies, the God and the Goddess. I thank you for your great acts, your assistance, and your love. This day my petition for (name what you received) has been granted. I therefore raise my own energy so that it may become one with the universe and help another who is in need. As I will, so mote it be!

The Seals

As mentioned earlier, *The Sixth and Seventh Books of Moses* and *The Key of Solomon the King* carry a set of intricate seals (round sigils with various magickal symbols and letters). These seals are purported to be extraordinarily powerful in ceremonial magick and you can still purchase copies of them today in various occult stores. They are important to the study of Pow-Wow because they were used a great deal by its modern students. Basically the seal is either drawn or purchased, then anointed for a specific purpose. Magickal oils (the choice was up to the Pow-Wow) were carefully dabbed around the edges of the sigil to seal in the magick that was about to be performed. Candles were also anointed and set over the top of the seal before a specific ritual was done. With the ritual completed and the candle burned down to the end, the seal was carried in the pocket or hung in one's home to manifest the purpose for which it was called forth.

Below is a list of some of the seals and their general uses.

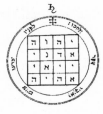

The First Seal of Saturn: Submission of spirits; used in exorcisms.

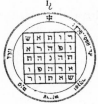

The Second Seal of Saturn: Talisman against all adversities.

The Third Seal of Saturn: Used only in a magickal circle when invoking the spirits of Saturn.

The Fourth Seal of Saturn: Helps invoke the spirits of the south for news; also a seal of destruction.

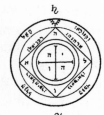

The Fifth Seal of Saturn: Chases away spirits that guard treasures.

The First Seal of Jupiter: Helps to find buried treasure or valuable things that are hidden.

The Second Seal of Jupiter: Brings all things good—glory, honor, peace.

The Third Seal of Jupiter: Defends and protects those who conjure spirits.

The Fourth Seal of Jupiter: Untold wealth.

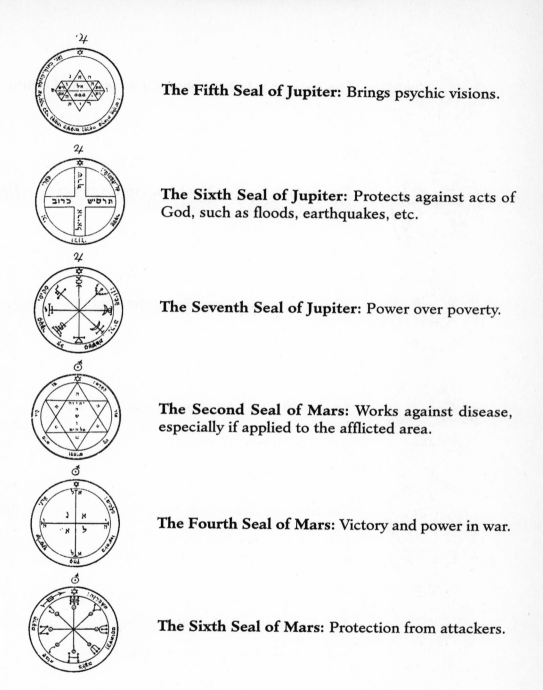

The Fifth Seal of Jupiter: Brings psychic visions.

The Sixth Seal of Jupiter: Protects against acts of God, such as floods, earthquakes, etc.

The Seventh Seal of Jupiter: Power over poverty.

The Second Seal of Mars: Works against disease, especially if applied to the afflicted area.

The Fourth Seal of Mars: Victory and power in war.

The Sixth Seal of Mars: Protection from attackers.

The Third Seal of the Sun: Gives glory and riches.

The Fourth Seal of the Sun: Grants the eyes of the spirit to see hidden influences.

The Fifth Seal of the Sun: Astral and time travel.

The Sixth Seal of the Sun: Grants invisibility.

The Seventh Seal of the Sun: Freedom from imprisonment.

The Second Seal of Venus: Brings love everlasting.

The Second Seal of Mercury: Helps to find difficult answers; used in research.

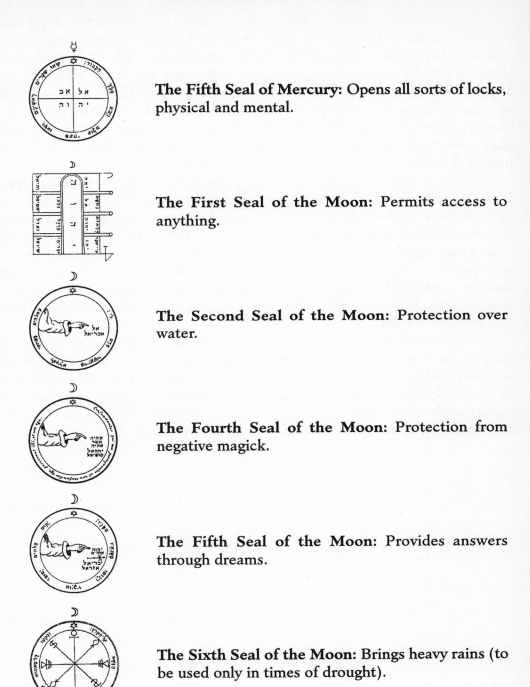

The Fifth Seal of Mercury: Opens all sorts of locks, physical and mental.

The First Seal of the Moon: Permits access to anything.

The Second Seal of the Moon: Protection over water.

The Fourth Seal of the Moon: Protection from negative magick.

The Fifth Seal of the Moon: Provides answers through dreams.

The Sixth Seal of the Moon: Brings heavy rains (to be used only in times of drought).

In actuality, the seals are talismans. A talisman is considered "big guns" magick because it takes you a while to make it (therefore instilling a great amount of will and effort), and magickal symbols and sigils are placed upon them to pull in extraordinary energies. Talismans are in the realm of the angels. When you work with an amulet, you are pulling in practical earth energy, which is powerful in its own right, but does not focus on cosmic energy. When you work with talismans, however, you are truly working with angelic energies, and this is an entirely different form of energy. It is vibrant, powerful, and packs one heck of a magickal punch.

Seals created on wood or metal last longer than those scribed on paper. Paper does not hold talismanic forces for a long time and requires you to be quite studious during the creation process. Unlike an amulet, which can be empowered without a ritual, the talismanic seal should be empowered within a fully cast magick circle. Talismans can be left on your altar or carried on your person. A talisman should be fingered occasionally to keep its energy flowing smoothly. When you have finished with the seal/talisman, the angelic energies should be drained from it in ceremony, then the talisman can be destroyed or buried.

Talismans/seals take a great deal of thought in creation. The color of ink used to the exact planetary alignments are important. For more information on talismans and the seals, one should purchase the book *The Key of Solomon the King*, by S. Liddell MacGregor Mathers, published by Samuel Weiser. It is suggested that you make your own talismans, rather than buy pre-drawn ones. This book shows the seals in detail for copying freehand.

Epilogue

Well, folks, this is the end of the line. I hope that the information gathered here has helped you. I pray that you will learn from and benefit from the ideas here, as I have.

Pow-Wow does not have to be a dying art. It is not difficult to learn; it takes patience, and of course, that illusive state of mind called "belief." You don't have to memorize this book to practice Pow-Wow. Over the years I have found that people stick with the things that work best for them. For example, if someone suffers a burn, a Pow-Wow has one chant he or she uses and doesn't bother with other chants unless the first one didn't work. Pow-Wows chose what worked and discarded what didn't. You can, too. Most of all, remember that if you argue for your limitations, they truly are yours.

Maybe he wouldn't be like the messiah on the oil-streaked grass-stained pages of my journal, maybe he wouldn't say anything this book says. But then again, the things this one told me: that we magnetize into our lives whatever we hold in our thought, for instance—if that is true, then somehow I have brought myself to this moment for a reason, and so have you. Perhaps it is no coincidence that you are holding this book; perhaps there's something about these adventures that you came here to remember. I choose to think so. And, I choose to think my messiah is perched out there on some other dimension, not fiction at all, watching us all, and laughing for the fun of it happening just the way we've planned it to be.

—Richard Bach
Illusions

Blessed be, and happy "trying!"

Appendix

This rite is from *The Sixth and Seventh Books of Moses*. The words here are of Hebrew origin.

The Cross of the Qabalists is the equal-armed "Greek Cross" of the four elements and the four directions, which are like the Crux Ansata of Egypt. The words are the Hebrew Qabalist formula of invocation of the Creator, which is our Lady and our Lord together. They mean "for thine is the kingdom and the power and the glory forever," later used by the Hebrew teacher Yehshuah.

The names intoned toward the four directions are mighty and powerful names. AGLA is believed to be a combination of initials of invocation, representing a powerful formula of invocation of the Qabalists.

The Archangels are the rulers of the directions of the elements in the magickal traditions. The totems of the four directions may be summoned as the protectors as well.

The Lesser Banishing Ritual of the Pentagram

There are four parts to the rite.
1. The Qabalistic Cross of the Hebrew Sages
2. The Pentagrams and Sacred Names
3. The Invocations of the Archangels of the Directions
4. The Qabalistic Cross, repeated

It is an article of faith among the Witches of England that at the time the King did expel the Jews from England, the Witches of the countryside did shelter many of them, wherein certain sacred Names and chants were taught by the Jews' sages to us for our use, and rudiments of their system of Magick, which they call Qabalah. Herein is one such part.

The Qabalistic Cross of the Four Elements

With the fingers of the right hand drawn from the heavens into the forehead, say:

Ah-tah

Touching the chest or stomach below the heart, say:

Mal-koot

Touching the right shoulder, say:

Ve-geh-boorah

Touching the left shoulder, say:

Ve-ged-oolah

Clasping hands at heart, say:

Lay-olam

Amen.

The Pentagrams and Sacred Names

Facing East, trace the Banishing Pentagram of Earth with hand or athame and say:

Yod-hay-vow-hay (YHVH or Tetragrammaton)

Facing South, trace the Banishing Pentagram of Earth and say:

Ad-do-noy

Facing West, trace the Banishing Pentagram of Earth and say:

Eh-ay-eh

Facing North, trace the Banishing Pentagram of Earth and say:

Ah-gee-lah

The Invocations of the Archangels of the Directions

Facing East, extend the arms to the sides to form a cross with the whole body and say:

> *Before me, Raphael*
> *Behind me, Gabriel*
> *On my right is Michael*
> *On my left is Auriel*
> *Before me (or around me) flames the Pentagram*
> *And above me shines the Six-Rayed Star*
> *Shekinah descend upon me now!*

The Qabalistic Cross

Repeat Qabalistic cross, as before. The banishment is completed.

Bibliography

Adams, Charles J. III. *Pennsylvania Dutch Country Ghosts, Legends, and Lore.* Exeter House Books, 1994.

Aurand, A. Monroe, Jr. *Popular Home Remedies and Superstitions.* The Aurand Press, no date.

Aurand, A. Monroe, Jr. *The Realness of Witchcraft.* Aurand Press.

Calvocoressi, Peter. *Who's Who In The Bible.* Penguin, 1987.

Campanelli, Dan and Pauline. *Ancient Ways.* Llewellyn Publications, 1991.

Campanelli, Dan and Pauline. *Circles, Groves and Sanctuaries.* Llewellyn Publications, 1991.

Castleman, Michael. *The Healing Herbs.* Rodale Press, 1991.

Culpepper's Color Herbal. David Potternton, editor. Sterling Publishing Company, 1983.

Cunningham, Scott. *Encyclopedia of Magickal Herbs.* Llewellyn Publications, 1985.

Cunningham, Scott. *The Art of Divination.* Crossing Press, 1993.

Erichsen-Brown, Charlotte. *Medicinal and Other Uses of North American Plants.* Dover Publishing, 1979.

Fell, Barry. *America B.C.* Pocket Books, 1976, 1989.

Flowers, S. Edred. *Fire & Ice.* Llewellyn Publications, 1990.

Frater, U. D. *Practical Sigil Magic.* Llewellyn Publications, 1990.

Gamache, Henri. *Mystery of the Long Lost 8th, 9th, and 10th Books of Moses.* Original Publications, 1983.

Gardner, Gerald. *The Meaning of Witchcraft.* Magickal Childe Publishing, 1959.

Gonzalez-Wippler, Migene. *The Complete Book of Amulets & Talismans.* Llewellyn Publications, 1992.

Hohman, John George. *Long Lost Friend.* 1820.

Hohman, John George. *Long Lost Friend,* introduction by William Keisling. Yardbird Books, 1992.

Huson, Paul. *Mastering Herbalism.* Scarborough, 1974.

Hutchens, Alma R. *Indian Herbalogy of North America.* Shambhala, 1973.

Hymenaeus, Beta X. *The Equinox,* Volume III, Number 10. O.T.O. Thelema, 1986.

Intercourse News (periodical). "Jacob Zook Hex Shop teams up with Ivan Hoyt." Vol. 26, No. 5, June 17, 1994.

Kauffman, Henry J. *Pennsylvania Dutch American Folk Art.* Dover Publications, 1946.

King, Francis. *Modern Ritual Magic.* Prism Press, 1989.

Lessons In Sympathy. No author listed, no publishing company or date. (Published around 1860; found at the Cumberland County Historical Society.)

Lewis, Arthur H. *Hex.* Trident Press, 1969.

Magnus, Albertus. *Egyptian Secrets.* No publisher, no date.

Ossman and Steel. *The Guide to Health or Household Instructor.* 1894.

S. Liddell MacGregor Mathers. *The Key of Solomon the King.* Samuel Weiser, 1972.

Sabrina, Lady. *Reclaiming the Power.* Llewellyn Publications, 1992.

Sfhah, Sayed Idries. *The Secret Lore of Magic.* The Citadel Press, 1958.

Sheil, Thor and Audrey. *Old Norse Charms, Spoken Spells and Rhymes.* Trollwise Press, 1992.

Sheil, Thor and Audrey. *Advanced Spoken Spellcraft.* Trollwise Press, 1992.

Sheil, Thor and Audrey. *Old Norse Runecraft and Spellcraft.* Trollwise Press, 1992.

Bibliography

Smith, Elmer L. *Hex Signs and Other Barn Decorations*. Applied Arts Publishers, 1965.

Snellenburg, Betty. "Four Interviews With Pow-Wowers." *Pennsylvania Folk Life* (periodical). 1969, pgs. 40-45.

The Sixth and Seventh Books Of Moses. Dover Publishing, no date.

Thorsson, Edred. *Northern Magic*. Llewellyn Publications, 1992.

Tyson, Donald. *Ritual Magic*. Llewellyn Publications, 1992.

Vogel, H. C. A., Ph.D. *The Nature Doctor*. Instant Improvement, Inc., 1952, 1993.

Westkott, Marcia. "Pow-Wowing in Berks County." *Pennsylvania Folk Life* (periodical). 1961, pgs. 2-9.

Williams, Jude C. *Jude's Herbal Home Remedies*. Llewellyn Publications, 1992.

Zook, Jacob and Jane. *Hexology*. Jacob Zook's Hex Shops, Inc., 1962.

Index

Index

Index

Index

schnitzel beans, 67

schtanna, 244

Shamans, 26

shapeshifting, 217-218, 220

Sixth and Seventh Books of Moses, The, 27, 244, 256-257, 260, 262, 269

Skuld, 223-224, 230

skunk cabbage, 147, 188

slippery elm, 141, 152, 160, 187-188

smierkase, 67

Solomon's seal, 153, 160, 181

Somerset, England, 5

Sowilo, 228, 231

Springett, Gulielma Maria, 6

St. Joseph's wort, 152

Star of David, 244

stars, 16, 25, 61, 108, 170, 184, 203, 242-245, 268

Sun, 47, 121, 128, 135, 138-139, 146-148, 150, 153-154, 156, 176, 203, 207, 214, 231, 245-247, 251, 258, 264, 272

sunflower, 141, 153, 160, 177

Susquehannock, 14-15

takinoff, 205-207

Teutonic, 112, 224

The Burning Times, 11

Theosophical Society, 21

thief, to catch, 39, 61, 147, 203

Thompson, C. J. S., 58

Thorsson, Edred, 253

Thurisaz, 228-229

tincture, 124-125

Tiwaz, 228, 231

Triple Goddess, 224

triple charms, 113, 179, 204, 223

trying, 28, 33, 40, 90, 97, 105, 115, 123, 156, 176, 196, 210, 275

tuberculosis, 139, 144, 148

twisting vine spell, the, 199

unicorn, 62, 215, 220, 239, 242

Urd, 223-224, 230

Uruz, 228-229

valerian, 138, 153-154

Venus, 78, 129, 140, 142, 149-150, 152-156, 272

Verdandi, 223-224

vervain, 46, 51, 53, 140, 153-155, 160, 181, 189-191, 196, 202

vultures, 2, 218, 220

Waite, Arthur Edward, 21

warding, 46, 136, 167-169, 171, 173, 175, 177, 179, 181, 183, 185-189, 191, 196

Water, 16, 18, 24, 36, 42, 45, 47, 49-55, 58, 62-64, 67-68, 71, 76, 80, 83, 89, 92, 100, 107, 109-111, 116-117, 119, 121-124, 129-132, 135-143, 145-147, 150, 152-157, 159, 168, 176, 179, 181, 186, 199, 216, 232-234, 244, 246, 251, 253, 258, 266, 273

Web of the Wyrrd, 223, 225, 227, 229, 231, 233, 235

Wescott, Dr. William Wynn, 21

wild fire, 41

win (games), 204

witch's mannikin, 145

Witchcraft, 5-11, 13, 17, 20, 23, 27, 34-36, 159, 210, 224, 229-230, 244, 256-258

wolves, 19, 26, 62, 151, 177, 218, 221

Wunjo, 228, 230

Wyrrd, Sisters of the, 113, 148, 190, 199, 223-224, 230, 233, 248

yarrow, 148, 155, 160, 196

York, 7, 16, 19, 21, 24, 27-29, 33, 35, 42, 111, 150, 170-171, 200, 246

Zerbe, Preston, 38, 42, 54, 57, 74-75, 95, 97, 99, 261

Zook, Jacob and Jane, 242, 246, 253

Stay in Touch. . .

Llewellyn publishes hundreds of books on your favorite subjects!
On the following pages you will find listed some books now available on related subjects. Your local bookstore stocks most of these and will stock new Llewellyn titles as they become available. We urge your patronage.

Order by Phone

Call toll-free within the U.S. and Canada, **1–800–THE MOON**.
In Minnesota call **(612) 291–1970**.
We accept Visa, MasterCard, and American Express.

Order by Mail

Send the full price of your order (MN residents add 7% sales tax) in U.S. funds to:

Llewellyn Worldwide
P.O. Box 64383, Dept. K723-4
St. Paul, MN 55164–0383 U.S.A.

Postage and Handling

- ◆ $4.00 for orders $15.00 and under
- ◆ $5.00 for orders over $15.00
- ◆ No charge for orders over $100.00

We ship UPS in the continental United States. We cannot ship to P.O. boxes. Orders shipped to Alaska, Hawaii, Canada, Mexico, and Puerto Rico will be sent first-class mail.
International orders: Airmail—add freight equal to price of each book to the total price of order, plus $5.00 for each non-book item (audiotapes, etc.). Surface mail—Add $1.00 per item.
Allow 4–6 weeks delivery on all orders. Postage and handling rates subject to change.

Group Discounts

We offer a 20% quantity discount to group leaders or agents. You must order a minimum of 5 copies of the same book to get our special quantity price.

Free Catalog

Get a free copy of our color catalog, *New Worlds of Mind and Spirit*. Subscribe for just $10.00 in the United States and Canada ($20.00 overseas, first class mail). Many bookstores carry *New Worlds*—ask for it!

To Ride a Silver Broomstick
New Generation Witchcraft
Silver RavenWolf

Throughout the world there is a new generation of Witches —people practicing or wishing to practice the craft on their own, without an in-the-flesh magickal support group. *To Ride a Silver Broomstick* speaks to those people, presenting them with both the science and religion of Witchcraft, allowing them to become active participants while growing at their own pace. It is ideal for anyone: male or female, young or old, those familiar with Witchcraft, and those totally new to the subject and unsure of how to get started.

Full of the author's warmth, humor and personal anecdotes, *To Ride a Silver Broomstick* leads you step-by-step through the various lessons with exercises and journal writing assignments. This is the complete Witchcraft 101, teaching you to celebrate the Sabbats, deal with coming out of the broom closet, choose a magickal name, visualize the Goddess and God, meditate, design a sacred space, acquire magickal tools, design and perform rituals, network, spell cast, perform color and candle magick, divination, healing, telepathy, psychometry, astral projection, and much, much more.

0-87542-791-X, 320 pp., 7 x 10, illus., softcover **$14.95**

To Stir a Magick Cauldron
A Witch's Guide to Casting and Conjuring
Silver RavenWolf

The sequel to the enormously popular *To Ride a Silver Broomstick: New Generation Witchcraft*. This upbeat and down-to-earth guide to intermediate-level witchery was written for all Witches—solitaries, eclectics, and traditionalists. In her warm, straight-from-the-hip, eminently knowledgeable manner, Silver provides explanations, techniques, exercises, anecdotes, and guidance on traditional and modern aspects of the Craft, both as a science and as a religion.

Find out why you should practice daily devotions and how to create a sacred space. Learn six ways to cast a magick circle. Explore the complete art of spell-casting. Examine the hows and whys of Craft laws, oaths, degrees, lineage, traditions, and more. Explore the ten paths of power, and harness this wisdom for your own spell-craft. This book offers you dozens of techniques— some never before published—to help you uncover the benefits of natural magick and ritual and make them work for you—without spending a dime!

Silver is a "working Witch" who has successfully used each and every technique and spell in this book. By the time you have done the exercises in each chapter, you will be well-trained in the first level of initiate studies. Test your knowledge with the Wicca 101 test provided at the back of the book and become a certified Witch! Learn to live life to its fullest through this positive spiritual path.

1-56718-424-3, 288 pp., 7 x 10, illus., softcover   **$16.95**

Beneath a Mountain Moon
A Novel by Silver RavenWolf

Welcome to Whiskey Springs, Pennsylvania, birthplace of magick, mayhem, and murder! The generations-old battle between two powerful occult famlies rages anew when young Elizabeyta Belladonna journeys from Oklahoma to the small town of Whiskey Springs—a place her family had left years before to escape the predatory Blackthorn family—to solve the mystery of her grandmother's death.

Endowed with her own magickal heritage of Scotch-Irish Witchcraft, Elizabeyta stands alone against the dark powers and twisted desires of Jason Blackthorn and his gang of Dark Men. But Elizabeyta isn't the only one pursued by unseen forces and the fallout from a past life. As Blackthorn manipulates the town's inhabitants through occult means, a great battle for mastery ensues between the forces of darkness and light—a battle that involves a crackpot preacher, a blue ghost, the town gossip, and an old country healer—and the local funeral parlor begins to overflow with victims. Is there anyone who can end the Blackthorns' reign of terror and right the cosmic balance?

1-56718-722-6, 360 pp., 6 x 9, softcover $15.95

To order, call 1–800–THE MOON
All prices subject to change without notice

Angels
Companions in Magick
Silver RavenWolf

Angels do exist. These powerful forces of the Universe flow through human history, riding the currents of our pain and glory. You can call on these beings of the divine for increased knowledge, love, patience, health, wisdom, happiness and spiritual fulfillment. Always close to those in need, they bring peace and prosperity into our lives.

Here, in this complete text, you will find practical information on how to invite these angelic beings into your life. Build an angelic altar ... meet the archangels in meditation ... contact your guardian angel ... create angel sigils and talismans ... work magick with the Angelic Rosary ... talk to the deceased. You will learn to work with angels to gain personal insights and assist in the healing of the planet as well as yourself.

Angels do not belong to any particular religious structure—they are universal and open their arms to humans of all faiths, bringing love and power into people's lives.

1-56718-724-2, 288 pp., 7 x 10, illus., softcover   **$17.95**

Leaves of Yggdrasil
Runes, Gods, Magic, Feminine Mysteries, Folklore
Freya Aswynn

Leaves of Yggdrasil is the first book to offer an extensive presentation of Rune concepts, mythology and magical applications inspired by Dutch/Frisian traditional lore.

Author Freya Aswynn, although writing from a historical perspective, offers her own interpretations of this data based on her personal experience with the system. Freya's inborn, native gift of psychism enables her to work as a runic seer and consultant in psychological rune readings, one of which is detailed in a chapter on "Runic Divination."

Leaves of Yggdrasil emphasizes the feminine mysteries and the function of the Northern priestesses. It unveils a complete and personal system of the rune magic that will fascinate students of mythology, spirituality, psychism and Teutonic history, for this is not only a religious autobiography but also an historical account of the ancient Northern European culture.

0–87542–024–9, 288 pp., 5¼ x 8, softcover   **$12.95**

Green Witchcraft
Folk Magic, Fairy Lore & Herb Craft
Aoumiel

Very little has been written about traditional family practices of the Old Religion simply because such information has not been offered for popular consumption. If you have no contacts with these traditions, *Green Witchcraft* will meet your need for a practice based in family and natural Witchcraft traditions.

Green Witchcraft describes the worship of nature and the use of herbs that have been part of human culture from the earliest times. It relates to the Lord & Lady of Greenwood, the Primal Father and Mother, and to the Earth Spirits called Faeries.

Green Witchcraft traces the historic and folk background of this path and teaches its practical techniques. Learn the basics of Witchcraft from a third-generation, traditional family Green Witch who openly shares from her own experiences. Through a how-to format you'll learn rites of passage, activities for Sabbats and Esbats, Fairy lore, self-dedication, self-initiation, spellwork, herbcraft and divination.

This practical handbook is an invitation to explore, identify and adapt the Green elements of Witchcraft that work for you, today.

1-56718-690-4, 6 x 9, 288 pp., illus.   **$14.95**